"Charles Cochrane's contribution to scholarship endures because he was willing to go behind the texts to the animating experiences from which they arose. It was in this way that he put us in touch with an ancient world whose problems were not so remote from our own. His guide to those common challenges was the inexhaustible mind of Augustine who taught us to see everything in relation to the mind of God. To have, besides the towering achievement of *Christianity and Classical Culture*, the companion pieces that David Beer has so expertly edited here, is an occasion for considerable rejoicing. It is a welcome resource for all of us who must continue to reflect on the role of Christianity within the history of order."

—**David Walsh**
The Catholic University of America

"Although sometimes overshadowed by his Toronto colleagues, including Harold Innis, Frank Underhill, and Donald Creighton, Charles Cochrane was a brilliant classicist whose 1940 book, *Christianity and Classical Culture*, enriched our understanding of Western history. His sudden death five years later robbed the academic world of an important thinker at the height of his career. Representing years of love and scholarly labor on the part of David Beer, *Augustine and the Problem of Power* brings that powerful mind to a new generation of leaders. We are in Professor Beer's debt."

—**Donald Wright**
author of *Donald Creighton: A Life in History*

AUGUSTINE
AND THE
PROBLEM OF POWER

AUGUSTINE
AND THE
PROBLEM OF POWER

The Essays and Lectures of Charles Norris Cochrane

Charles Norris Cochrane

Edited with an introduction by David Beer

CASCADE *Books* • Eugene, Oregon

AUGUSTINE AND THE PROBLEM OF POWER
The Essays and Lectures of Charles Norris Cochrane

Copyright © 2017 David Beer. All rights reserved. Except for brief quotations in critical publications or reviews, no part of this book may be reproduced in any manner without prior written permission from the publisher. Write: Permissions, Wipf and Stock Publishers, 199 W. 8th Ave., Suite 3, Eugene, OR 97401.

Cascade Books
An Imprint of Wipf and Stock Publishers
199 W. 8th Ave., Suite 3
Eugene, OR 97401

www.wipfandstock.com

PAPERBACK ISBN: 978-1-4982-9424-9
HARDCOVER ISBN: 978-1-4982-9426-3
EBOOK ISBN: 978-1-4982-9425-6

Cataloguing-in-Publication data:

Names: Cochrane, Charles Norris. | Beer, David, editor.

Title: Augustine and the problem of power : the essays and lectures of Charles Norris Cochrane / Charles Norris Cochrane ; edited with an introduction by David Beer.

Description: Eugene, OR : Cascade Books, 2017 | Includes bibliographical references.

Identifiers: ISBN 978-1-4982-9424-9 (paperback) | ISBN 978-1-4982-9426-3 (hardcover) | ISBN 978-1-4982-9425-6 (ebook)

Subjects: LCSH: Augustine, Saint, Bishop of Hippo. | Christianity and politics. | Christian civilization. | Civilization, Greco-Roman. | Cochrane, Charles Norris, 1889–1945.

Classification: BR65.A9 C579 2017 (paperback) | BR65.A9 C579 (ebook)

Manufactured in the U.S.A.   11/14/17

Contents

Acknowledgments | vii
Note on Citations, Editions, and Translations | ix

Introduction | 1

1 Augustine and the Problem of Power | 26
2 The Latin Spirit in Literature | 103
3 The Classical Idea of the Commonwealth | 119
4 *Pax Romana* | 134
5 Revolution: Caesarism | 148
6 Niccolò Machiavelli | 166
7 The Mind of Edward Gibbon | 210

Bibliography | 249

Acknowledgments

THE APPEARANCE OF THIS volume provides the opportunity to acknowledge and thank many people who have provided assistance, encouragement, resources, and support towards its completion. The small seed for this project was first laid when I was an undergraduate at Georgetown University working on a senior honors thesis on Augustine. My dear friend Rouven Steeves suggested that I read Cochrane's *Christianity and Classical Culture* as part of my literature review, and I was immediately enthralled. It was later when I was in graduate school at the Catholic University of America that I returned to Cochrane and, while I should have been working on my dissertation, I discovered that he had delivered lectures that were never published. I cannot overstate the debt of gratitude that not only I, but the entire world owes to Margaret Phillips, Charles Norris Cochrane's granddaughter, who went to considerable lengths to save Cochrane's papers from being lost when her uncle Hugh David Cochrane passed away. Without her efforts, as well as those of her extended family, nothing that follows in this book would have been possible.

Margaret Phillips tracked down Cochrane's papers and arranged for their donation to the University of Toronto Archives at the Thomas Fisher Rare Book Library. University Archivist Loryl MacDonald and Special Media Archivist Marnee Gamble deserve special praise for their work not only in cataloging and sorting Cochrane's papers, but also for assisting in research within the holdings and for granting permission to publish. My research has also been assisted by capable archivists at Dalhousie University, the Library and Archives of Canada, and Oxford University Press Archives. The staff at these institutions assisted in navigating their institution's collections and locating materials for the biographical and introductory sections.

I also want to gratefully acknowledge the grants of financial support that provided the resources for several aspects of this project. Malone University approved summer research grants in 2013 and 2014 providing funds to travel to Toronto and work in the archives. A Charles G. Koch Foundation grant in 2014–2015 provided student assistants the opportunity to engage alongside my research and editing, and I happily thank Marissa Bennett and Rachel Jenkins for reviewing the manuscript, and Katie Karkoska for assistance with the ancient Greek texts. This grant also created a reading group of faculty and students who spent a year meeting regularly to discuss Cochrane's *Christianity and Classical Culture*, and I particularly want to thank the students who brought their questions and professors Jay Case, Jacci Stuckey, and Scott Waalkes for their faithful commitment and valuable perspectives. Another summer grant from Malone University in 2016 supported the final preparation of the manuscript for publication and brought Zachary Murray on board as a student-research assistant.

A small army of student workers in Malone University's Department of History, Philosophy, and Social Sciences, too many to name in entirety, have toiled on this project. They each spent hours trying to decipher and transcribe handwritten notes, foreign languages, and blurred copies, but I particularly want to thank Kaitlyn Stump and Christina Stump for their work, and Becky Albertson, for many years my department's administrative assistant, for molding this group of students into a valuable academic support service.

As the project was reaching its final stages, versions of the introductory chapter benefited from the comments and suggestions of many colleagues. I would like to thank the Malone University Writers Group, particularly Jay Case, Bryan Hollon, Steve Jensen, Matt Phelps, and Scott Waalkes, as well as Scott Dill and Steve Moroney for all generously giving of their time.

In very personal ways my family has been involved with this project from its earliest days. My parents provided some of the earliest transcriptions of blurry copies of Cochrane's manuscripts and handwriting to allow me the freedom to pursue other avenues of investigation, but it is my wife who has given the greatest sacrifice. My wife has patiently tolerated my absences for research trips and conferences in the summers, and my long hours at the office and at home on the computer during the school year. Her tolerance has been stretched by the fact that the research and editing of this work began before we had children, and now that it is completed we have four. Her love and support have sustained me through college, graduate school, and now the rigors of academic life, and I cannot thank her enough.

Note on Citations, Editions, and Translations

THE AIM OF ANY editor should be to present the best and most faithful version possible of the work in question. This task is complicated here by the space of time from Cochrane's life and requirements of contemporary scholarship. Even in essays Cochrane published in his lifetime, he was not compelled to provide citations to many canonical works referenced, or to provide translations for quotations from original languages. This has required the editor to balance being helpful to the modern reader and being faithful to Cochrane's writing style. In order to align with current scholarly expectation, I have supplied citations where Cochrane omitted them, and corrected any small errors where Cochrane did provide citations. It should be noted, however, that Cochrane provided his own translations to all French, Greek, and Latin texts quoted in this volume. In these cases, there is a citation supplied to help locate the referenced text, but Cochrane's translation will be different from that in the edition identified in the bibliography. This is particularly true of the Greek and Latin texts and terms he uses. Cochrane had such a grasp of these ancient languages that he constantly sprinkles his writing with ancient terms and ideas. However, Cochrane never enslaved his comprehension and use of texts to a formulaic sense of literalness. At times he will be quite loose in his rendering or utilization of an ancient text in order to inspire the contemporary reader, and at other times he will use the closest English derivative word to simply connect the ancient understanding to our present age. Fluency in Greek and Latin is not required to understand Cochrane's work, but rather Cochrane intends references to ancient authors and texts to prompt the reader for further investigation and engagement with the classical world and late antiquity.

Introduction

I

CHARLES NORRIS COCHRANE'S DEATH in 1945 at the age of fifty-six cut him down in his academic prime. The University of Toronto classicist, historian, and philosopher, was an internationally recognized scholar of the ancient world and early Christianity. Oxford University Press had recently reprinted in a second, American edition his magnum opus *Christianity and Classical Culture: A Study of Thought and Action from Augustus to Augustine*, a book Jaroslav Pelikan once called, "The most profound book I know on Augustine,"[1] and W.H. Auden had recently exclaimed in the pages of *The New Republic*, "I have read this book many times, and my conviction of its importance to the understanding not only of the epoch of which it is concerned, but also of our own, has increased with each rereading."[2] Princeton University, where he had previously been an invited guest lecturer, was recruiting him for an appointment as a visiting professor as soon as the war ended. More importantly, Cochrane only months earlier had delivered the Nathaniel William Taylor Lectures at Yale University. Cochrane's four lectures at Yale, "Augustine and the Problem of Power," were meant to condense the argument of his famous book and to extend its analysis of the late antique world into the development of a specifically Christian political philosophy. In a sense, Cochrane was laying the foundation that could serve as the basis for a sequel to *Christianity and Classical Culture*. After his return from Yale in the Spring of 1945, unfortunately, Cochrane suffered a heart attack that weakened him to the point that he passed away a few months later without ever having recovered. The academic obituaries and notices of his death in the learned journals of the day not only acknowledge the great ac-

---

1. Pelikan, "Writing as a Means of Grace," 176.
2. Auden, "Augustus to Augustine," 373.

complishment of Cochrane's scholarly contribution to the understanding of Western civilization, but also lament the lost promise of even greater future achievements that would have come from his pen.[3]

The tragedy of Cochrane's untimely death was compounded as over time his scholarly contribution has slowly faded from view because of undeserved neglect and the prejudice for the new over the old that C.S. Lewis termed "chronological snobbery."[4] His diminished reputation was further hindered by the absence of a posthumous publication of his remaining manuscripts and uncollected works. In 1946 the Royal Society of Canada took the extraordinary step of posthumously awarding Cochrane the Lorne Pierce Medal in Literature, despite the academic and historical nature of his subjects and prose. The address delivered in conferring the award anticipates that his Nathaniel William Taylor Lectures delivered at Yale would soon be published as a successor to his previous work. The project, however, never came to fruition. It was only after Cochrane's son, Hugh, died in 2002 that his grandchildren, who had only ever known their grandfather from familial stories, recovered his papers hidden among Hugh's possessions and donated them to the University of Toronto archives to be made available for scholarly access.

The present volume of Cochrane's shorter writings corrects the long neglect of Cochrane's thought by disseminating the writings that were left unpublished or uncollected at his death. Though Cochrane's great work, *Christianity and Classical Culture*, remains unrivalled as his masterpiece, its sheer magnificence in scope and weight of scholarship can be a hindrance to its reception. The essays and lectures represented here provide an accessible introduction to Cochrane's thought and can either stand alone or serve as an inducement to make the leap into his monumental work.

Cochrane's scholarly life was devoted to the period that stretched from classical Greece to the late antique world of the Roman Empire. The writings included in this volume encapsulate the whole range of Cochrane's development and maturation. Some early essays were unpublished and show the development of his thought and his early approaches to important questions. Some chapters were published in a Toronto journal and represent a middle point of his career. His Yale lectures were the final work of his life, and they display the fruits of his best achievements. The most significant contribution of Cochrane's scholarship focused on the transition in culture and philosophy that occurred with the advent of Christianity. This general

---

3. See among others: Innis, "Obituaries: Charles Norris Cochrane, 1889–1945"; A.S.P. Woodhouse, "Charles Norris Cochrane, 1889–1945"; and M.D.C. Tait, "Charles Norris Cochrane, 1889–1945."

4. Lewis, *Surprised by Joy*, 206.

theme unites the included essays and lectures that cover Augustine, Edward Gibbon, Machiavelli, and Roman political history.

The appearance of Cochrane's "lost works" also provides the opportunity to make the case for Cochrane's continuing relevance. Cochrane likely would not have claimed personal originality for himself, so the question ultimately resolves itself into an investigation of how Cochrane is able to elucidate the thinkers he draws on from the classical and late antique period, particularly Augustine, and suggestively apply this to the modern world. In many ways we must consider the grounds for Auden's and Pelikan's praise, noted above, of Cochrane's interpretation of Augustine and its relevance to our own era, as well as how these are extended in his forthcoming essays and lectures.

The simplest way to approach the continuing value of Cochrane's interpretation of Augustine is to start with what is taken for granted about Augustine's view of Christianity and politics. The common way to summarize Augustine's *City of God*, is to outline his development of the two-cities model that makes a clear distinction between the earthly city of man and the heavenly city of God. The earthly city is the realm of conflict and imperfection, while the heavenly city is divinely perfect and knows no pain or sorrow. The two-cities model provides a fundamental Christian view of politics and an insight into the necessarily limited nature of what any government will be able to accomplish on earth. Cochrane's thought is important in two ways that I will preview here, but expand at greater length below. In the first place he elucidates Augustine's two-cities model by situating its development amidst a comprehensive treatment of the Greek and Roman political philosophy that preceded Christianity's advent. In so doing, Cochrane coined the phrase, "creative politics," to describe the view of classical thinkers regarding the role of politics in human life. Creative politics sets for itself the task of completing all of humanity's aims in the public sphere through political action, or in other words, realizing perfection on earth. Against these arrogant pretensions of classical thinkers, at its most basic level Augustine's two-cities model resisted the idea that heaven can be created on earth.

Secondly, and more importantly, Cochrane's interpretation of Augustine is profoundly original because it does not simply leave off with the limits of politics. A typical assessment of Augustine's political contribution is essentially negative in character as it simply critiques political efforts, and focuses on politics strictly as a restraint on sin. In line with this negative assessment, the attention is almost exclusively focused on Augustine's exposition of original sin. Cochrane is different here in that he is not content to treat Augustine's view of original sin without also developing his treatment of grace and God's superintendence of his creation. By including grace in his treatment of Augustine, Cochrane does not restrict our view to a negative vision of politics and human history, but provides a hope beyond the unrealistic aspirations of creative politics. Cochrane's nuanced interpretation of Augustine accounts for both sin and grace in human life and politics and is the enduring contribution of Cochrane's work.

The intention of this introduction is to provide a brief biographical context for Cochrane's life and work and adumbrate the outline of how each chapter fits into the scope of his project of chronicling the momentous affect Christianity and its new concepts of sin and grace had on the classical and late antique world and their continuing importance to this day. This aspect of contemporary relevance should not be missed in reading his work today. Cochrane was not an ivory-tower academic aloof from the events surrounding the two great wars of the twentieth century and the ideological conflicts that underlay them. Instead, Cochrane argued that Augustine's contribution was necessary for his "distracted age," and by implication our own similarly distracted age, because Augustine provided "the preface to an original and distinctively Christian philosophy of power."[5] This Augustinian Christian political philosophy still offers the same promise of an illuminating vision of reality and human action that serves as a helpful corrective to the distortions of contemporary ideologies.

II

Charles Norris Cochrane was born on August 21, 1889, the son of Charles Edward Cochrane, a rural physician, and Anne Charlotte (née Norris) Cochrane, herself the daughter of a physician. Cochrane spent his early childhood in Omemee, Ontario near the Kawartha Lakes until, after his father's early death and a fire tragically burned the family's home, Cochrane moved with his mother and older sister to Toronto. After two years at Lindsay Collegiate Institute, he enrolled at University College within the University of Toronto taking the honors course of English and History with the classical option. Despite his familial connection with medicine, Cochrane was singled out for his facility in classical history and literature during college. After being awarded the McCaul Medal in Classics in 1911, special funds were raised to send Cochrane to Corpus Christi College at Oxford University.[6] After two years of study, Cochrane received an additional Bachelor of Arts degree as was common for colonial students studying in England, and

---

5. See below, 32.
6. Friedland, *University of Toronto*, 177.

he was called back to Toronto and appointed a lecturer in Ancient History for University College under his teacher W.S. Milner in 1913.

As with so many of his age, Cochrane was drawn into the service of his country and the British Empire during World War I. Prior to his enlistment in the Canadian Expeditionary Force in 1916, Cochrane was active in the formation of the Canadian Officer Training Corps at the University of Toronto, as well as in promoting Canadian involvement in World War I, particularly through the promotion of recruitment efforts. Canadians were recruited largely as infantry troops and often served under British officers, and so there were fewer opportunities for a college-educated Canadian to lead his own men as Cochrane had done as a Captain in the Canadian Officers Training Corp in charge of the cadets of Victoria College. Unable to quickly secure an officer's commission in either the British or Canadian regular armies, Cochrane turned to other areas of war service. He first served as secretary for the Speaker's Patriotic League and was later appointed by Prime Minister Robert Borden as organizing secretary of the Soldier's Aid Commission in Ontario. After unsuccessful attempts to be deployed with the Canadian army and unable to gain an imperial commission in the Royal Flying Corp, he finally found an opportunity for overseas deployment with the newly created 1st Canadian Tank Battalion where he served as a lieutenant. The Canadian Tank Battalion sailed to England for training, however, it never saw action because the battalion's training was not completed before the Armistice was signed.

Cochrane returned to Toronto after the war and resumed his position as lecturer teaching ancient history until he succeeded his old teacher and was promoted to associate professor of ancient history when W. S. Milner retired in 1924. He was also named the first Dean of Residence for University College and published his first book, *David Thompson: The Explorer*, the same year. In 1926 Cochrane co-authored with W.S. Wallace, *This Canada of Ours*, a secondary-school textbook for Canadian civics.

Cochrane's works on Canadian history and civics were published exclusively for the small Canadian market and aimed at secondary school students, and so it was not until he published his first major academic work in 1929, *Thucydides and the Science of History* with Oxford University Press, that Cochrane began to gain a scholarly reputation. In this work Cochrane argued against the contemporary interpretation of Thucydides put forward by F.M. Cornford that Thucydides's account of the Peloponnesian war did not reach the level of scientific history, but was more closely related to the writing of Greek myth.[7] Cochrane's unique interpretation of Thucydides

---

7. See F. M. Cornford, *Thucydides Mythistoricus*.

turns on showing his connection to the Hippocratic view of medicine, and that Thucydides applied this early scientific method to the study of history with regards to questions of causality. Cochrane's concern to place Thucydides in the scientific tradition, however, was not an antiquarian controversy, but had profound implications for the emphasis on the scientific progress of society being advocated in his own day.

Cochrane more clearly explains himself in a letter he sent to Maurice Hutton, another of his former professors, after the book was published:

> If I am right in connecting [Thucydides] with the Hippocratics, then his real achievement was the discovery of a method which may for our purpose be called scientific. This means that it is no more than a method or as I say somewhere a way of looking at the world ... But absolutes are not to be grasped by such processes of reasoning, they are, as you I think, admit intuitive and all the realm of absolutes belongs to "religion and philosophy" (and poetry & myth). I did not mean to set [Thucydides] on a pedestal further than in crediting him with the application of this idea to the study of society and the net result is to show the very definite limitation of the scope of science and to widen immensely the field which belongs to faith. I have been greatly troubled for example by a good deal of modern science, and I think the source of the confusion in my mind and in the mind of many others is that what is merely a way of looking at the world is by many scientists taken to be *the* way of looking at the world, all others being ruled out.[8]

Cochrane's concern regarding a scientific outlook is particularly focused on those trying to extract from history "a general law of progress," and, who, on the basis of this view of progress, claim exclusive right to truth, and will tolerate no opposition. He sees the same spirit animating the social reform movements of his day. "There are the prophets of politics who are no less dogmatic and assured than those of religion, for indeed their politics are really religion and often bad religion at that. They are all out to realize the kingdom of the Saints and they are sure that this can be done by prohibitions and vetos such as those so familiar in this continent today."[9] While it is only implicit in his academic text, in Cochrane's mind he is laying the groundwork for a critique of the petty moralization of politics in his own day that among other efforts sought to prohibit alcohol and other social ills. Cochrane's critique of social reformers probably combined with the con-

8. Cochrane, "Extract from Letter to Hutton."
9. Ibid.

temporary rise of fascism in Italy to suggest his next avenue of exploration, namely Machiavelli.

About the same time he was finalizing the Thucydides manuscript, Cochrane was also developing an interpretation of Machiavelli. He worked on the long essay included in this volume at least between 1928 and 1930, going through multiple drafts, and this essay and the work on Thucydides must be viewed together to explain his transition to the thought of St. Augustine and development of Christian political philosophy. It is not clear what kept him from publishing any of the different versions of the Machiavelli manuscript during his lifetime, but the work helps illustrate the transition in Cochrane's intellectual development.

Cochrane's aim in the Machiavelli essay is to examine his whole corpus in perspective rather than simply focusing on *The Prince*. Cochrane draws out Machiavelli's republicanism and scientific outlook as a two-pronged argument; first, against the contemporary claims Mussolini was making about Machiavelli as he led Italy into fascism, and second, against those who failed to "understand the scope and limitations" of this scientific outlook.[10] Without meaning to denigrate Machiavelli's achievement, Cochrane rejects the perception that Machiavelli is truly original by connecting him to the classical sources from which he drew inspiration, and demonstrating that he turned to classical sources in "revolting" from the metaphysics of the Christian view.[11] Cochrane further claims that this is directly relevant to the political philosophy of Western liberalism. Cochrane writes,

> Machiavelli has been described as the conscience of the Renaissance and of modern times; but it is truer to say that he represents the revival of an old point of view or rather that in his case the old and the new are one. "The wisdom of this world is foolishness to God" was the cry of Christianity; and Medievalism was an attempt (successful or not depending on the point of view) to substitute the divine wisdom for the human, and for the will of man the will of God. But that hardly is the modern attitude, and it was certainly not the attitude of the Greco-Roman world upon which no light of revelation broke. Thus, in the history of the West, Medievalism is an interlude; and Machiavelli, looking forward and backward like Janus, and finding in the old world doctrine for the new, demonstrates the essential affinity between us and the classical antiquity.[12]

---

10. See below, 173.
11. See below, 175.
12. See below, 207.

Machiavelli helps to demonstrate the presuppositions of scope and method upon which political science is generally based and how arguments about ends must be prior to the assumptions of method. From the perspective of Cochrane's development, it is clear how his work on Thucydides and Machiavelli laid the groundwork for his investigation of the advent of Christian philosophy in the development of Western culture and particularly Augustine's monumental role. As Cochrane notes in concluding his treatment of Machiavelli, "We may admit that the issue is still unsettled, that there is something to be said for the saint as well as for the sinner, and that the task of the future will be to judge the claims of Augustine and Machiavelli."[13] Cochrane set himself just such a task for the remainder of his life, as he notes in his letter to Hutton which was written after both the Thucydides and Machiavelli works were complete, "As soon as I can I am going to try an essay on the political science in [Augustine's *City of God*] . . . Most writers on S. Augustine have concentrated on his philosophy and I have come across none of them who seems to appreciate the nature of his political ideas or understand their source. Indeed it is a vein that can be worked for a good deal of ore."[14]

Cochrane spent the better part of a decade writing *Christianity and Classical Culture* in the attempt to come to terms with the philosophic assumptions that vivified the Greco-Roman and Christian traditions. His earliest published survey of the field was an essay on "The Latin Spirit in Literature," published in the *University of Toronto Quarterly* in 1933, and reprinted here. This early article particularly demonstrates that Cochrane's command of the ancient world sources extends from philosophy and politics all the way to literature, rhetoric, and satire, and it is also his first attempt to argue against separating Roman and Christian sources since Latin Christianity contained Roman characteristics and addressed practical Roman concerns. This ultimately forms the basis of his complaint in the preface to *Christianity and Classical Culture* that "classical and Christian studies have become dissociated with consequences which are, perhaps, unfortunate for both."[15] Cochrane works to view these fields in comparison by showing how the classical world had failed to answer the question of "material (or social) peace," and how "Latin Christianity was to widen and deepen the spiritual foundations of a material life which it refused either to repudiate or deny," by supplying an "antidote to the pessimism of classical antiquity by

---

13. See below, 209.
14. Cochrane, "Extract From Letter to Hutton."
15. Cochrane, *Christianity and Classical Culture*, vii.

stripping life of all vague idealism and sentimentalism and representing it as something to be remade by a radical remaking of character."[16]

In "The Latin Spirit in Literature" Cochrane demonstrates the approach he continued in *Christianity and Classical Culture* when he asserts that the various elements and thinkers of the classical world, despite certain differences, all share definite assumptions and aims that can be unified into a coherent classical worldview. He develops this claim and its demonstration by monumentally surveying the canonical classical authors and outlining their position within what he broadly refers to as classicism through the demonstration of their shared vision of life in this world. The shared understanding of the aim of life in this world and the transitions that attend the advent of Christianity marks the rudimentary structure of Cochrane's magnum opus.

Christianity and Classical Culture is divided into three main parts: "Reconstruction," "Renovation," and "Regeneration." He takes Augustus as the high-water mark of classicism and begins his first section there because after the turmoil of his ascendance to power Augustus sought to reconstruct the Roman Empire from the best of late antiquity's tradition. The political problems the Roman Empire suffered after Augustus, therefore, are all at root problems that arise because of the defects of classical culture and its view of the world. The classical world could not successfully be reconstructed on its familiar foundation, and leaders turned to stronger medicine to revive its failing position.

In moving into his renovation section, Cochrane credits the Emperor Constantine for grasping the possibilities for the improvement of classical society that were presented by the advent of Christianity, but it is important from the beginning to understand the limitations of this renovating project. Constantine and his successors could not simply patch the foundations of the classical world. Constantine's limitation was the assumption that the classical world required only a reworking on slightly more Christian lines. According to this view, Christianity was useful for social policy and, therefore, implicitly was subordinated to the political.

For Cochrane, Athanasius and Augustine, however, developed the larger project of a truly Christian philosophy that recognized that Christianity called not for a slight repair or shifting of classical ideas, but for a complete regeneration and transformation of all aspects of human existence. As Cochrane writes of the opposition between classicism and Christianity:

> The choice for man, as Augustine sees it, does not so much lie between science and superstition as between two kinds of faith,

---

16. See below, 117.

> the one salutary, the other destructive, the one making for fulfillment, the other for frustration. Of these alternative faiths, the former saves by illuminating experience and giving it value in terms of an absolute standard of truth, beauty, and goodness. To pledge allegiance to this faith is thus to experience no sense of limitation, but only a feeling of enhanced freedom and power. The latter may well be described as Promethean. Based as it is on a distorted or partial apprehension of ultimate reality, its character is necessarily felt as oppressive; and the sense of oppression bears its inevitable fruits in defiance and revolt to be followed by confusion, defeat, and despair.[17]

Here we see the connection with Cochrane's previous work on Thucydides, Machiavelli, and their development of a scientific approach to politics. Cochrane goes on to demonstrate that Christianity provided fresh impetus to thought and action by contributing such new ideas as grace, original sin, and the trinity in order to build on new foundations. Even where Christian thinkers borrowed existing Greek vocabulary, Cochrane explains how the terms are used in new ways to express new variations on the original concept.

In the era of the ideological conflicts between liberalism, fascism, and communism, Cochrane insisted on recovering Augustine's contribution of the two-cities model. The early Christian emperors of Rome had thought that Christianity could serve their political needs instead of realizing that "Christianity ... concerned itself with the problems of economic and cultural life only in a secondary sense; despite the fumbling and uncertain character of its efforts, its real object was still to build the Kingdom of God."[18]

At the urging of Oxford University Press, Cochrane spent the 1938–39 academic year in Oxford editing the manuscript so that it could quickly be brought into print despite the rising tensions of war. As with most academic publishing, Cochrane was forced to remove a large amount of material in order to whittle the manuscript to a more manageable size. Cochrane ultimately removed ancillary chapters on the Roman political situation leading up to Augustus from the manuscript. These chapters, "The Classical Idea of the Commonwealth," "*Pax Romana*," and "Revolution: Caesarism," included in the present collection, all provide a greater level of detail to the general sketch than Cochrane was able to include in the finished manuscript.

The book, however, was unfortunately timed with its first edition appearing in 1940 as the conflict of World War II was escalating. Oxford

---

17. Cochrane, *Christianity and Classical Culture*, 456.
18. Ibid., 392.

University Press faced difficulties in printing and distribution because of the war time rationing and restrictions in England as well as problems in trans-Atlantic shipping. Despite the difficulties in production and distribution, and a rather high purchase price for such a large book, *Christianity and Classical Culture* was well received in the academic communities of Canada, England, and the United States. *The American Historical Review*, *The Classical Review*, *The Journal of Biblical Literature*, *The Journal of Roman Studies* and other newspapers, periodicals, and magazines in North America and England carried reviews of the work. The book's international reception may actually have been helped by the fact that the manuscript bore no reference to Canada or Cochrane's position at the University of Toronto. The manuscript's title page had originally included Cochrane's affiliation to University College, Toronto, but it was removed prior to publication. According to Harold Innis, this was done in order to guard against the decreased sales that might arise from bias against a Canadian scholar.[19]

Cochrane's position in Canada became an asset, however, during the war. Cochrane had far more freedom than English and European academics since he was free from fear of air raids or advancing armies. Cochrane used his position in Toronto and the connections from his recent trip to Oxford to help his old friend Kenneth Bell relocate the children of many Oxford professors out of harm's way and settle them in Canada or the United States.[20] Cochrane also benefited from the difficulty of trans-Atlantic travel because unlike his English and European colleagues he could freely accept offers to deliver guest lectures. He availed himself of opportunities to lecture at Princeton on Edward Gibbon and at Yale on Augustine, and both lectures are included in this volume.

Cochrane visited Princeton University on December 9, 1941, one day after the United States declared war on Japan. In what was likely a dress rehearsal for a future appointment to Princeton, given that Cochrane later received an offer to serve as visiting professor at Princeton whenever the war would come to a conclusion, Cochrane discussed "The Mind of Edward Gibbon," by which he meant the assumptions that undergirded Gibbon's account of the decline of the Roman empire and his critique of Christianity's part in that decline.

Cochrane first began to outline his analysis of Gibbon when he was invited to lecture at Queen's University on October 31, 1941. He had been invited to present his previously published essay "The Latin Spirit in

---

19. Innis, "Obituaries: Charles Norris Cochrane, 1889–1945," 96.

20. See Bell, *Thank You Twice*, for a narrative account from English children Cochrane assisted.

Literature," but after reviewing the article he decided to shift the direction slightly and titled the lecture "The Spirit of Latin Letters." This led to a discussion of what Gibbon had received from his intense study of the classical world. Weeks later he expanded his treatment of Gibbon in his Princeton lectures, and eventually published the material in two articles in the *University of Toronto Quarterly*.

In the first article Cochrane charts Gibbon's methodology and philosophical assumptions borrowed from Bacon, Locke, Hume, and Montesquieu, which "determine[d] his attitude to the problems raised by the collapse of ancient civilization," and his "preconceptions (whether implicit or explicit) which govern[ed] his thought."[21] Once again, Cochrane returns to the theme of the basic assumptions that color and shape how the questions of life are considered, and this allows him to make a pointed examination of the source material of the classics that Gibbon chose to quarry for his great work and the uses to which he put it.

In part two of "The Mind of Edward Gibbon," Cochrane begins "to consider how skeptical philosophy is applied by Gibbon, and to examine its value as a principle of historical interpretation."[22] Here Cochrane demonstrates that the same principles that lead Gibbon to rank Christianity as "a type of superstition,"[23] with no real difference from barbarism, also lead him to entertain "little sympathy for the idea of progress."[24] This leads Cochrane to estimate that for Gibbon, "the defense of civilization means, in substance, a defense of the *status quo*."[25] However, Gibbon's commitment to the status quo is vitiated by his faith in the protection of the techniques of civilization against barbarism. Cochrane writes, "Despite his professed skepticism, Gibbon after all has his own gods, though their vast potential, whether for good or evil, was in his day but dimly suspected. They are our gods also, the gods of the industrial revolution and of the machine age. From this standpoint, all this is needed for the defense of civilization is to command, if possible to monopolize, the techniques. But, as we are now being painfully reminded, this is a game at which others, in whose purposes and methods we find something lacking, can also play."[26]

21. See below, 210.
22. See below, 227.
23. See below, 230.
24. See below, 240.
25. See below, 240.
26. See below, 240–41.

Against Gibbon's historical "idolatry" that is "blind to the true issues of history,"[27] Cochrane counsels focusing on the "creative principle" in history that allows for an "intelligible account of that sense of orderly movement in which the substance of personality is disclosed."[28] Clearly borrowing from R.G. Collingwood, Cochrane suggests it is possible to reject the assumptions of Gibbon's rationalism, and "to make a fresh beginning from a less inadequate starting point," and, through "the aid of sympathetic imagination," to "enter into and recover what it can of past experience . . . and this experience it will seek to 'represent' in such a way as to convey something, at least, of its meaning to contemporaries."[29]

Cochrane received the invitation to give the Nathaniel William Taylor Lectures as part of the yearly convocation at Yale's Divinity School in May 1944, and used this opportunity to evaluate his past work and develop a new presentation of Augustine's philosophy. The Yale lectures seek to outline the argument of Augustine's *City of God* in a way that was not possible in *Christianity and Classical Culture* as well as to account for the broader context of Augustine's polemics with Manichaeism and Pelagianism that are embedded in his work. Here again Cochrane has one eye on history and one eye towards the present. Cochrane aims "to throw light on the resources (moral and intellectual) with which Augustinian Christianity addressed itself to problems originating in the social order: in other words, to indicate something of the social significance of the Evangel as it presented itself to the mind of the early fifth century."[30] "But this, in itself," Cochrane continues, "is far from exhausting the meaning and value of Augustine's achievement. For the issues raised by the collapse of the Roman order remain to this day of vital importance; what they involve is nothing less than a question of the nature and source of genuine power in human life."[31] Cochrane's focus on power is not unrelated to the events of his day and the political controversies leading to the second great war of his lifetime. Cochrane argues that Augustine's contribution is necessary for his "distracted age" because Augustine provides "the preface to an original and distinctively Christian philosophy of power,"[32] as well as a vision for how the question of power connects with human imperfection and the historical nature of humanity.

---

27. See below, 244.
28. See below, 244–46.
29. See below, 246.
30. See below, 32.
31. See below, 32.
32. See below, 32.

Cochrane had obviously been reflecting on the problem of power for some time. In remarks he delivered at the fourth Conference on Science, Philosophy, and Religion in Their Relation to the Democratic Way of Life at Columbia University in September 1943, Cochrane noted, "It is a weakness of contemporary political liberalism that it shrinks so painfully from the problem of power. And it is precisely this weakness which has exposed liberal democracies to the crisis of our time, a crisis from which they can escape only as they succeed in facing the duty of making a fresh analysis of this—perhaps the most baffling—problem of human life."[33]

This indictment necessarily leads us to consider what Cochrane means when he invokes the "problem of power." At its broadest meaning, Cochrane uses power as a shorthand term for the existence of civilizational order and stability and its necessary components of liberty, security, peace, and prosperity. Power here does not mean simply the ability to do something, but the total account of human relations that provides for the possibility of human life together in community. In *Christianity and Classical Culture*, Cochrane had connected Rome's decline with classicism's defective view of power. After surveying competing scholarly narratives of Rome's decline, he writes:

> The debacle [of Rome], however, was not merely economic or social or political, or rather it was all of these because it was something more. For what here confronts us is, in the last analysis, a moral and intellectual failure, a failure of the Greco-Roman mind... Nor is it unreasonable to suggest that the defect in question was intimately connected with the classical *logos* of power. Classicism, as we have seen, resolved the concept of power into a subjective and an objective factor; the former, character (art and industry); the latter, circumstance (fate and fortune of the gods); tracing its genesis to a combination or, at least, a coincidence of the two. But, as must be evident, this solution was no solution at all. For, in this combination, no intelligible relationship could be established between the two component elements.[34]

The great virtue of Cochrane's *Christianity and Classical Culture* is the exhaustive documentation he provides of classical thought and action in relation to the problems of reconciling the individual's subjective virtue and the claims of an external objective fate or fortune. The detail with which he catalogues these problems, however, often masks a more straightforward account of Christianity's compelling alternative concepts of nature and grace. Cochrane's "Augustine and the Problem of Power" provides a direct

---

33. Cochrane, "Response to Federalism in Antiquity," 47.
34. Cochrane, *Christianity and Classical Culture*, 171.

platform for developing the Augustinian account of nature and grace within which humanity thinks and acts. This account of the power of God's supervision of creation and humanity's moral responsibility in action provides a superior treatment of civilization that was not dependent on achieving perfection in this life as creative politics had required.

The first lecture in the Yale series, "The Augustinian Prognostic," demonstrates the competing interpretation of power that developed out of the presuppositions of classicism, and contrasts this vision with the Christian prognostic that develops from its original concepts of nature and grace. He writes, "What we may venture to call the Augustinian prognosis of power claimed to be . . . both critical and constructive."[35] That is to say that it can account for both the "grandeur and decadence of imperial Rome."[36] It is important to remember that all falsehoods must be based on some aspect of truth in order for anyone to conceivably accept them. Therefore, while the classical struggle between virtue and fortune may be defective, it did animate the creation of one of the greatest political organizations the world has ever seen. Which is simply to acknowledge that while classicism could carry forward life for a time, its inevitable failure was still a result of its presuppositions. Cochrane approvingly references R. G. Collingwood's judgment that "the disease of pagan philosophy was metaphysical, and further that this disease of pagan metaphysics meant death to pagan civilization."[37] Therefore his intention in this first lecture is simply to indicate that "the problem, as it had been posed by classical speculation, was so formulated as to be quite incapable of a satisfactory solution. And for the simple and obvious reason that what philosophy asked for was the impossible, viz., a program of perfection in a radically imperfect world."[38]

Acknowledging the imperfections of the world, however, was not meant to be an indictment of nature. "There are many passages scattered throughout the works of Augustine . . . in which he gives expression to the Christian sense of nature as a realm of bodies in orderly motion, each and every one (no matter how huge or how diminutive from the human standpoint) exhibiting the divine principles of number and proportion; the whole, despite its immensity, designed and governed in such a way as to maintain its equilibrium, thereby manifesting the power and glory of a Creator."[39] The implication for this changed view directly affects human ex-

35. See below, 32.
36. See below, 31.
37. See below, 38.
38. See below, 38.
39. See below, 39.

istence. Cochrane writes, "Augustine envisages nature, neither as chaos nor mechanism, but as a spacious and hospitable abode provided by God for the human spirit."[40] In other words, humanity has many positive possibilities for action and accomplishment in this life according to the Augustinian vision.

This leads Cochrane into his second lecture, "Natural Necessity and Human Freedom," where he develops Augustine's original treatment of human will. Cochrane asserts that, "Under God, man himself is the one efficient cause of his own activity."[41] Thus, Augustine "provided a fresh vindication, in terms of Christian principles, for that sense of moral freedom and responsibility" that underlay the very foundations of human political life.[42] Counterintuitively, by exalting the human mind and locating the roots of corruption in the natural world, classicism had shackled human life in this world, and by accepting the corruption of the "total man," Christianity could offer "regeneration," that is, "a radical change in attitude and outlook of the total man (appetite, sense, *and* reason) as a necessary prelude to the genuine reformation and perfection of his nature."[43]

The implications of Augustine's theology of grace were necessarily political because classical philosophy had been political in nature. Cochrane rightly points out, "If Plato is right in what he has to say about the nature and conditions of perfectibility, then obviously the question resolves itself into one of politics, i.e., it is a question of the possibility of redemption from ignorance and error through νομοθεσία, legislation or (in the terminology to be employed by Christianity) through 'law.'"[44]

Accordingly, Cochrane's third lecture, "The Imperfection of Politics," returns him again to the limits of politics. Such repetition is necessary because of the profound claims put forward by the Greeks and Romans. Cochrane writes, "The Roman experiment emerges as the last and greatest effort of creative politics to implement those ideals of liberty, security and prosperity projected by the Hellenic genius into the consciousness of antiquity. And, from this standpoint, the Roman order claimed to provide a complete and final solution to the problem of power in human life."[45] The Roman order had completely accepted the "logic of creative politics" in its view of virtue and fate translated into the terms of art and nature. Cochrane writes that Roman thought assumed "that what 'nature' did was to supply

40. See below, 39.
41. See below, 44.
42. See below, 45.
43. See below, 52.
44. See below, 54.
45. See below, 68.

to man the raw materials (in Augustinian terminology a pure *possibilitas* or potentiality) for τελείωσις or *perfectio*; [further] it implied that the responsibility and privilege of man was, on the basis of this pure *possibilitas* or potentiality, to 'complete' his nature by means of arts or techniques devised by himself."[46] Cochrane elaborates on the implications of this view, "Secular perversity thus uncritically assumed that, if indeed there existed some 'flaw' or 'fault' operating to prevent the fulfillment of the human potential, the place to look for such a fault was in 'nature' (envisaged as the sphere of incompletion) when, in point of fact, the fault was not in 'nature,' but in the construction placed upon it by the human mind. To make this assumption was to suppose that man begins, so to speak, where nature leaves off; that the human task is to perfect the imperfection of nature's handiwork. In other words, it is idolatry in its most subtle and seductive manifestation, the worship by man of himself."[47]

In this regard it is helpful to see Augustine's preface to the *City of God* in a fresh light. Augustine is certainly not being superficially pious when he references James's quotation of Proverbs 3:34, "God resists the proud, but to the humble he giveth grace."[48] This reference explicitly connects Cochrane's themes of limited politics and the political possibilities of grace. As Cochrane explains, "Christianity is in full accord with classicism in defining the criterion of perfection as 'security.' In this connection it is important to note that the word *securitas*, as it is used by both parties to the controversy, indicates a condition of the spirit, 'freedom from care or anxiety' (*se* + *cura*; *se* being privative), in the absence of which it is agreed that genuine perfection is unthinkable. The question thus arises: how is such perfection to be attained? To this question Christian faith had, of course, its answer, an answer which was determined by its acceptance of Christ as the Messiah, and by the consequent assurance of perfect felicity in the 'life to come.'"[49] In contrast to secular perversity, "Christian faith perceives that the task of mankind is emphatically not one of 'creation,' as secularism in its arrogance has supposed, but rather one of 'construction,' in humble and patient submission to divine will. The prerequisite to this task must therefore be a complete reversal of the attitude characteristic of secularism, an acknowledgement that the *sine qua non* for genuine perfection must be a rebirth, renewal or renovation of the human spirit."[50]

46. See below, 70.
47. See below, 75.
48. Jas 4:6.
49. See below, 79.
50. See below, 78.

Cochrane's culminating lecture is titled "Personality and History." This movement to the individual in relation to history was a movement that Cochrane also signaled years earlier in *Christianity and Classical Culture*. While Greco-Roman thought had stalled at an insurmountable obstacle between what individuals could accomplish through their own virtue in relation to the determinism of fate in history and nature, Christianity presented a new vision of the possibilities of human life. In *Christianity and Classical Culture*, Cochrane outlined the importance of Christianity's view of personality first in its freedom from the consequences of classical thought, "The integration of personality . . . means, in the first place, emancipation from erroneous and muddled conclusions such as must inevitably result from the acceptance of a vicious starting-point. It thus levels ideological stone walls which, so long as they stand, constitute an insurmountable obstacle to truth . . . it makes possible, but in a significantly new sense, the classical ideals of freedom and detachment [from fate]."[51] The Christian insight into personality subsumed the classical search for peace, but directed it along different lines. "It points to a realization of the classical ideal of peace, not through the mortification of the flesh but through the regeneration of the flesh. And finally, in the achievement of freedom and peace, it discovers the meaning of true felicity, the sovereign good, so far at least as this may be attained under the conditions of morality. This it does by revealing a vision of personality which is not truncated at any point and in which self-consciousness has at last ceased to be the blight of life."[52]

In his final lecture at Yale, Cochrane carries his reflections on Christianity and personality into their "applicability to the interpretation of history."[53] Classical history had attempted to abstract from history the important aspects from the trivial and meaningless, and in doing so had drawn upon the perfection of humanity that classicism had presented. Christianity's transformed conception of human perfection, therefore, did not just change the view of politics, but also changed the view of history. "There is not and cannot be any finality to human history, no city of refuge in which historical man may rediscover the security of his lost Eden and protect himself from the impact of change and novelty; but the life of historical man is in very truth a *peregrinatio*, pilgrimage or trek through the wilderness, a trek which must continue until, as Christianity puts it, the consummation of all things. To such an experience and such a history mankind is committed by the law of his being as a free agent. By the selfsame law of his human

---

51. Cochrane, *Christianity and Classical Culture*, 502.
52. Ibid.
53. See below, 84.

freedom he is, indeed, in a position to reject his destiny, but, in so doing, he merely stultifies himself and his humanity, and deliberately paves the way for his own destruction."[54] Cochrane's judgment drawn from Augustine applies not only to the late antique period, but also to the authoritarian, communist, and fascist governments of Cochrane's day and to the distractions of our own age.

The rejection of limited, but true human freedom for an illusionary vision of human perfection through human means is not simply a mistake, but a conscious decision that can only be explained by reference to the sin of pride. Cochrane writes, "In the life of history, secular pride emerges as the antithesis of Christian humility; and on the interplay of these two antithetic principles, both of which are real because they are the expression of real though opposing wills, depends . . . the Augustinian dialectic of history."[55] This opposition was not original to the beginning of human existence, but developed as a result of original sin and its rejection of the "bounds fixed by the Creator as the norm or standard for human nature."[56] Here he demonstrates again the proposition that he stated in *Christianity and Classical Culture* that, "The doctrine of sin and grace marks, in its most acute form, the breach between Classicism and Christianity."[57] The development of new concepts, however, did not immediately dispense with older competing notions, and classicism and Christianity continued to struggle at least until the time of Augustine.

Augustine's insistence on Christianity's break from classical thought is evidenced, according to Cochrane, by his conflicts with both the Manicheans and the Pelagians.

> The fundamental truth to which Augustine clung so tenaciously throughout the storms of controversy was that of moral freedom and responsibility, otherwise of personality expressing itself through the autonomous self-determination of will. And from this standpoint the error of Manichaeism was that it annihilated personality by resolving the human impulse to sin into terms of an irresistible physical or physiological necessity from which there was thus not the remotest possibility of escape. On the other hand, as against the Pelagians, Augustine argued with equal insistence that their particular version of secular error . . . was equally fatal to the Christian concept of personality. For Pelagius contended that vice was nothing but an error of

54. See below, 94.
55. See below, 94.
56. See below, 94.
57. Cochrane, *Christianity and Classical Culture*, 498.

judgment, and this implied that it was purely 'personal' or individual, since only individuals enjoy the capacity of forming judgments, whether right or wrong.[58]

Where both Manicheans and Pelagians had claimed to be protecting Christianity from error or laxity in its development of original sin, Augustine argued against both because they actually attempted to salvage classicism from the departure of Christianity's new philosophy. In trying to work against the negative vision of Augustine's view of sin, his opponents missed how they impaired the good news of grace. As Cochrane notes, "The sentence of death thus passed on human life is not unconditional."[59] Just as the denial of original sin has consequences for the meaning of grace, the exposition of original sin loses its meaning if it does not include the possibility of grace. In the same way that this is true for theology, it is also true for political philosophy.

Politically speaking, it is because of original sin that man's political existence is vitiated, even though human sins also drive the greatest political accomplishments. As Cochrane summarizes towards the end of his final lecture, "[The] passion for freedom and security manifests itself in an unquenchable thirst for power. From this standpoint, the human quest for power is seen for what, in fact, it is, viz., the real *hormé* or dynamic of all secular endeavor, the impulse which serves to explain the most splendid and impressive achievements, as well as the most abject failures of the race. Thus envisaged, the problem of power emerges as the crucial problem of human history."[60] However, humanity is not left in sin, but is offered a "genuine Savior with an efficacious program of fulfillment."[61] Cochrane continues, "However tenacious the grip of sin, it has ultimately no power to hold mankind in bondage; that, in fact, the perfection to which mankind aspires is not an historical impossibility, but, on the contrary, the goal of history itself."[62] Here Cochrane is not falling once again into the errors of the classical period because the perfection offered by Christian grace also includes an understanding of eschatology that keeps humanity in a patient attitude of dependence and waiting.

---

58. See below, 96–97.
59. See below, 100.
60. See below, 100–101.
61. See below, 101.
62. See below, 101.

III

Cochrane suffered a major heart attack shortly after his return from Yale in the Spring of 1945. His obituary for the Royal Society of Canada written by his colleague A.S.P. Woodhouse relies on the medical conceptions of the day in asserting that Cochrane had worked himself to the point of exhaustion in preparing and delivering the Yale lectures and that this induced his heart attack.[63] At our present distance, it is impossible to claim with certainty anything about Cochrane's actual medical condition. Cochrane lingered for some months in a weakened condition after the onset, and there was initially some hope that he would recover at least some strength. The University of Toronto's board of governors granted Cochrane a three-month leave of absence from the university, and we can conclude from Woodhouse's mentioning that Cochrane was considering a new project on Greek jurisprudence in his last days that Cochrane himself may have anticipated at least a partial recovery and continuing ability to write. However, this was not to be.

A wide section of the North American academic community mourned Cochrane's passing. Academic obituaries appeared in journals such as *The Canadian Journal of Economics and Political Science*, *Phoenix*, *The Classical Journal*, and the *Proceedings of the Royal Society of Canada*. The notices of his death are consistent in their regard for the accomplishments of his scholarly career and their sense of the great loss that scholarship had suffered from Cochrane's early demise. His fellow academics also shared the hope that his occasional works would be collected and published posthumously, a hope that, though only now realized, remains justified in its estimate of his contribution and worth.

Over seventy-five years after its initial publication, *Christianity and Classical Culture* remains in print, and has been translated into multiple languages. This publication record is particularly amazing given the relatively short shelf life of most modern works of history and deserves some comment as well as defense. Historical scholarship is often the product of specialized concern to develop some identified trend within a given time period. Such works are quickly dated when the academic community moves beyond this particular theme. If this is the case, why has Cochrane's work commanded interest over a sustained period? The strength of Cochrane's work is its suggestive nature. In fact, this is no new revelation; contemporary reviews of *Christianity and Classical Culture* bear this out. Paul Oskar Kristeller's review for *The Journal of Philosophy* criticizes Cochrane for unifying the "entire body of ideas" of the various philosophic and rhetorical

---

63. Woodhouse, "Charles Norris Cochrane, 1889–1945," 84.

schools in the classical world under the overarching rubric of "classicism."[64] Kristeller, however, also notes that Cochrane's methodology is based on his view of the philosophical, political, and social problems of his day and his endorsement of what we may call Christian anthropology.[65] It is here that Cochrane is at his strongest, despite the era of his investigation and focus.

Cochrane did not survive to witness the transition from the end of World War II to the Cold War, the collapse of the Soviet Union that followed, or the rise of radical extremism that concerns us today. Nonetheless, the questions that animated his study still remain relevant because he is concerned with the relationship of Christianity to culture, whether ancient or modern. His colleague in classics, M. D. C. Tait, noted of Cochrane, "He had nothing but contempt for the type of research which consists in the mere amassing of insignificant facts. Always he sought some principle of understanding, some unifying point of view by which the manifold data under his observation were rendered intelligible and significant. One might disagree with his synthesis, but a synthesis he always provided, and an illuminating one."[66] Here Cochrane fits alongside his Canadian contemporary and friend, Harold Innis, in using the medium of historical investigation to make suggestive comments about the contemporary world. However, Cochrane's presentation is nuanced and sophisticated enough that it is not marred by the years that have elapsed since its writing.

Cochrane's work has also survived the passage of time better than most because of its monumental effort to bring together material from the various scholarly disciplines that are commonly held apart by contemporary scholarship. Despite being a classicist, Cochrane's work is not philology and naturally stretches into history, philosophy, politics, and theology. The modern compartmentalization within the scholarly discourse did not exist to the same extent for the world of academia in Cochrane's day. While this in some sense bodes well for Cochrane's contribution, it has also hindered continued appreciation of Cochrane's work because it crosses so much different territory that no single field claims it as its own and builds upon his work. The grand scope of his project, however, does serve as entry point for continuing conversations and greater depth in all of these fields. By displaying the connections between history, philosophy, politics, and theology during the transition from the Roman Empire to the early church, Cochrane's broad vision serves both the general reader and the scholar as either a foundation or a channel. Neither the general reader nor the academic scholar is

---

64. Kristeller, Review of *Christianity and Classical Culture*, 578.
65. Ibid., 580.
66. Tait, "Charles Norris Cochrane, 1889–1945," 1–2.

served well by the artificial divisions of the humanities into separate spheres and Cochrane continues to appeal as a counteraction to the limitations of such divisions.

There are many fine biographies and critical accounts of historians and philosophers that serve the two-fold purpose of developing the intellectual history of their respective periods and honoring the position that many scholars have played in the development of their particular fields. Cochrane, however, is incredibly neglected among his contemporaries. This can only be explained in part by his nationality. Canadians pay respect to many other historians, but still neglect Cochrane. This may be partly explained in that, unlike his more famous contemporaries such as A. L. Burt, Harold Innis, Frank Underhill, or George Wrong, Cochrane was not focused on writing Canadian history or philosophy with an immediate eye on the limited scope of Canada's developing position as a nation in its own right. For example, A. B. McKillop notes, "English-Canadian historians in the twentieth century have consistently been moral critics as concerned with telling Canadians how the Canadian past ought to have been or in what direction the future ought to go as with dispassionate historical analysis."[67] While other contemporaries were concerned with Canada and its nascent place in the modern world, Cochrane was focused on the development and continued existence of Western culture. A limited inquiry into Canada seems fairly parochial in light of the great upheavals of the twentieth century, and can only be countenanced on the assumption that since Western civilization survived two world wars and the Cold War that the underlying problems of those great conflicts must certainly have been resolved.

Reading Cochrane today is far more edifying than any of his better-known contemporaries because Cochrane reminds us that our modern world has developed upon a pre-modern foundation that it did not build and we continue to wonder if it can be assured of lasting stability upon such terms. Perhaps no one knew this better than his friend Harold Innis, who, though more prominent in his day than Cochrane, credited Cochrane with influencing his work. Writing an obituary for Cochrane, Innis declares him to have made "the first major Canadian contribution to the intellectual history of the West."[68] Similarly, M. D. C. Tait noted of Cochrane's intellectual achievements, "This would be a matter of pride to Canadians if Canadians generally took pride in such matters."[69] Since Canadians have not reminded the world of Cochrane's contribution to the understanding of Western

---

67. McKillop, *Disciplined Intelligence*, 231.
68. Innis, "Obituaries: Charles Norris Cochrane, 1889–1945," 96.
69. Tait, "Charles Norris Cochrane, 1889–1945," 1.

culture, it remains for outsiders to take up the work. Reviving Cochrane's legacy, however, is not a project for national patriotism, but for a broader audience that must wrestle with Augustine and the political implications of his inquiry into the foundations of Western culture that we take for granted in the modern world.

Since the midpoint of the last century, there has been a discernable growth in the popularity and weight of Augustinian studies. Seminal thinkers as diverse as Hannah Arendt,[70] Albert Camus,[71] and Joseph Ratzinger[72] devoted extended study to Augustine during their formative years. This is no doubt a response to the existential anxiety generated by the confrontation of the totalitarian crisis of the last century. Through the recovery of his arguments against what Cochrane called creative politics, Augustine was a valuable resource in the fight against ideological and utopian dreams that sought to coerce reality through violent political means during this period. This valuable insight, however, should not over-shadow the rest of Augustine's corpus or even the broader context within which his argument against creative politics was formulated. It is a shame that Cochrane's legacy as an Augustinian thinker has been diminished and neglected since his death because Cochrane provides a rich picture of Augustine. Ironically, in so far as Cochrane is still remembered today, it is almost exclusively for the elucidation of creative politics, and never for the glimpses of grace in politics that he develops from Augustine.

In order to revive Cochrane's Augustinian legacy, we must remember that Augustine provides both a negative message against the pretensions of creative politics, and also a positive message about human action in this life. As Cochrane explains, Augustine's message is not strictly negative; and, in fact, he provides a path to affirm much of the good humanity has always sought politically. Remember again Cochrane's claim from *Christianity and Classical Culture*:

> The choice for man, as Augustine sees it, does not so much lie between science and superstition as between two kinds of faith, the one salutary, the other destructive, the one making for fulfillment, the other for frustration. Of these alternative faiths, the former saves by illuminating experience and giving it value in terms of an absolute standard of truth, beauty, and goodness. To pledge allegiance to this faith is thus to experience no sense of limitation, but only a feeling of enhanced freedom and power.

---

70. Arendt, *Love and Saint Augustine*.
71. Camus, *Christian Metaphysics and Neoplatonism*.
72. Ratzinger, *Volk und Haus Gottes in Augustins Lehre von der Kirche*.

> The latter may well be described as Promethean. Based as it is on a distorted or partial apprehension of ultimate reality, its character is necessarily felt as oppressive; and the sense of oppression bears its inevitable fruits in defiance and revolt to be followed by confusion, defeat, and despair.[73]

Since the end of the Cold War the conflicts of ideology have not seemed as pressing in our modern politics, and Augustine has lost some of his appeal, but we cannot forget that less virulent forms of ideology still inhabit our political sphere and still persist in "defiance and revolt" that lead to "confusion, defeat, and despair."

Cochrane's Augustinianism reminds us that we should not only speak against the errors of politics, but also speak to the goods that are realizable through human will that acknowledges its limits and the order of created existence. In so far as today's politics often turns to the rhetoric of "hope and change," simply relying on Augustine's negative critique will not be widely efficacious. However, attempting to develop the possibilities of politics without addressing Augustine's foundational position risks leaving him forever in an opposing stance. It is imperative to root the development of a positive vision for politics with Augustine because of his unique position as the original expositor of the two-cities model, which continues to set the boundaries of Christian political discourse. Christian thinkers other than Augustine can open themselves to his foundational critique if they seek to reformulate Christianity's traditional understanding of political action without addressing the concepts Augustine first elucidated. From the Christian standpoint, Augustine's criticism of earthly politics cannot be disproved, so it remains to use Augustine's own work to provide the needed nuance for further development. Cochrane's exposition of Augustine serves both the traditional function of limiting political projects because the division between the two cities remains intact, but Cochrane also suggests how Augustinian theology offers continuing resources to political theory by developing the political implications of Augustine's doctrines of grace.

---

73. Cochrane, *Christianity and Classical Culture*, 456.

I

Augustine and the Problem of Power

The Nathaniel William Taylor Lectures,
Yale Divinity School, April 3–5, 1945

The Augustinian Prognostic[1]

THE PROBLEM OF POWER is one of perennial interest and importance in human life, but at no period in history has it presented itself with greater urgency and insistence than in the days of St. Augustine. For, during his manhood, the Empire, which for so many centuries had guarded the frontiers of organized society, was tottering to its fall. Everywhere there were signs of disintegration and decay, and the world appeared to be headed for one of those periodic cataclysms such as had been envisaged by Plato in the *Laws*—a cataclysm from which, as he put it, a mere fraction of the human race was destined to survive, condemned to eke out a miserable existence as hunters and herdsmen until, with the slow multiplication of population and the rediscovery of the arts, the forms and practices of "political" or civilized life should eventually be renewed.[2]

In the year 410 the threat to civilization was signalized by an event which shook the Roman world to its foundations. This was, of course, the occupation of the Eternal City itself by Alaric and his Goths. For the first time in precisely eight hundred years, i.e., since the Gallic raid under Brennus in

---

1. [Charles Norris Cochrane, "The Augustinian Prognostic," Charles Norris Cochrane Fonds. University of Toronto Archives, B2003-0011/006 (16).]

2. Plato, *The Laws*, 677.

390 BC, the proud capital, "venerable mother," as the poets called her, "of civilization and law," lay helpless at the feet of a barbarian conqueror. The sack which followed was attended by all the usual circumstances of horror and destruction; and it served to provoke a vast flight of the civil population from Italy to places of refuge across the Mediterranean.

The rape of the Eternal City was no isolated incident. On the contrary, it was but the culmination of a long series of defeats and disasters which had marked the declining fortunes of *Romanitas* since the fatal battle of Adrianople, some thirty years before. Adrianople has been described as the "second Cannae" of the empire. But this time, despite the valiant efforts of the Emperor Valentinian and Theodosius, there was to be no real recovery for Rome. Four years or more before the Gothic occupation of the city, the few legionary formations which remained to garrison Britain and the Germanies had been withdrawn to Northern Italy for the protection of the peninsula. The consequences were soon to be apparent. On New Year's Eve of the year 406, a mixed horde of Teutonic warriors swarmed across the ice of the undefended Rhine, to establish themselves permanently and without more than local resistance in the provinces of Gaul. But even worse was in store. Spoliation of the ancient capital, itself crammed with the rich spoils of secular conquest, was to be followed within less than two decades by the loss of Spain and Africa, and in 430 Augustine himself was to perish during the Vandal siege of Hippo Regius, his episcopal seat, while ministering to the spiritual needs of the defending imperial troops. The picture thus presented throughout the West was that of a vast and complex society in rapid dissolution. On every hand the lights of civilization were flickering out, and nothing that human ingenuity could accomplish by way of reform or reconstruction seemed adequate to restore the imperial power.

The shock caused by such a train of uninterrupted calamity was universal and profound. As early as 396, the year following the death of Theodosius, St. Jerome, from his monastic retreat at Bethlehem, gave utterance to a sense of distress and apprehension such as must have been experience by all who permitted themselves to reflect on the position and prospect of the Empire. "The mind shudders," he declares, "to contemplate the havoc of our time. For the last twenty years, the blood of Romans has drenched the lands between Constantinople and the Julian Alps, where countless numbers of ferocious barbarians spread devastation and death . . . The bodies of freemen and nobles, of matrons and maidens have become the prey of lust. Bishops are imprisoned; churches plundered; horses stabled at the altars of Christ; the bones of martyrs are flung out of their coffins . . . Everywhere sorrow, everywhere lamentation; everywhere the shadow of death."[3]

3. Jerome, *Epistle* 60.16.

The emotions thus excited manifested themselves in diverse ways. On the one hand, they served to engender in many a mood of lassitude, apathy and cynicism, the consequence of a situation felt to be well-nigh desperate. *Ridens mortua est*, "the Roman world went laughing to her doom." Like all generalizations, this familiar aphorism contains no doubt an element of exaggeration, yet it will suffice to describe the behavior of all who abandoned themselves to this mood. Among others, the tendency was to provoke a violent resurgence of *religio*, that powerful and sinister impulse of the pagan mind for the workings of which there is ample evidence to be found in the literary and archaeological remains of classical antiquity. Pagan *religio* found expression *inter alia* in what St. Augustine calls "unusually virulent attacks" upon the Christian faith and its adherents, attacks in which the misfortunes that had overtaken the empire were attributed to the anger of the offended pagan deities at the prohibition recently imposed by Theodosius on their cults.

To add to the perplexity of the situation, so far at least as thoughtful Christians were concerned, there was the fact that the empire thus apparently doomed to extinction was itself formally and officially Christian. This position had been reached by a series of imperial measures beginning in A.D. 313 with the Protocol of Milan and culminating in the revolutionary legislation of the Theodosian house for the suppression of paganism and heresy. By the former, Constantine and Licinius had broken with the Roman past and accorded to Christianity the status and privileges of a *religio licita* or "licensed cult," thereby inaugurating the new order to be extravagantly hailed by Eusebius and other politically-minded ecclesiastics of the day as the "millennial kingdom." By the latter, Theodosius had made the formal profession of Trinitarianism the prerequisite to imperial citizenship, thus completing the structure of a wholly novel type of polity, the "orthodox state." Thenceforth, the full resources of the imperial power had been invoked to extirpate all manifestations of dissent, and various devices of legal pressure, ranging from civil excommunication with the loss of property rights to the most atrocious forms of capital punishment, such as burning alive, or consignment to beasts, were used in a concerted and systematic attempt to enforce spiritual conformity. This last desperate expedient of statecraft proved, however, to be futile. Its failure marked the final eclipse of hopes cherished during the century which had elapsed since the first Christian emperor had taken the *Labarum* as his personal standard and assumed the motto, *hoc signo vinces*.

The Roman Empire was the most extensive, most enduring and, measured by the standard of its economic, social and cultural achievement, unquestionably the most beneficent power-structure thus far erected by human hands, the instrument whereby, as Augustine puts it, "it had pleased God to subdue the whole world and, by drawing it into a single community united in the bond of common interest and law (*in unam societatem rei publicae et legum*) to pacify it far and wide."[4] Its collapse was thus an occasion for reflection and, more particularly, because of the historical situation to which I have just alluded, a challenge to Christian thought. Nor was this challenge to be evaded, since it was notorious that the faith of many professing Christians had been gravely shaken by the events of the time. It was, indeed, precisely to such persons that Augustine addressed himself, a task to which he set his hand in the *De Civitate Dei*.

In considering (as I proposed to do in these lectures) the argument of the *De Civitate Dei*, we may begin by noting that, as Augustine freely admits, the Roman Empire had implemented, so far as was possible in view of the intellectual and moral resources at its command, the legitimate demands of secular order or peace (*pax terrena*). Augustine does, indeed, permit himself a certain degree of misgiving as to the ethics of Roman empire-building. "Did the Romans" he asks, as though to discount their secular effort of world-conquest and world-organization, "do any real harm to the peoples they subjected to their sway, apart, that is, from the slaughter which resulted from their wars? Could the same object have been attained by peaceful agreement (*concorditer*), it would have been even more gratifying." "But in that case," he grimly observes, "there would have been none of the glory of conquest."[5] On the other hand, he entertained no doubt whatever as to the efficacy of Roman methods, "the arts," as he puts it, "by which, as though along a direct path, the Romans have climbed to honor, empire and glory, by which they have earned regard throughout the earth and have imposed the law of their empire upon many nations, until today they are glorified in the history and literature of virtually every people."[6]

We may go further and assert that Augustine does not deny or minimize the genuine value of Roman achievements in the establishment and maintenance of a secular world order. "The really significant point," he declares, "for the generosity and humanity of which the world has reason to be thankful, is that, when once Mars and Bellona had played their part, all who belonged to the empire were taken into full association with it and granted citizenship, so that what had once been the privilege of a few became in the end a possession common to all."[7] And, with respect to political power in general, "humanly speaking," he adds, "there can be no greater good fortune

---

4. Augustine, *City of God*, 18.22.
5. Ibid., 5.17.
6. Ibid., 5.15.
7. Ibid., 5.17.

than this that, through the mercy of God, those who are endowed with true piety, provided they have the necessary competence, should exercise authority over their fellows."[8]

Augustine was most emphatically no Christian "anarchist" or "theocrat;" men being what they are, he never supposed that the forms and procedures normal to organized society could be dispensed with. As he observed in a familiar passage from the *Letters*: "Clearly these institutions have not been devised in vain, the authority of the sovereign, the sword of the law, the hooks of the executioner, the might of the armed forces, the discipline of the landed proprietor, even the strictness of the good *pater familias* in his household. Each and all these have their own modalities, their own causes, their own justification in reason and utility. And, when such agencies are respected, the dispositions of evil men are kept in check, so that the good may live more tranquilly among them."[9]

This being so, we may dismiss as merely malicious the insinuation of Gibbon that "while professedly justifying the ways of Providence in the destruction of Roman greatness, Augustine celebrates with peculiar satisfaction this memorable triumph of Christ."[10] True indeed that, in his references to secular order, Augustine seems on occasion to speak the language, if not of active hostility, at any rate of utter indifference; as when, for example, he asks, "with respect to the life of mortal man, limited as it is to a few brief days, what difference does it make under what regime he lives, provided the authorities do not compel him to act in a manner contrary to faith and morals?"[11] It should, however, be remembered that to indict the spirit of secular order is not necessarily to proclaim oneself the enemy of organized society; it is merely to expose the vanity of its pretensions. And the vanity of Roman pretensions, as Augustine saw them, may be stated in a word; it was to have mistaken relatives for absolutes, to have put forward its finite, partial, "man-made" insights and aspirations as though they were the truths of God. In this respect, indeed, the imperial city had been the chief of sinners, and her sin was epitomized in the formula *aeternitas populi Romani*, the claim to eternity made on behalf of the Roman people. For in this claim there was implicit the assumption that the Romans had solved, once and for all, the problem of human relationships, and that the solution was embodied in the structure and objectives of imperial society in accordance with the celebrated maxim of the Roman jurists, *suum cuique reddere*, "render to each man his due."

8. Ibid., 5.19.
9. Augustine, *Epistle*, 153.16.
10. Gibbon, *Decline and Fall*, 2:984.
11. Augustine, *City of God*, 5.17.

It is, however, precisely this assumption which Augustine is concerned to repudiate. "Wretched is the people," he declares, "which is alienated from the justice of God. Yet even they enjoy a kind of order of their own, an order which is not to be despised, although indeed they will not maintain it in the end, seeing that they have failed to utilize it properly before the end. It is, nevertheless, to our interest also that they should maintain it provisionally in this life; because, so long as the two societies are intermingled, we also utilize the order of Babylon, from which indeed the people of God are set free by faith (and so, in principle), save that meanwhile they sojourn therein like resident-aliens."[12]

From this position of relative, if not absolute, detachment Augustine propounded what he felt to be the real question raised by the grandeur and decadence of imperial Rome. That question, as he puts it, is why God, who has the power to bestow goods of the kind human beings may possess even though they themselves fall short of (true) goodness and so of (true) felicity, should have willed that the Roman Empire be so vast and so long."[13] In other words, his problem was to discover the hidden springs alike of Roman strength and Roman weakness, in the light of which it might fairly be said of the Romans, that they had no reason to complain of the justice of the one supreme and just God; *they had, in fact, received their reward.*[14]

The thought just expressed is further developed in a subsequent passage:

> In an empire so extensive and so enduring, and in the distinction conferred upon it through the virtues of so many of its sons, the Romans for their part have reaped the reward of their consistent purpose. At the same time, they have provided us with the exemplar we need to warn us that, should we in our battle for the society of God fail to manifest the qualities shown by them on behalf of the terrestrial society, we ought to be stricken with shame . . . For while, to quote from the Apostle (Romans 8:18), *the sufferings of this present time are not to be compared with the glory destined to be revealed in us*, nevertheless, by every criterion of strictly human and temporal glory, their life has been adjudge to be worthy enough.[15]

Thus far, our main concern has been to dispose of possible misconceptions with respect to Augustine's attitude toward the Roman Empire, such

12. Ibid., 19.26.
13. Ibid., 5. Preface.
14. Ibid., 5.15.
15. Ibid., 5.18.

as might interfere with a correct appreciation of his argument in the *De Civitate Dei*. By doing so, I hope we have cleared the ground for a further investigation into the argument. The interest of such an investigation is, as I see it, two-fold. In the first place, it helps to throw light on the resources (moral and intellectual) with which Augustinian Christianity addressed itself to problems originating in the social order: in other words, to indicate something of the social significance of the Evangel as it presented itself to the mind of the early fifth century. But this, in itself, is far from exhausting the meaning and value of Augustine's achievement. For the issues raised by the collapse of Roman order remain to this day of vital importance; what they involve is nothing less than a question of the nature and sources of genuine power in human life. Accordingly, in undertaking to explore those issues, Augustine in effect addressed himself not only to his own generation, but to posterity as well; and not least, perhaps, to our own distracted age. And what he sought to put forward for the consideration of his readers was, we suggest, the preface to an original and distinctively Christian philosophy of power.

This is not to suggest (as might be supposed) that what is sometimes called the message of ancient wisdom, whether classical or Christian, may be taken to provide a ready-made solution for historical problems which are more or less specific to the twentieth century. Indeed, we need no authority beyond that of Augustine himself for rejecting the notion that, in the sense just indicated, there is and can be any historical "recurrence" or "return." "Christ," he assures us, "died once and for all for our sins." Accordingly, it is no part of my intention to elaborate a comparison between the events which have shaken the foundations of modern society and those which marked the decline and fall of ancient Rome, and to palm this off as a significant contribution to understanding. But it is one thing to recognize that historical events, considered as such, are each and every one unique in its time and circumstances; quite another to imagine, with more extreme exponents of historical relativism, that the experience of those events recorded in contemporary literature and art, is devoid of meaning for future generations; since it is, in fact, precisely this experience which raises events from the plane of brute fact and gives them the character of history. To recover and re-present that experience, so far as may be possible in view of the obvious barriers to understanding, is the task of historical investigation. This must be my excuse for embarking on a discussion of issues that were debated in the Roman world more than fifteen hundred years ago, in the last decades of the Western Empire.

What we may venture to call the Augustinian prognosis of power claimed to be and—in form at least—really is, both critical and constructive.

It is this fact which determines the general direction and scope of the argument in the *De Civitate Dei*. The immediate purpose of Augustine, as he himself informs us, was "to defend the faith against the blasphemies and errors of those who contended that the origin and diffusion of current evils was a direct consequence of the ban imposed on the official cults."[16] This was paganism on what Augustine designates as the vulgar or popular level, i.e., as it had been enshrined in the *ius divinum* or *constitutio religionum*, the attempt to consecrate the material, moral and intellectual values of secular life conventional to the classical *polis*. As such, he points out, it rests upon the essentially superficial assumption that the value of religion is primarily economic or utilitarian, i.e., that it somehow serves to guarantee temporal or worldly success. But, as he argues, this assumption, however congenial to the secular mentality (whether ostensibly Christian or pagan) does not find the slightest warrant in history or experience. On the contrary, the evidence suggests that, in the hidden wisdom of his omnipotence, God bestows the elements of secular prosperity alike on the just and the unjust; and we can only suppose that He does so in order that we should learn not to overvalue temporal felicity.[17] It is with this thought in mind that Augustine denounces the pragmatism of conventional secular ethics; winding up with a criticism of the Emperors Constantine and Theodosius in the so-called Mirror of Princes with which he concludes the first section of his work.[18]

But what of the rationalizations (*interpretationes physicae*) which, as Augustine says, underlay the practice of secularism and with which philosophy sought, "under color of a loftier teaching, to whitewash the ugliness of secular error?"[19] To deal with these was, as he recognized, a much more arduous and hazardous enterprise. For what it involved was nothing less than the refutation of "every error perpetrated by every philosopher," a task which, within any reasonable limits, was quite impossible. He therefore proposed to confine his attention to such opinions as bore directly on "theology" or, as we should say, metaphysics; in other words, to the efforts of philosophic paganism to relate experience to some "divine center," a cosmic principle of order and value in terms of which it might be rationalized and justified.[20]

It is important to notice the limitations of the program thus enunciated by Augustine, since this is bound to affect our judgment regarding

16. Augustine, *Retractations*, 2.43.
17. Ibid., 2.23.
18. Books 1–5, esp. 5.24–25.
19. Ibid., 7.5.
20. Ibid., 8.1.

the effectiveness of his polemic on both the critical and constructive levels. What it means is that his attention was directed primarily to questions of first principle, such, e.g., as the Platonic Idea of the Good, or the Peripatetic and Stoic concept of nature, and the claims put forward on behalf of them as possible principles of integration for the individual and the community. Theoretically, the proposed limitations do not preclude a consideration of secondary factors, for example, the *tributaria sollicitudo* or "fiscal grief" referred to by Orosius and by him put forward as one of the chief causes making for the disintegration of Greco-Roman society.[21] But what it does most emphatically suggest is that such factors have, and can have, significance only in so far as they are referred to principles which comprehend much more than any mere question of economics, considered in the abstract and without reference to its character as an ingredient in the determinations of what Augustine calls "the total man." For while, indeed, as he remarks, the maxim "buy cheap and sell dear" (*vili emere, caro vendere*) may well be accepted as a formula to describe and account for the wealth of individuals and peoples, its usefulness in that regard is qualified by its relevance to criteria of value which are not necessarily or exclusively those of "economic" or, indeed, of "political" man.[22]

The importance of these considerations, as they affect the argument of St. Augustine, will be readily apparent. His concern, as an exponent of Christian wisdom, is not so much with the positive findings of classical *scientia*, as with the presuppositions, whether explicit or implicit, which underlay them; in other words, with the fundamental postulates upon which rested the thinking of classicism in relation to the great issues of contemporary experience and which determined its interpretation of those issues. To those who have been nourished on the conventions of modern historiography, Augustine's position may come with something of a shock, and they may be inclined to dismiss it out of hand, as "a theological straight-jacket" which takes all meaning out of history. I need hardly comment on the intellectual arrogance concealed in such an attitude. It may be challenged as nothing but the reflection of a prejudice which has survived from the seventeenth century, a prejudice in favor of methods of enquiry indigenous to the field of natural philosophy or science and subsequently applied, with indifferent success, to the study of human nature and human history. On the other hand, it is possible to argue, with a distinguished modern writer, "All historical judgments are based upon an explicit or implicit assumption about the character of history itself; and there can be no judgment about the character

---

21. Orosius, *Against the Pagans*, 7.41.7.
22. Augustine, *On the Trinity*, 13.3.6.

of history which does not rest upon a further assumption about the relation of history to eternity."²³ From this point of view, the question is not whether we are to approach history without presuppositions or preconceptions, but rather what presuppositions and preconceptions it may be legitimate and profitable to entertain. To recognize the truth of this proposition is to take the first step toward a sympathetic and intelligent appreciation of Augustine, who is thus to be seriously regarded as the earliest, but by no means least considerable, of the long line of thinkers, ancient and modern, who have set themselves to investigate the decline and fall.

Augustine's position was, no doubt, imposed upon him largely by the exigencies of the situation with which he was confronted. For if he was to face and overcome the challenge of classical practice and classical theory, it was necessary for him to meet classicism on its own ground. And that ground was, as I have already stated, "theological." But since he himself was (at least to begin with) a characteristic product of classical life and discipline, with all that this implies, there is not the slightest reason to suppose that he would have been under temptation to do otherwise, even if this had been historically possible. We may therefore assume (as the text of the *De Civitate Dei* suggests) that the main interest of Augustine as a controversialist was in what may be called the classical idea of the commonwealth, or rather in its claim to be a means, indeed (as at least one eminent classical authority had maintained) the only possible means to τελείωσις or *perfectio*, a complete fulfillment of the human potential for development. Over against the pretensions of the classical commonwealth it was the task of Augustine, as a Christian, to set the alternative program proposed by Christianity. And his point of departure was, no doubt, the so-called Christian counsel of perfection, put forward by the Master himself in the injunction, *Be ye perfect, even as your Heavenly Father is perfect*,²⁴ together with the promise of illumination and power held out to the faithful. But for a fuller understanding of the nature and conditions of perfection, as these were set forth in the Evangel, Augustine drew upon the general body of Christian thought, especially perhaps as it had been expounded by St. Paul in his Epistles to the Romans and the Galatians. Certainly, his references to the Apostle are endless; the anti-Pelagian treatises, in particular, are little more than a commentary on various Pauline texts.

To accept the Pauline version of Christian doctrine with respect to human nature and destiny was to adopt concepts of interpretation original to Christianity but largely, if not wholly, foreign to the classical or secular

---

23. Niebuhr, *Nature and Destiny of Man*, 1:146.
24. Matt 5:48; the word used in the Greek text is τέλειος.

mind. The language used to express these concepts was, however, classical Greek or Latin and, thus, historically determined. Hence the possibility of grave misunderstanding as to the precise significance to be attached to old words in the new context of thought. Of this possibility Augustine himself appears to have been fully aware. "Moses said this and passed on," he somewhere remarks, "what did he really mean?" The danger was particularly acute with respect to terminology which had been consecrated by centuries of usage in the ancient philosophic schools. In this, as in other aspects of their activity, the problem of the Christians was to spoil the Egyptians. This involved a radical revision in the use of terms. Some were eliminated as meaningless or misleading except in relation to the discarded ideology of classicism; others as totally incompatible with the premises of Christian faith. Still others were taken over and utilized, but to these a fresh significance was imparted in keeping with the intellectual and moral demands of the Christian order. From this point of view the Christian revolution emerges primarily as a revolution in thought. What it thus involved was, in the first place, a radically new and specifically Christian picture of nature, and of the status therein of mankind. This picture was, of course, derived from the Scriptures, more especially from the Book of Genesis, accepted as a revelation of the creative activity of God and, so, the basis for a distinctive cosmology and anthropology. These, in turn, served as the starting-point for a fresh diagnosis of the human situation, particularly as it related to the ancient classical problem of τελείωσις or *perfectio*. The result was a complete restatement of the problem, as this had been formulated by the classical mind. This included a fresh vision of the end or goal (the classical *summum bonum*), together with a fresh examination of the means by which it was to be attained, and of the conditions which governed its attainment. And, in order to convey precisely what it meant in this connection, Christian thinking invoked its own original concepts of "nature" and "grace."

In the *Retractations*, the last work of his life, Augustine reviews the process by which he gradually emancipated himself from the vestiges of classical ideology, the *damnosa hereditas* of his early life and upbringing, while, at the same time, he strengthened his grip upon the Christian concepts of understanding, and developed their implications both for theory and practice. To trace the process under his guidance would be an interesting and profitable task. But I shall here refer only to one point, since it has a direct bearing on the attitude to be assumed by Christian thinking to the problem of perfection for mankind. This has to do with the classical notion of τύχη, *fortuna*, or, as we should say, contingency or luck.

No one familiar with the literature of classical antiquity will question the importance of the role ascribed to fortune in both popular and philosophic thought. Indeed, it is hardly too much to say that it constituted a crucial difficulty for the classical mind. In a reference to the *De Academicis*, the earliest of his published essays, Augustine takes occasion to regret that, owing to the immaturity of his thinking at the time it was written, he had so often used the word, *fortuna*, not indeed in the sense in which it was personified and worshipped as a god, but in the sense of luck or chance, the contingent, the accidental. Words like *forte, forsan, fortisan, fortasse, fortuito*, he observes, have no place in the vocabulary of a Christian, since to use them is to deny by implication the universal power and providence of the Creator. The conclusion follows: "that which is commonly designated *fortune* is in all probability subject to a hidden order, and we use the word *chance* only with reference to events, the reason and cause of which is not disclosed to us."[25]

To reject the concept of fortune was to identify oneself with a sentiment long since expressed by Cicero when he described it as nothing but a word invented by men to cover up their ignorance. But what was for Cicero a mere *obiter dictum* was with Augustine translated into a matter of fundamental conviction. And what troubled Augustine was not so much the popular tendency of the pagan mind to deify personifications like *Fortuna* and *Felicitas*, as the admission of pagan metaphysics which made such deifications possible. In this connection we may recall the so-called "errant cause" (πλανωμένη αἰτία) of Plato in the *Timaeus*, the "disorderly and discordant motion" of primordial matter, upon which Plato argues, the demiurge seeks, so far as possible (κατὰ δύναμιν) to impose the pattern of the Eternal Ideas—a theory of creative activity yielding a picture of nature as subject to the necessary imperfection of a process of becoming which, however, never attains the status of complete finality (γιγνόμενον μὲν ἀεί, ὂν δὲ οὐδέποτε). Or, to put the point otherwise, Platonic cosmology includes an element of blind necessity, by virtue of which chance and circumstance (τύχη and καιρός) play a part coordinate with that of the gods.

The difficulty of Plato originated no doubt in a characteristic vice of Greek speculation, viz., its inability to establish an intelligible relationship between order and process. Nor did Aristotle, despite his unique gift for analysis, succeed in finding a way of escape from conclusions hardly less fatal to an adequate theory of nature than those of Plato. In this connection, we may perhaps be permitted to repeat the words of an eminent contemporary authority:

> For Aristotle, chance or the contingent is not conceived as a pure indeterminism, that is to say as something which might

25. Augustine, *Retractations*, 1.1.2.

occur without any reason and, in this sense, he does not create a breach in an (otherwise) universal determinism; but it is the incompletely determined; that which, in relation to the efficient cause, is accidental, because it has not been produced by the efficient cause with a view to any end, or because it is not the end for the sake of which the efficient cause acts. The fortuitous then, in nature, is that which has no end.[26]

Aristotle's recognition of a metaphysical contingency is the direct and inevitable outcome of his notion of the Deity as Prime Mover, and of the relation between the Prime Mover and the cosmos. But for Augustine, in the light of a revelation whereby God was disclosed as a genuine creator, creating *ex nihilo*, there was no need to accept any such conclusion. To return once more to my authority:

> Nothing which occurs escapes Divine providence; even matter, since it is created, cannot introduce into the cosmos an element of blind necessity, nor play the role of accidental cause which it played in the uncreated world of Aristotle.[27]

But how, it may be asked, do these considerations, interesting and important as they may be in themselves, bear on the question of the Augustinian prognostic, i.e. the concepts of interpretation which Augustine employs? And even if it were true, as has been asserted,[28] that the disease of pagan philosophy was metaphysical, and further that this disease of pagan metaphysics meant death to pagan civilization, in what sense could it properly be maintained that Christian thinking offered to humanity the promise of a new and more abundant life? These are precisely the questions with which I shall try to deal in the present course. Here I wish merely to suggest that one result of accepting Christian faith was to bring about a radical change in perspective. In the light of that faith, it became evident that the problem, as it had been posed by classical speculation, was so formulated as to be quite incapable of a satisfactory solution. And for the simple and obvious reason that what philosophy asked for was the impossible, viz., a program of perfection in a radically imperfect world.

Hence, we may infer, the characteristic difficulties of classical *scientia* in its secular effort to work out a doctrine of perfection which would do justice to the legitimate demands of reason and sense. Hence also the atmosphere

---

26. Gilson, *L'Espirit de la Philosophie Mediévale*, 164–65; [Cochrane's translation; see Gilson, *Spirit of Mediaeval Philosophy*, 367].

27. Gilson, *L'Espirit de la Philosophie Mediévale*, 166.

28. Collingwood, *Essay on Metaphysics*, 223–24.

of ineradicable pessimism which cast its blight upon the fairest promise of classical achievement, as well as on its most impressive performance—a pessimism which has often been noted, but seldom adequately explained. In the lectures to come it will be my task to examine certain of the more fundamental difficulties encountered by classical theory (as Augustine saw them) and to expose their fatal consequences for practice. Here I need only remark that, if these difficulties were in fact radical (as he contended), then the only thing for them was a radical cure; no mere palliative was worth a moment's consideration. And such a cure he found in the article of faith, "God created the world." Envisaged in terms of this proposition, the classical antithesis of "body" and "mind," of κόσμος αἰσθητός and κόσμος νοητός, proved to be illusory; and, with this discovery, it was seen that most of the historic ἀπορίαι debated by classicism were mere shadow-boxing, as also were most of its solutions; in other words, that they hardly touched the real problems of human existence, of motion and order, of time and eternity, of nature, man and God.

Positively, the first fruits of Christian doctrine were to be found in a refreshingly novel attitude toward nature. There are many passages scattered throughout the works of Augustine (notably in the *Confessions* and the *De Civitate Dei*) in which he gives expression to the Christian sense of nature as a realm of bodies in orderly motion, each and every one (no matter how huge or how diminutive from the human standpoint) exhibiting the divine principles of number and proportion; the whole, despite its immensity, designed and governed in such a way as to maintain its equilibrium, thereby manifesting the power and glory of a Creator who, as he puts it:

> does not withhold, even from the lowliest of his creatures, its specific power and dominion; who produces the seeds and nourishment of mortals, dry or liquid, which their natures require; who founds and fructifies the earth; who dispenses its fruit alike to man and beast . . . who so administers everything he has created, as to permit it to enjoy and exercise for itself the motions proper to it.[29]

Thus, in a mood which is almost, if not quite, romantic, Augustine envisages nature, neither as chaos nor mechanism, but as a spacious and hospitable abode provided by God for the human spirit. Accordingly, there is nothing for surprise in his warning that, remembering that she is the world of an omnipotent and beneficent creator, we should approach the mysteries of nature in a spirit, not of dogmatism, but of enquiry.[30] In the attitude this

---

29. Augustine, *City of God*, 7.30; cf. Books 11–12 as a whole and, above all, 22.24.
30. Augustine, *Retractations*, 1.18; *non affirmando, sed quarendo tractandum est*.

recommended, it is hardly too much to see an anticipation of all that is finest and best in the spirit of modern experimental science. Certainly it indicates the spirit in which Augustine embarks on one of the great controversy of his life, viz., that with the Manicheans.

This debate, as we may learn from the *Retractations*, was provoked "by the boasting of the Manicheans regarding the false and deceptive abstinence by which they mislead the ignorant, an abstinence which bears no relation whatever to the principles of true Christian asceticism."[31] But the discussion, which thus began as a simple question of ethics, presently expanded to include the broadest issues of metaphysics and cosmology. That it should have taken this course will astonish no one who is acquainted with the *Retractations*. For the basic problem raised by the disputants was soon perceived to be the origin of evil (*unde sit malum*); and, on this question Augustine was at one with orthodox Christian thought when he ascribed moral evil purely and simply to the free self-determination of the human will.[32] The Manicheans, on the other hand, rejected the Christian doctrine of evil and contended that, if it were valid, this would mean that God, as the architect of all natures, was radically at fault. And, in order to avoid this conclusion, they went on to postulate a principle of evil in nature, independent of and coeval with the Creator. By so doing, they introduced into the concept of nature an absolute dichotomy, represented in the imagery of the sect by two cosmic souls or spirits, the one supposed to be a part of God, the other belong to the realm of darkness (*de gente tenebrarum*) which, they held, God never created and which was opposed to him as darkness to light.

As applied in practice, this dualistic version of classical naturalism entailed the most disastrous consequences. Its effect was to subvert *in toto* the notions of freedom and responsibility, to resolve human life into the theater of an endless and indecisive conflict between opposing natural forces, the one good, and the other evil.[33] At the same time, by an equally hypothetical identification of darkness or evil with the life of sense, it promoted a horror and loathing of the body far beyond anything proposed even by the Neo-Platonist Porphyry with his *omne corpus fugiendum est* and, in extreme cases, amounting to sheer insanity. Accordingly, it is no matter for surprise to learn that Manichean asceticism should, on occasion, have stood on its head, finding a relief from its program of unreasonable and excessive repressions (the three "seals" of the head, the heart and the belly) in spasmodic

---

31. Ibid., 1.6.81.

32. Ibid., 1.8; commenting on the *De Libero Arbitrio*.

33. Ibid., 1.14, commenting on the *De Duabus Animis*; cf. 1.6, commenting on *De Moribus Ecclesiae* and 1.15 on *Contra Fortunatum Manicheum*.

outbursts of unbridled lust which it thus sought to justify, so to speak, on homeopathic principles. But, in so doing, it succeeded merely in illustrating the truth of Augustine's maxim that, without correct belief about God, a good life is impossible.[34]

The picture of Manichaeism, as we have it from Augustine, was that of a loudly-advertised rationalism which, notwithstanding its pretensions to certitude, ended in sheer intellectual and moral chaos; and, from this point of view, it presents itself as the *reductio ad absurdum* of classical *scientia*. But how to avoid the conclusion to which Manichean science pointed, viz., that God and Devil ride mankind?—this was the question of practical importance. Two possibilities were open. One was to fall back upon Academic skepticism or suspension of judgment, the method of philosophic doubt. The other was frankly to adjure reason and abandon oneself to the sway of irrational animal impulse. From either of these alternatives Augustine was saved by faith. "Academic doubt," he protests, "is Academic madness."[35] And, as far any of the various forms of irrationalism current in antiquity, to accept them would have been to admit a radical imperfection of the instrument which was wholly incompatible with belief in God as the principle of order in an orderly world. In these conclusions we may discern a practical application of the well-known Augustinian precept: "believe in order that you may understand."

It should further be noted as a conviction from which Augustine never wavered, that the order in which he thus asserted his belief was in no sense incongruous with freedom and responsibility; on the contrary, the absolute sovereignty of God, so far from nullifying the possibility of voluntary self-determination, was its surest guarantee. In defending this characteristically Christian paradox, Augustine took issue with an opinion deeply rooted in the tradition of classicism and, in fact, enjoying an unbroken descent from Homer. The *locus classicus* for the problem, as it presents itself to the poetic imagination, consisted of the Homeric couplet: τοῖος γὰρ νόος ἐστὶν ἐπιχθονίων ἀνθρώπων οἷον ἐπ' ἦμαρ ἄγῃσι πατὴρ ἀνδρῶν τε θεῶν τε,[36] with which may be compared the turn that Seneca gives the same idea, *ducunt volentem fata, nolentem trahunt*.[37] But while, on a question of this kind, refusing to concede any authority to the poets, Augustine thought it necessary to refute this opinion in the form in which it appeared to be endorsed by philosophy. This he did in a passage of the *De Civitate Dei*

---

34. Augustine, *City of God*, 5.10; *male vivitur, si de Deo non bene creditur.*
35. Ibid., 19.18.
36. Homer, *Odyssey*, 18.136–7.
37. Seneca, *Epistle* 107.11.

which recapitulates and reaffirms the substance of his *De Libero Arbitrio*, pronounced by the commentators to be a landmark in the development of his thought.[38]

The problem of liberty and necessity served to create an apparently irreconcilable dilemma for classical humanism. Augustine refers to this dilemma only in its Ciceronian version, although actually it may be traced back in philosophic thought at least as far as Plato, with whom, indeed, it emerges in a singularly acute form. Nor did Plato, for all his intellectual acumen, succeed in resolving the dilemma in question; as may be judged from the fact that, all efforts at a scientific explanation failing, he ultimately had recourse to myth. The myths of the *Gorgias*, the *Phaedo*, the *Politicus* and the so-called "Choice of Lives" at the end of the *Republic* represent a succession of attempts to deal with the difficulty. Mythology, however, served merely to illustrate; it did not dispose of the dilemma, which thus survived to constitute a stumbling-block for scientific thought until Augustine found a way of escaping from the impasse. This he did by challenging the presuppositions upon which scientific thought proceeded; thereby giving a wholly new turn to the problem of human freedom. I shall come back to this point in my next lecture. Meanwhile, I can only record his conviction that, by divine fiat, the human will is so constituted as to be capable of free self-determination and, further, that this capacity for self-determination original to the will is not and cannot possibly be lost, despite the notorious truth that, as a matter of historical record and universal experience, it has in fact been enfeebled and impaired throughout the whole course of secular history. But, in seeking to account for this deterioration in the will of historical man, Augustine refused to resort to mythological "explanations" such as had been proposed by poetry and philosophy. Rejecting every such hypothesis as "fate" and "fortune," "natural necessity," or the "gods," he fell back in the spirit of Christian realism upon the Biblical doctrine of original and actual sin. In the position which he thus adopted we may discern the grounds of the controversy on which he was to embark with Pelagius.

To grasp the significance of the Pelagian controversy, we should understand, to being with, that Pelagius considered himself a perfectly good Christian and, in this regard, he enjoyed the support of many churchmen who found his sentiments impeccable. Indeed, in the heat of his debate with Augustine, he went so far as to denounce the latter as a Manichean. Yet, if we look beneath the surface, we shall, I think, discover that Pelagius was little better than a wolf in the sheep-fold. For, couched though it was in the language traditional to Christianity, his thought was, in reality, cast in the

---

38. Augustine, *City of God*, 5.8–9.

ancient mold of classical humanism and, for this reason, it fairly bristled with terminological pitfalls. And it was for precisely this reason that Augustine deemed it essential to expose him; any failure to do so would, he was convinced, seriously imperil the future of a cause on which depended the hope of the human race. Accordingly, he set himself to oppose the heresies of Pelagianism by throwing the spot-light on the inner meaning of the sentiments which it so plausibly and engagingly expressed.

Of such sentiments we need for the moment consider but two: the one contained in the celebrated Pelagian maxim, "I ought, therefore I can"; the other in the theory of grace according to merit (*gratia secundum merita nostra*). In putting forward these sentiments, Pelagius professed merely to combat a disposition toward moral indolence and laxity on the part of Christians who, relying on the assurance of an all-sufficient grace, were inclined to discount the part played by works in the Christian scheme of perfection. And, on the face of it, the sentiments in question appeared to be innocuous; indeed, in certain respects, wholly admirable. Nevertheless, Augustine was quick to detect in them implications of the most subversive character; behind the former, as he saw it, here lurked the specter of Aristotelian and Stoic self-sufficiency (αὐτεξούσια, αὐτάρκεια); while in the latter he discerned nothing but a pseudo-Christian whitewash for the traditional classical doctrine of ἀρετή or *virtus*, that "strictly human excellence" which, as is generally recognized, underlay the pretensions of the classical commonwealth.

In these circumstances it is not surprising that Augustine should have perceived in the Pelagian movement the demons of civilization emerging once more from their tombs. Nor yet that, in his effort to discount the "virtue" and "self-sufficiency" preached by classical humanism, he should have stated in such unequivocal terms as he did the prerogative claims of divine grace.

The Pelagian controversy brought to a focus all the fundamental issues which divided the classical from the Christian apparatus of thought. Its implications were thus profound and far-reaching; notably as they affected the program of τελείωσις or *perfectio* proposed respectively by classicism and Christianity. And in this fact we may see the measure of its importance in the intellectual development of Augustine. Together with the Manichean controversy, it served to clarify his thinking and provide him with the concepts of understanding in terms of which he was to offer his interpretation of the existing situation in the Greco-Roman world. Our next task will be to consider how he applies these concepts and what light he succeeds in throwing on the malady of imperial Rome.

Natural Necessity and Human Freedom[39]

In my introductory lecture, I began by offering some account of the historical situation with which Augustine and his contemporaries were confronted in the first decades of the fifth century, and then went on to discuss the elements of what I conceive to have been the Augustinian prognostic, the concepts of Christian wisdom or *sapientia* in terms of which Augustine undertook to read the meaning of the situation for the benefit of those who were dismayed and bewildered by what they felt to be the inexorable march of doom and who, in their perplexity, looked to him for guidance. I shall now proceed to examine the use to which Augustine put those concepts in his effort to assess the position and prospects of the Empire, together with the idea of civilization for which it stood. And I shall argue that they provided him with the material he needed for a realistic assessment of the situation, the originality of which lay in the treatment accorded to the will. We might, indeed, go further and suggest that the notion of will, as it presented itself to Christian realism, was the point of departure for revolutionary developments to be brought about by Christian thinking in relation to the traditional Greco-Roman problems of ethics, politics and (above all, perhaps) the philosophy of history. These developments, which were to be in large measure the work of Augustine, were all implicit in his challenging proposition, "*voluntas est quippe in omnibus; immo omnes nihil aliud quam voluntates sunt*"—"will is present in all men; nay, at bottom, they are nothing more or less than wills."[40]

To accept this proposition of Christian realism was to assert that, under God, man himself is the one efficient cause of his own activity. It was thus to cut loose, at a stroke, from all the manifold varieties of diabolism which had been latent in the naturalism of pagan antiquity. These would include the "one big devil" of Manichean science, as well as the innumerable demons, great and small, for which the earlier and more strictly classical versions of pagan speculation had provided such ample hospitality. One and all, these were liquidated in the sweeping formula, *non dei sed verba*—"they are not gods but words." And, in so far as those words pointed to any concrete (physical or mental) reality, it was that merely of *figmenta imaginaria*, "creatures of the imagination." The purge was thus at once thorough and complete, for the demons eliminated comprised those of all three types catalogued by the antiquarian Varro:

---

39. [Charles Norris Cochrane, "Natural Necessity and Human Freedom," Charles Norris Cochrane Fonds. University of Toronto Archives, B2003-0011/006 (17).]

40. Augustine, *City of God*, 14.6.

1. those of vulgar or poetic fancy
2. the so-called *di selecti*, the "official" or "political" deities recognized pragmatically in the *constitutio religionum*, the religious establishment set up by law (*ius divinum*)
3. the deities of "natural" or "physical" philosophy

To this achievement of Augustinian realism must be added another, not less significant. This was to have provided a fresh vindication, in terms of Christian principles, for that sense of moral freedom and responsibility which, as we may well believe, underlay the whole concept of the *polis* and of political or civil discipline as a means to the realization of virtue and felicity, but of which Greek thought had never been able to provide an adequate account.

That such a sense did, in point of fact, exist among the Greeks, as it has among all men, cannot well be doubted. To be assured of this, we need go no further than the lexicographers, from whom we may discover that it finds expression in at least two words, βούλομαι and ἐθέλω, the distinction between them being nicely indicated in the Platonic sentence, εἰ βούλει, ἐγὼ ἐθέλω, "if you desire, I for my part am willing," or "if it be your will, I agree or consent."[41] Of these two words, the former, together with its correlates βουλή and βουλεύομαι, appears to have been the more common in early epic and, so we are informed, it ordinarily takes the place of ἐθέλω when used with reference to the gods, since with them to wish was to will.[42]

The noun βουλή employed occasionally in the plural as well as in the singular, and normally translated "counsel," "design," "scheme," "purpose" or "plan," connotes an act of decision, the result of deliberation and choice, especially when (as has already been said) it is used in relation to the gods, as, in the opening lines of Homer's *Iliad*: Μῆνιν ἄειδε θεὰ Πηληϊάδεω Ἀχιλῆος οὐλομένην ... Διὸς δ' ἐτελείετο βουλή.

One further point before we leave the question of etymology. The word βούλομαι (root: βολ-) appears to be related through the strengthened root ϝελ- (Latin *volo, velle*) with ἐέλδομαι, ἔλπομαι, and in these latter forms it bears the connotation of "wish" or "desire"; thus conveying the sense of emotional urge rather than intellectual decision, i.e., precisely the sense which attaches to the noun ἐλπίς in Thucydides, that of a blind, irrational and, we may add, dangerous impulse or appetite. These distinctions, a product of the vulgar or popular mentality, were to survive in common usage throughout the classical centuries. In them we may discern the source of ideological difficulties such as were to confront the Greek poets and philosophers when

---

41. Plato, *Gorgias*, 522E.
42. See Liddell and Scott, *sub. voc.*

they addressed themselves to the problem of moral freedom or the freedom of the will.

It will be remembered that, in my first lecture, I referred briefly to this problem and to the dilemma it served to create for the Greco-Roman mind. I also referred to the wholly new turn given to the problem by Augustinian Christianity and promised that, at an appropriate point in this course, I should have something further to say on the matter. The time has now come to discharge that promise.

The problem of freedom had been the theme of constant preoccupation and thought in Greece from earliest times. We shall, I think, best understand it if we consider it historically and genetically, i.e., as it emerged in the consciousness of Hellas. For this purpose we must go back to the early theological poets, especially to Hesiod, in whose works we may encounter the first serious, if not very effective, effort to grapple with it, as he does in the myth of Prometheus and Pandora.

For us, the significance of Hesiod's effort does not, of course, lie in his positive findings, so much as in the light it throws on the characteristic processes of the Greek mind. Hesiod starts from the grim actualities of contemporary history, the Age of Iron when, as he puts it, "men never cease by day from toil and anguish, nor from death by night; when strife divides brothers in fierce contention; might is taken to be right, and there is no respect one for another; when the daimonic powers of Reverence and Righteous Indignation (Αἰδώς and Νέμεσις) forsake this world to join the company of the deathless gods, and bitter sorrows are left for mortals, and there is no support against evil."[43]

Such being the picture of human experience as Hesiod sees it, the question arises: how is it to be explained? The answer—for Hesiod, an easy and natural inference, no doubt, from his own observation—is that the gods are determined to withhold from mankind the wherewithal of life.[44] To illustrate and account for this hypothesis he has recourse to a cosmological myth, which we must now briefly examine.[45]

In the Hesiodic cosmos, Zeus "the wise," son of Cronos and Rhea, installed by virtue of a successful usurpation of his father's power as autocrat of the universe, is envisaged as a principle of limitation and control, and, as such, his chief preoccupation is to maintain his sovereignty against all comers, notably against the earth-born Titans, the unruly vitalities of physical life, whose aid he had invoked in the hour of his own rebellion against his

---

43. Hesiod, *Works and Days*, 11.176–201.
44. Ibid., 1.42.
45. Hesiod, *Theogony*, 11.453.

father, but whom he is now concerned to hold in subjection to his sway. Of these superhuman natural forces, two are personified as Prometheus and Epimetheus, i.e., as different aspects of cosmic mind. To the former, Prometheus or "Providence," with the help of his "scatter-brained" brother (ἁμαρτίνοος Ἐπιμηθεύς) the poet ascribes the mission of creating man, and of providing him with what he needs to secure his existence. And it is in this connection that Prometheus is said to have perpetrated the act of pious fraud for which he was to suffer at the hands of a resentful Zeus, by stealing from heaven the fire (basis of the creative arts) required by man, if he was to overcome the handicap of his physical weakness and to perfect his life as a civilized being.

The consequences, as portrayed by Hesiod, are remarkable, both as they serve to demonstrate the relentless operation of natural forces, and as they provide material for the characteristically Greek prognosis of civilization to be ventured by the poet. Civilization is depicted as a more or less continuous regress, punctuated by periods of crisis and mutation, from the so-called Age of Gold through successive stages of increasing corruption, culminating in a final catastrophe (Deucalion's flood), to be followed by a fresh start, but only for those who are prepared to conform with the righteousness of Zeus by observing the limits set by his sovereign will; and the poet does nothing to indicate his sense of the *hormé* or impulse which actuates the social process beyond throwing out the suggestion that, in each successive phase, there are engendered the seeds of another and a worse; which is as much as to say that civilized society carries within itself the germs of its own dissolution.

Hesiod succeeds but imperfectly in rationalizing and moralizing this picture of cosmic and human order. Accordingly (not without reason) the figure of Prometheus has been take to symbolize the superhuman qualities of pride and endurance needed to resist the crushing weight of unmerited suffering through divine oppression. As one of our own romantic poets, from this point of view, so vividly puts it:

> Titan! to whose immortal eyes
> The sufferings of mortality,
> Seen in their sad reality,
> Were not as things that gods despise;
> What was thy pity's recompense?
> A silent suffering and intense;
> The rock, the vulture, and the chain;
> All that the proud can feel of pain;
> The agony, they do not show;
> The suffocating sense of woe …

> Titan! to thee the strife was given
> Between the suffering and the will,
> Which torture where they cannot kill;
> And the inexorable Heaven,
> And the deaf tyranny of Fate,
> The ruling principle of Hate,
> Which for its pleasure doth create
> The things it may annihilate,
> Refuse thee even the boon to die...
>
> Thy godlike crime was to be kind;
> To render with thy precepts less
> The sum of human wretchedness,
> And strengthen man with his own Mind.
> But baffled as thou wert from high,
> Still, in thy patient energy,
> In the endurance and repulse
> Of thine impenetrable spirit,
> Which Earth and Heaven could not convulse,
> A mighty lesson we inherit.[46]

On the other hand, in his attitude to men, the sovereign deity is represented as hardly less vindictive than he shows himself toward their superhuman benefactor. For the countless evils (physical and moral) with which they are afflicted are described as a gift provided by the immortals, to be sent along with the seductive Pandora, bride of Epimetheus and the blight of his foolish life, so that for every good thing which men enjoy, they may suffer a commensurate ill.[47] Since thus only, as Hesiod puts it, will they come to realize that "there is no way to escape the will of Zeus."[48]

It would be impossible, within the limits of available time, to deal adequately with subsequent efforts of the poetic imagination to dispose of the legacy of moral and intellectual difficulties it inherited from the earlier theologians, Homer and Hesiod. Pindar and the dramatists did, to be sure, succeed in some degree in refining upon the rudimentary notions of cosmic order and justice put forward in the epic, but without however (and this is the point to be noticed) daring to challenge the fundamental assumptions on which those notions were based. Indeed, there is not the slightest reason to suppose that it even occurred to them to do so; a fact which, given the

---

46. Byron, "Prometheus," 191.
47. Hesiod, *Works and Days*, 11.60–105.
48. Ibid., 1.105.

Augustine and the Problem of Power

ideological limitations within which their minds operated, is not hard to understand. Thus, for example, the tragedians, preoccupied with the task of reconciling cosmic law with cosmic justice, devoted their energies to discovering and exhibiting some fault or flaw (ἁμαρτία) in the character of the typical tragic hero, such as might serve to explain and justify the ἄτη or doom by which he was overwhelmed, or would at any rate be accepted as the "proximate cause" of his downfall.[49] But, in order to succeed in this purpose, they were compelled to pay a terrible price in terms of realism. For, as Aristotle naively observed, if tragedy was to evoke the appropriate emotions of pity and terror (i.e., to commend itself to the popular Greek consciousness), then two possibilities were automatically excluded. On the one hand, the downfall of the hero must not be ascribed to an ἀτύχημα (a piece of bad luck), i.e., to anything that involved the notion of spontaneity or chance,[50] or (to put the point otherwise) originated in the area of matter which, though admittedly operating as a cause,[51] is, in terms of Aristotelian metaphysics, devoid of design (τὸ ἕνεκα του) and even of regularity (ὡς ἐπὶ τὸ πολύ) and so, utterly irrational (ἄλογον).[52] The other possibility to be excluded was that of ἀδίκημα, the crime or wickedness of the man who deliberately takes evil to be his good, the ἀκόλαστος of the *Nicomachean Ethics*. But to eliminate these possibilities was (if Aristotle here correctly interprets the mind of Hellas) to be left only with a third, viz., the ἁμαρτία. This word, as it was employed by the epic poets, indicates what we should call a "mistake" or "mishap," and more or less the same sense clings to it in Attic usage, both poetry and prose.[53] What the word thus points to is an error of judgment or opinion (ἁμαρτία δόξης), as when, for example, the tragic hero fails to formulate correctly the minor premise of the practical syllogism and suffers in consequence. In this sense, as has been remarked, "it would cover any error . . . arising from a nasty or careless view of the special case; *an error which is in eerie degree morally culpable, since it might have seen avoided*"![54] It would also apply to any act which, while admittedly conscious and intentional, could not properly be described as deliberate, the agent being thus absolved from blame, because what he did was the result of

---

49. Butcher, *Aristotle's Theory*, 302–34.
50. Aristotle, *Poetics*, 9.12.
51. Aristotle, *Metaphysics*, 1027a13; ἡ ὕλη . . . αἰτία.
52. Butcher, *Aristotle's Theory*, 181.
53. See Liddell and Scott, *sub. voc.*
54. Butcher, *Aristotle's Theory*, 318; emphasis added.

passion.⁵⁵ Finally, it would include any general frailty or weakness of character, where the fault in question was not tainted by a vicious purpose.⁵⁶

To make these admissions with respect to tragic poetry is to recognize that it failed as "an interpretation of life," whatever may be thought of its possible utility as an instrument of catharsis. It is also to perceive the reason for its failure. This was because tragedy could not hope to discharge its cathartic function except by excluding from its purview much of what was genuinely historical in human experience, and that (as Aristotle is at pains to inform us) on the ground that it was "too horrible" to contemplate. The failure of poetry was confessed, at least by implication, by Aristotle himself when he perversely declared that it was "more philosophical and serious" than history, precisely because of its generalized and unhistorical character, presumably because he felt that for this very reason it provided better access to reality and truth.⁵⁷

In view of the evident inability of poetry to vindicate the human sense of freedom and responsibility, it is not surprising that philosophy should, sooner or later, have initiated an investigation of its own into the same problem—an investigation which aimed to avoid the characteristic error imputed to poetry, viz., its mythologism. The question at once arises: did the philosophers, in their quest for an ethic based on "the really real," fare any better than the poets? To this the answer must emphatically be that they did not! So far at any rate as concerns the pre-Socratics, all they succeeded in accomplishing was to "construct," by the aid of the scientific imagination, a terrifying picture of nature as a mechanism in which, theoretically, there was no piece left, however restricted, for the independent activity of spirit. Nor, if we may believe Aristotle, did Anaxagoras, the contemporary and friend of Pericles, in any way improve the situation by his attempt to insinuate into an (otherwise) closed system of mechanical causation a quite hypothetical Νοῦς or *Intellectus*, to serve as a principle of organization and intelligibility. On the other hand, nothing was ultimately to be gained for freedom by falling back, with certain of the Sophists, upon dogmatic humanism, as Protagoras did, when he propounded the entirely unsupported thesis that man is the measure of all things, of those that are that they are, and of those that are not that they are not. Yet this was the total achievement of Greek speculation, in ethics at least, until the time of Socrates.

55. Aristotle, *Nicomachean Ethics*, 5.8; τὰ ἐκ θυμοῦ οὐκ ἐκ προνοίας κρίνεται—"in acts committed from passion there is no presumption of malice."

56. Aristotle, *Poetics*, 13.3; ὁ . . . μήτε διὰ κακίαν καὶ μοχθηρίαν μεταβάλλων εἰς τὴν δυστυχίαν.

57. Aristotle, *Poetics*. 9.3; cf. *Analytica Posteriora*, 1.31; τὸ δὲ καθόλου τίμιον, ὅτι δηλοῖ τὸ αἴτιον.

To Socrates, the problem of freedom presented itself as, in the first instance, a simple question of knowledge. To know the right is, he asserted, to do it; and this is moral freedom in the only intelligible sense of the word. Yet, in this apparently simple proposition, there were concealed a whole tissue of metaphysical and cosmological assumptions which it was the historic mission of Plato to bring to light. Of these assumptions, perhaps the most fundamental was that whereby the "rational" was identified with the "real." And, from this point of view, the cosmos or world of nature was envisaged as a composite (σύνθετον) of elements or parts equally original and originally discrete. The parts in question were (following a clue derived perhaps from the speculations of Pythagorean philosophy) variously distinguished as higher and lower, spirit and body, mind and sense, form and matter; and, in one of its more extreme manifestations, the supposed antithesis between these "parts" or "elements" found expression in the Pythagorean or Orphic proposition that "body" was the tomb of "soul." (σῶμα σῆμα) It was further assured that, to these antitheses in nature, there existed corresponding antitheses in knowledge, i.e., between two opposing worlds of "being" and "not-being," or of intelligibility and sensibility; and that the former was the world of science (ἐπιστήμη), the latter of mere opinion or belief (δόξη). From this point of view, Platonism is perhaps to be best understood as an attempt to find a middle path between Parmenides and Heraclitus, between a position which denied all reality to the phenomenal world of matter-in-motion, and one which insisted that the one indefeasible reality was the universal and ever-lasting flux. Thus Plato, in his effort to steer between these two extremes, put forward the idea that knowledge or science, properly so called, was limited to those exalted planes of cosmic being which, standing at the opposite pole from "matter," exhibit the character of pure form. As for this sub-lunary world, the world of inorganic and organic life, he regarded it as susceptible, not of true science, but merely of an opinion or belief which, as he puts it, "tumbles about" between "being" and "not-being"; in other words, as a world in which, because of the fact that it is tainted with matter, there remains an irreducible residuum of metaphysical unreality to mark its permanent and necessary imperfection.

It would be difficult to exaggerate the importance of these ideas in their application to Platonic ethics. To begin with, the principle of evil and corruption in human life was identified, not with what Augustine calls the "total man," but with a specific element in his nature, viz., the element of matter, conceived as that which is essentially unintelligible and unreal. On the other hand, the perfection of human nature was envisaged as the perfection of mind or reason; as Cicero, in a characteristic echo of Platonic doctrine, was to put it, *virtus perfecta ratio*.[58] This means that the problem of perfection was taken to be, at bottom, a problem of transcendence; it was to escape from the limitations of the sensible and the tangible, in order to emerge into the clear and undiluted light of pure Being, Mind or *Nous*. Hence (we may infer) the peculiar and distinctive features of what Plato was to promulgate as his *ascesis* or discipline, and therewith, if it is not too bold to hazard the suggestion, the program of perfection through the medium of liberal arts (*artes liberales*), as this was to be practiced for centuries in the schools of the Roman Empire. The central idea of Platonic *ascesis* was that of emancipation; its professed object was to "liberate" the human mind from whatever might obscure the clarity of its vision, or interfere with what was conceived to be its natural propensity to turn toward the light of reality and truth, as toward the very principle of its own being. Translated into terms of practice, this pointed to (a) the subjugation of animal impulse, emotion and desire, the so-called lower elements or parts of the soul and (b) the progressive cultivation through appropriate disciplines of those elements which, while themselves devoid of reason, were nevertheless deemed to be capable of hearing and obeying its dictates. As for reason itself, the highest and noblest part of the soul and that which in nature constitutes the link between the human and the divine, there was no suggestion that it needed to be in any way chastened or kept within bounds, for the simple reason that its native potentialities were held to be essentially and exclusively good. Accordingly, the problem was merely to ensure that those potentialities should be duly cultivated by receiving the proper stimulus for their development, whether by way of literature, or through mathematics and dialectic. In other words, the aim was to establish and secure the "independence" of the mind, and this independence was equated with freedom. So far was Platonism from grasping the need for what Christianity was to describe as "regeneration," i.e., for a radical change in the attitude and outlook of the total man (appetite, sense, *and* reason) as a necessary prelude to the genuine reformation and perfection of his nature.

Plato's concern, with the problem of freedom and perfectibility is, as I pointed out in my previous lecture, illustrated by the attention he gives it in various myths and, of these, one of the most interesting and important for our purpose is the myth of Er at the conclusion of the *Republic*.[59] In this myth Plato undertakes to elucidate the thesis that the Deity is in no sense responsible for the failures and shortcomings of mankind, but that these are the result of his own deliberate preference and choice.[60] It is not (as one

58. Cicero, *De Legibus*, 1.45.
59. Plato, *The Republic*, 614B–621D.
60. Ibid., 6227E; αἰτία ἑλομένου θεὸς ἀναίτιος.

authority suggested) merely a question of showing that "great decisions have to be made in life which, once made, are irrevocable and dominate the man's whole career and conduct afterwards"[61]; but, rather of how, in view of the (to Plato) obvious fact that an element of law or "necessity" enters into human life which is evidently beyond control, any significant decision on the part of man is even possible. What Plato has in mind is clearly the Homeric concept of μοῖρα or destiny, envisaged as a complex of necessity (ἀνάγκη) and chance (τύχη); and this, we should note, he accepts without question. Accordingly, the problem, as he sees it, is to demonstrate that, notwithstanding the intervention of μοῖρα, there is still room for "free" decision and choice. To make good this contention, Plato argues that, in the types or patterns of life made available by "necessity," there is an ample range of selection[62] and while, no doubt, something depends upon the order in which the lots are cast, and while this is a matter of sheer luck, or chance,[63] it still remains possible at the very end of the draw to make an excellent choice, so that the chooser may well say with Odysseus, "Had my turn come first, I would not have done otherwise."[64]

But, granted the very generous scope for selection which Plato here postulates, what has he to say about the actual question of choice? It is clear that, as he sees it, the goodness or badness of a man's decision is contingent upon his knowledge,[65] and that his knowledge, in turn, is conditioned by his apprehension of the eternal Ideas emanating from the Idea of the Good. Otherwise, it would appear that Plato is committed to the notion of an infinite regress, in which the lot chosen by a man in any particular life would depend upon the quality of his experience in some previous incarnation. And since that experience is, on the face of it, partial and limited, the choosers would inevitably be impelled to hasty and ill-considered decisions. This Plato himself readily concedes when he declares that it is "at once a pitiful, a ridiculous, and an amazing spectacle" to watch them making their choice.[66] But, if this be so, then it is evident that Plato has failed to resolve the antinomy with which he started, the antinomy between freedom and responsibility on the one hand, and, on the other, determinism and irresponsibility. As a recent student of Platonism has put it:

61. Stewart, *Myths of Plato*, 172.
62. Plato, *The Republic*, 618A; τῶν βίων παραδείγματα . . . πολὺ πλείω τῶν παρόντων.
63. Ibid., 619D; διὰ τὴν τοῦ κλήρου τύχην.
64. Ibid., 620D.
65. Ibid., 619C.
66. Ibid., 620A.

> Whatever [the course taken by the chooser], he will be conscious that he was entirely free to exercise his will to refrain, or the inner check, and will hold himself responsible for his happiness or misery. But *he will also know that at the moment of action his positive will was bound to follow the predominant inclination,* and that, as the *physical craving* and the *weight of experience were determined by causes not entirely within his jurisdiction, he is not fully responsible for the contingencies of pleasure and pain . . . [and] any philosophical statement of the problem must close with this admission of an irreconcilable paradox.*[67]

From which, we may conclude, the sense of freedom imputed to the chooser at the moment of his choice is, in point of fact, utterly illusory—a conclusion which, given the ideological limitations of Platonism, is, we may agree, quite inescapable.

But if this be the conclusion to which the logic of Plato drives him, it then becomes easy to understand why he should have had no alternative but to accept its ultimate implications, as he does in the concept of the philosopher-king. The demand for the philosopher-king is nothing less than the demand for an earthly providence; for some superhuman or daemonic power capable of intervening to rescue mankind from the vicious circle to which fate or destiny has condemned him by saving him (as he cannot conceivably save himself) from the inevitable consequences of his ignorance and error. That such intervention should ever, in fact, occur, is, Plato concedes, a matter of divine good fortune (θεία μοίρα). It is nonetheless indicated as the one possible means whereby the life of man can be secured from the contingencies of history (ἀνάγκη and τύχη). In the establishment and maintenance of such security, and in this alone, Plato sees a real prospect for the perfection of human life in virtue and felicity. And this is why he is such a fervent believer in the *polis*.

This brings me to a further implication of Platonism and that of fundamental importance for our understanding of the classical doctrine of perfection, and of the indictment to be leveled against it by Augustine. For, if Plato is right in what he has to say about the nature and conditions of perfectibility, then obviously the question resolves itself into one of politics, i.e., it is a question of the possibility of redemption from ignorance and error through νομοθεσία, legislation or (in the terminology to be employed by Christianity) through "law." And, in this connection, it is to be noted that the word "law," as applied to the Gentiles, i.e., to all not favored as the Jews had been by a special divine revelation, is taken to embrace those postulates

---

67. More, *Platonism*, 163–64; emphasis added.

of natural reason and equity by virtue of which (as St. Paul had put it) they are "a law unto themselves."[68] It is further to be noted that, the problem being conceived as political, the presumption was that it might be solved by the conventional methods of political and legislative action, viz., by persuasion and force. Thus, at any rate, in both the *Republic* and the *Laws*, Plato envisages the role of the νομοθέτης, or statesman. In this context, the lawgiver emerges as a man who is himself divine or divinely inspired. And, by virtue of the fact, he is invested with a mission and a responsibility in relation to his fellows. This mission is, admittedly, many-sided, but at bottom it is perhaps best described as one of instruction (διδαχή) and, from this point of view, instruction is envisaged as, next to warfare, the most important function to be discharged by the *polis*. In this fact, as we shall have occasion to notice, Christianity was to discover the essential deficiency of the Platonic and classical scheme of perfection; and, therewith, the need for what it accepted as a further and final revelation of divine order in the historical Incarnation of the Word, and in the assurance of divine grace thereby extended to mankind. For what Christianity here perceived and what classicism overlooked was the truth that, while it is one thing to desire and to decree perfection, it is quite another to mobilize the resources of moral energy necessary to ensure it. Indeed, as Christianity was to argue, mankind deludes himself if he imagines that, by his own unaided efforts, it is even possible for him to do so. This, however, was a truth which, as Augustine is concerned to point out, was revealed only to Christian humility: from classical and secular pride it was concealed.[69]

It would, I think, be generally agreed that, within the whole range of classical speculation on human nature and destiny, there is nothing which equals or even approaches the thought of Plato in profundity and insight. Accordingly, in our survey of classical effort, we could well afford to pass over developments of doctrine introduced, by Plato's successors, were it not for the possible exception of Aristotle. This is not to suggest that we shall encounter in Aristotle any radical divergence from the views which had been expressed by Plato with respect to the ideal of human perfection and the way it was to be realized. For him, as for Plato, the problem remained one of political and legislative action; indeed, it is Aristotle himself who describes the technique or art (τέχνη) of politics as "architectonic" and who declares that, while, to be sure, the *polis* is natural, nevertheless he who first invented it was the greatest of benefactors.[70] Accordingly, we may sum up

---

68. Rom 2:14.
69. Augustine, *City of God*, 1. Preface.
70. Aristotle, *Politics*, 1253a30.

the achievement of Aristotle in political theory by saying that what he has to offer is just another version of the classical idea of the *polis*, but on a rather less exalted and much more strictly human plane. This Aristotle manages by rejecting the elements of metaphysics and cosmology which had dominated the political thinking of Plato, and by substituting for them his own somewhat mystical conception of nature as a hierarchy of means and ends. Thus, in the light of his teleological physics, Aristotle undertakes a further effort to rehabilitate and reaffirm the classical idea of the *polis*.

In the version of politics thus proposed by Aristotelian naturalism, the problem of perfection is no longer envisaged as one which calls for the intervention of a lawgiver endowed with superhuman powers of leadership (intelligence and endurance). What Aristotle puts forward is rather a scheme of perfection on successive planes of strictly human excellence, which, taken together, comprise the whole nature of man; and, in this context, the word τελείωσις or *perfectio* is defined as a ἕξις or stable condition, whether of body (τὸ θρεπτικόν ον τὸ φυτικόν), spirit (τὸ ἐπιθυμητικόν καὶ ὅλως ὀρεκτικόν), or mind (τὸ νοητικόν ον τὸ λογικόν), in which these parts or elements of the human compound function without impediment, each according to its proper *areté* or virtue and in keeping with its maximum potential for development thereby, as Aristotle contends, achieving happiness or felicity (εὐδαιμονία); in other words, a fulfillment of the end (τέλος) appointed by *natura creatrix* as the goal and pattern of human life.

On the basis of an anthropology thus conceived, Aristotle proceeds to erect a hierarchy of natural values, in which the element of reason is somewhat arbitrarily identified as "the ruling element" (τὸ ἡγούμενον) and conceded an undisputed primacy in the human economy. And further, within the ruling element itself, the best and noblest part is identified with pure reason—a reason which, if only because it is concerned with sublime and divine objects, is itself held to be less strictly human than divine.[71] In the role thus ambiguously ascribed to what Aristotle calls the theoretic intelligence (διανοία) we may discern the vestige of an otherwise discarded Platonism. As for the practical reason (φρόνησις) i.e., the part which is organically related to the body, its impulses and passions, the activation of this part is the activation of the merely human and, so in Aristotle's hierarchy of natural values, it takes a secondary place. This classification is, however, merely formal, since, for all but the rare intellectual elite deemed capable of pure theoretic activity, the development of the strictly human elements of human nature is regarded as the normal end of τελείωσις or *perfectio*. Perfection thus means, in effect, the cultivation of φρόνησις (roughly *savoir*

---

71. Aristotle, *Nicomachean Ethics*, 10.7.

faire or knowing what to do), φρόνησις being envisaged as a principle of organization and control, designed as such to legislate for those aspects or parts of the soul whose perfection is realized in the relationships of society and politics. To illustrate what he has in mind, Aristotle offers a picture of what he conceives to be the *beau ideal* of such perfection in the concept of μεγαλοψυχία or magnanimity. It is a mistake to suppose, with at least one of his editors that, in his description of the *megalopsychos*, Aristotle is "half-ironical."[72] For this would be to attribute to Aristotle what he certainly did not possess, the editor's own Scotch sense of humor. Aristotle is here, we may be sure, perfectly serious: what he has before him is, no doubt, the pattern of behavior commonly credited to the Olympian Pericles, a pattern to be imitated and, in some degree, burlesqued by Alcibiades, his shameless successor in the leadership of the great Alcmaeonid house.

There is still a further point to be noticed in connection with the Aristotelian version of classical naturalism, and that of the highest importance, if we are to appreciate fully the protest to be made against it by Augustine. This concerns the relationship between what Aristotle distinguishes as "the irrational" and "the rational" parts of the soul.[73] Of these two parts, the former is conceived to experience "pleasures" and "pains" which, however ambiguous their connection with body, are nevertheless put down as carnal or physical in origin. At the same time, it is thought to be the *locus* of wish (βούλησις) and of desire or appetite (ἐπιθυμία); and, from this point of view, it is said to "partake of" reason in the sense that it is capable of listening to its commands, though it cannot properly be described as reasonable, since it does in fact struggle and fight against reason.[74] In this pronouncement of Aristotelian psychology, we have the clue to an understanding of one of the most significant aspects of Aristotelian ethics and politics. For, if Aristotle has correctly stated the relationship between the rational and the irrational parts of the soul, then it may be inferred that the function of φρόνησις or the practical intelligence is to act in a legislative capacity and to impose on the irrational or sub-rational part the practices and habits (ἐπιτηδεύματα) or "way of life" conventional to political or civilized man. And, in this connection, it is to be noted that Aristotle (no doubt as a consequence of his biological investigations) hit upon a most important discovery. This was that, since the human animal requires such a relatively long time to mature, the human soul is capable of almost infinite malleability through the process of habituation (ἐθισμός). In this undoubted truth of human biology we

72. Burnet, *Ethics of Aristotle*, 179 n. 3.
73. Aristotle, *Nicomachean Ethics*, 1.13.
74. Ibid., 1102b15–18.

may discern the secret which underlay most of the pretensions of "creative politics" in classical antiquity—a secret of which the modern European exponents of classical political technique have been quick to take the fullest possible advantage of in their schemes to "produce" moral and spiritual, as well as merely external "conformity." We mention it here, not merely as a time-honored device of political practice, but also because it provides such an excellent illustration of what Augustine was to denounce as "secular perversity" (*perversitas saeculi*).

From the standpoint of Augustine, there could be no clearer evidence of the deficiencies of classical naturalism as a basis for ethics than is to be found in the account which naturalism offers of the corruption of human nature through the "weakness" or "badness" of the will (ἀκρασία ον ἀκολασία). And here again, Aristotle may perhaps be held up as the horrible example, if only because, by virtue of his unique gift for clear and systematic exposition, he makes these deficiencies so apparent. Aristotle does, indeed, make a good beginning when he distinguishes the voluntary from the involuntary act as that which is not performed from external compulsion or through ignorance.[75] It is only when he comes to discuss the question of volition that the difficulties begin to emerge. In what is described by the editor as "the fundamental doctrine of the Ethics,"[76] volition (προαίρεσις) is defined as a "deliberative appetition of things in our power." But if so, how to account for any failure to achieve its object—that is the question. To this Aristotle answers that, if the problem under consideration be one of "impotence" or "lack of control," there are four possible solutions, the last of which provides the "true" or "natural" (φυσικῶς) explanation. This, he suggests, is that the pathology of impotence is by no means unique; the explanation is physiological and falls under precisely the same pattern as that which serves to account for drunkenness or sleepy-sickness.[77] Nor, in the last analysis, is that of "positive vice" essentially different, except for the fact that, in this case, the guilty party has so far departed from rational standards of conduct that he no longer even feels remorse for his acts.[78] The explanation here is also physiological, and the condition may be explained as a consequence either of "brutalization" or of "disease" and "injury," especially to the mind or brain of the victim.[79] Yet the beastliness or brutality of an animal (Aristotle, in a significant admission, adds) is not to be compared with that of a

75. Ibid., 3.1.
76. Burnet, *Ethics of Aristotle*, 132 n. 19.
77. Aristotle, *Nicomachean Ethics*, 3.3.
78. Ibid., 7.8.
79. Ibid., 7.5.

brutalized man, since the former is naturally devoid of reason, whereas in the latter reason has been destroyed (διέφθαρται); accordingly "a vicious man is capable of doing ten thousand times the damage of a brute beast."[80]

So much for what I have called the dilemma of classical naturalism and for the successive efforts of the classical mind to resolve it in such a way as "to save the appearances," i.e., to do justice to the facts of common experience, and especially that sense of moral freedom and responsibility which, as I suggested, is the necessary presupposition to classical and, indeed, to all human endeavor. I have dwelt at some length on those efforts and for a very good reason: it has been necessary to show that they were one and all vitiated and that, given the ideological limitations of the naturalistic approach, it was inevitable that this should have been the case. I have now only to add that, from the standpoint of Augustinian Christianity the secular effort of classicism constituted just so much evidence of secular pride; what classicism failed to perceive was that in seeking, to discover in what it called "nature" a solid and enduring foundation for a theory of practice or conduct, it was looking into the mirror of its own mind; in other words, it was guilty of idolatry. This, however, was precisely the truth which classical pride stubbornly refused to acknowledge. Accordingly, it persisted in the attempt to idealize its own abstractions; to endue them with a permanence which is denied to any merely historical artifact, whether of the human hand or the human mind. And this because it could not face the prospect that the objects of its own creation should sooner or later be obliterated by the relentless march of time. Thus classical pride bore its inevitable fruit in classical error, the error of identifying the merely temporal and ephemeral with that which is everlasting.

To the pride and error of classicism Christian faith proposed the rejoinder that "God created the world" and that "the world is in His keeping." So far as concerns the dilemma of naturalism, this was to attack it by recognizing frankly that it defied solution except in terms of first principles. And, in accepting these propositions of Christian faith, Augustine in effect declared that the concept of nature was not (as Greek speculative activity appears to have assumed) something to be composed or constructed by any effort of the scientific imagination; but that, on the contrary, it was itself presupposed in any attempt to think positively about nature, i.e., before the scientific intelligence could fruitfully go to work. This, we should now add, was to lay the foundation for a new approach to certain of the traditional problems of classical physics, notably the relationship between "order" and "motion." It was also to throw overboard the notions of "natural necessity"

---

80. Ibid., 1150a7.

and "chance" as these had been entertained by the Greeks and to assert, with Augustine, that all motion of whatever character, whether that which is designated as "voluntary" or that which is designated as "natural" (*motus voluntaries—motus naturalis*), is, under God, at one and the same time, both "determined" and "free." It was thus to deny that there exists in reality any fundamental opposition or antithesis, such as the Greeks had imagined, between the two kinds of motion, and so any problem of "reconciling" the one with the other. Quite the contrary, God, recognized as the creator of order, was, at the same time, acknowledged to be the creator of motion; "the one cause," indeed, as Augustine puts it, "which acts without being acted upon." But to say this was to assert that there is and can be neither order nor movement in the universe which divine providence does not make possible.

"Other causes," he proceeds, "both act and are acted upon; viz., all created spirits, more especially those which are rational. As for physical or corporeal causes, so-called, those which are acted upon rather than act, these are not to be rated as efficient causes, since they enjoy only such power as the wills of spiritual beings exert through them."[81]

This, we may suggest, was to provide a genuinely philosophical answer to the problem of order and motion in nature—a problem to which not even Aristotle had been able to offer anything more than a purely provisional and dogmatic solution; though Aristotle has, indeed, been hailed as "the inventor of the notion of intellectual development in time"; and of "the principle of organic development."[82]

So far as concerns the philosophy of nature in general, the contribution of Augustine was limited to indicating the possibility of a fresh approach in terms of the new *arché*, *principium* or philosophic starting-point. His interest in the matter was merely as it affected practice. Accordingly, he proceeded at once to ask what was for him the really significant question:

> How then should the order of causation, determined as it is by the prescience of God, force us to conclude that nothing, depends upon our wills, since our wills themselves occupy an important place in causal order? . . . It by no means follows that, because for God there exists a fixed order of causes, nothing is therefore contingent upon the decision of our wills. Our wills, indeed, are themselves included in the order of causation, an order determined by God and comprehended within His

---

81. Augustine, *City of God*, 5.9.
82. Jaeger, *Aristotle*, 3–7; see also the concluding chapter on Aristotle's *Physics*.

providence ... Wherefore also our wills enjoy such potency as God willed and foresaw they would enjoy.[83]

And, continuing the argument:

> But what, it may be asked, of the compulsions of our animal nature, particularly the necessity of death (*necessitas mortis*)?

To which the answer is given:

> Even if we identify the term necessity with what is not in our power, and if we admit that we are bound, whether we like it or not, to submit to the necessity of death, it is none the less apparent that the wills, by virtue of which we order our lives to righteousness or evil, are subject to no such necessity.
>
> There are many things we do which we should most certainly refrain from doing if we were unwilling. To go no further, the act of willing itself; for, if we will, there is an act of willing. And, *vice versa*, we should not will unless we were willing. But if necessity be defined as that according to which we declare it to be necessary that such and such a thing should be or should occur, I am at a loss to understand why we should be afraid lest this deprive us of our freedom of will. Assuredly, we do not suppose that the life and prescience of God is subject to any such necessity when we assert, as we do, that eternal life and complete prescience is *necessary* to God, nor do we imagine that His power is in any way diminished when we affirm that He cannot die or be deceived. The reason, indeed, why God cannot die or be deceived is that, if this were possible, He would certainly have less power than, in fact, He has. There are some things beyond His power, for the simple reason that He is omnipotent.
>
> So also when we declare it to be necessary that, when we will, we should exercise freedom of choice, we both assert what is indubitably true and we do not thereby submit our freedom of choice to any necessity such as would nullify its freedom.

The conclusion then emerges:

> We are thus in no way bound either to abandon the principle that the will is freely determined in order to retain the prescience of God or, if we retain the free determination of the will, to deny (as would be impious) that God has prescience of future

---

83. Augustine, *City of God*, 5.9.

events; but we embrace both, confessing both in the spirit of faith and truth.[84]

Or, as Augustine put the same point at a somewhat earlier stage of the discussion:

> As against these sacrilegious and impious adventures of thought (*ausus*), we both affirm that God knows everything before it happens and, at the same time, we know in our hearts (*sentimus ac novimus*) that we do by virtue of our will whatever we do not without willing.[85]

In this highly elaborated statement, as I think I hinted in my first lecture, Augustine recapitulates and reasserts the thesis of the *De Libero Arbitrio*, which has been described by the critics as a landmark in the development of his thinking. And, in the position he thus assumes, he receives a certain degree of support from modern philosophy. Thus a recent writer has asserted, "In choosing every man is immediately conscious of being free; free, that is, to choose between alternatives. Arguments as to whether this immediate consciousness is or is not to be trusted are futile ... The freedom of the will is, positively, *freedom to choose*, freedom to exercise a will; and, negatively, freedom *from desire*; not the condition of having no desires."[86] Yet it would hardly be accurate merely on this account to say of Augustine (as has indeed been said) that "he falls back upon the immediate consciousness of freedom as a sufficient vindication of its reality." For, in the context of Augustinian Christianity, the sense of freedom thus affirmed in consciousness is, at the same time, reinforced by authority, an authority derived from the Biblical account of Genesis and from the interpretation placed upon the genesis-story by orthodox Christian thought. This means that it was ultimately deemed to be a truth of the metaphysical, not the physical order; though, as such, it entailed conclusions of the utmost consequence for physics and anthropology. But to pronounce the truth in question to be such a truth was to declare that it is one which, properly speaking, can neither be affirmed nor denied on purely "physical" or "scientific" grounds.

At the beginning of my lecture, I indicated that, in the doctrine of moral freedom proposed by Augustinian Christianity, there were concealed implications of a revolutionary character for human thought. To begin with, it suggested a radically novel diagnosis of *vice*, the ἁμαρτία or *vitium*

---

84. Ibid., 5.10.
85. Ibid., 5.9.
86. Collingwood, *The New Leviathan*, 91; cf. MacIver, *Social Causation*, ch. 8, esp. 230–32.

to which classicism had pointed as the rock upon which humanity makes shipwreck, but of which it had failed to offer anything like an intelligible account. And, therewith, a fresh statement of the problem of τελείωσις or *perfectio*, including the conditions to be met, if the promise of human life was to be fulfilled. And finally, as an element, indeed the most essential element, of those conditions, it pointed to both the necessity and the possibility of divine grace as the *sine qua non* to all merely human effort of fulfillment. In what remains to me of time in this course, I shall attempt to discuss these profound issues of human destiny, beginning with the question of vice. And, for your comfort, I may remind you that these were the very issues which (according to Milton) were endlessly canvassed by the devils in Hell.

The Imperfection of Politics[87]

In my last lecture I attempted to show how the doctrine of human freedom (*liberum voluntatis arbitrium*) propounded by Christian realism served as a charter of emancipation from moral and intellectual difficulties inherent in the naturalism of classical antiquity—difficulties from which, within the self-imposed limitations of classical ideology, there does not appear to have been the slightest possibility of escape. And I further suggested that, in the Christian concept of freedom, there was implicit a wholly fresh approach to the question of τελείωσις or *perfectio*, the point of departure for which was the connotation attaching to the notion of will. My next task will be to examine the use to which Augustine puts these fundamentals of Christian doctrine (a) as an instrument of criticism in the light of which he undertakes to explore the maladies of classical society and (b) as a potential principle of integration, free from the deficiencies of classical speculation and thus, so he believes, adequate as a basis for the organization of human relationships in what he calls "the most glorious society of God."[88] I shall begin by considering how it serves as an instrument of criticism. Here the problem will be to show how, by making possible a genuinely realistic diagnosis of classical error, it enables Augustine to perceive the true reason for classical shortcomings, and therewith to expose the basic weakness which underlay the grandiose pretensions of creative politics, the program of perfection through political action advocated and practiced by classical antiquity.

---

87. [In a later draft of this chapter, Cochrane changed the title to "The State and Human Perfectibility." I have retained the original title of the lecture delivered at Yale. Charles Norris Cochrane, "The Imperfection of Politics," Charles Norris Cochrane Fonds. University of Toronto Archives, B2003-0011/006 (18).]

88. Augustine, *City of God*, 1. Preface.

In an interesting and provocative review of my last book, I have been accused of dwelling unduly upon "political thinking," "almost as though it had been the only aspect of classical culture with which Christianity had been concerned" and (specifically) to the "neglect of philosophy, rhetoric, literature, art and education."[89] This rebuke, I confess, leaves me somewhat bewildered. To go no further, it overlooks the fact that, in the classical world, "philosophy, rhetoric, literature, art, education" and, it should be added, religion itself, were normally conceived as functions of political life, at any rate during the earlier and more strictly classical centuries.[90] And in this connection, it may be pertinent to recall two considerations of profound significance with respect to the *polis* as an historical institution. The first is that it was peculiarly an Hellenic invention, a form of society unimagined before; the second that throughout the whole Greek world (wherever, at least, development was not delayed) the "salient feature was the city-state."[91] To appreciate the historical importance of this characteristic product of Hellenic genius, it must be envisaged over against the dark background of Asiatic despotism and European barbarism against which it emerged—a consideration to which, we need hardly say, the Hellenes themselves were fully alive. To which we may add that, however various the forms to be assumed by the actual city-states of history, they one and all embodied a certain notion of fulfillment for their members, crude and unsatisfactory as this might be from the standpoint of philosophy.

This is not to suggest that the achievement of the historical *polis* would have been recognized by Plato and Aristotle as marking anything more than a rough approximation to the demands of "right reason." Aristotle, for instance, both in the *Nichomachean Ethics* and in the *Politics*, expatiates on the relative importance of nature (intelligence and spirit), habituation and instruction in the manufacture of human virtue or excellence.[92] But he then goes on to remark that "Sparta is virtually the only state in Hellas where the legislator appears to have paid any attention to the question," adding that, "in the majority of states, considerations of the kind have been quite neglected and everyone lives according to his own fancy, laying down the law in Cyclopean fashion for his wife and children."[93]

---

89. Case, Review of *Christianity and Classical Culture*, 290.

90. See, e.g., Jaeger, *Paideia*, βίος πολιτικός.

91. See Adcock, "Growth of the Greek City-State," 687.

92. Aristotle, *Nicomachean Ethics*, 10.9; γίνεσθαι δ' ἀγαθοὺς οἴονται οἵ μὲν φύσει οἵ δ' ἔθει οἵ δὲ διδαχῇ.

93. Ibid., 1180a25–29.

But even of those Hellenic communities which diverged most sharply from the philosophical ideal, for example Periclean Athens, it still remains true to say that excellence was conceived to be essentially "political"—no less "political," in fact, than it was to be for Plato and Aristotle. In the Funeral Speech reported by Thucydides, Pericles commemorates the sacrifice of Athenian youth killed in the first year of the Peloponnesian War, and this he celebrates as at once the most splendid expression of and contribution to the *ethos* of democratic and imperial Athens. The key-note is struck when the orator invites his audience to consider, as he puts it, "the way of life, the constitution and manners by virtue of which we have achieved our present greatness."[94] This by way of preface to what has been called "the first philosophical vindication of political liberalism," the spirit which, according to him, issues in Athenian versatility (εὐτραπελία) rather than Spartan order (εὐνομία, εὐκοσμία). And yet, he claims, Athens enjoys an order of her own, and this order is unique, since it is wholly independent of religious sanctions such as the sense of reverence or holy awe (αἰδώς) embodied in archaic institutions like the pre-Periclean Areopagus. So far from this, Periclean order rests on two strictly human impulses, the one negative, the other positive in its working. The former is a novel kind of fear (δέος), the fear of lively and vigorous public opinion which, while it permits of the utmost latitude in matters of private conduct, nevertheless forbids Athenians to contravene in any way the demands of the public interest and, in particular, brands the man who refuses to accept his share of civic responsibility, not merely as inactive, but as totally worthless. The latter is a hitherto unheard of kind of affection, the affection of the citizen for a city in which high spirit (εὐψυχία) is equated with freedom (ἐλευθερία) and freedom with happiness (τὸ εὔδαιμον); a city which thus provides for its members the opportunity both to live and to end their lives in felicity.[95] The affection in question is depicted as so profound and so intense as to be almost personal in character, defying comparison except perhaps with the concept of romantic life in modern literature. Those who experience it, concludes Pericles, "need no arguments to convince them of what they stand to gain by taking up arms in defense of Athens." "Rather do they contemplate from day to day the might of the city until they fall in love with her, and when the sense of her greatness has dawned upon them, they lay to heart the truth that her citizens have deserved this greatness by knowing what to do and daring to do it, as well as by a sense of honor (αἰσχύνη) which sustains them in the

---

94. Thucydides, *Peloponnesian War*, 2.36; ἀπὸ δὲ οἵας τε ἐπιτηδεύσεως . . . καὶ μεθ' οἵας πολιτείας καὶ τρόπων.

95. Ibid., 2.44; ἐνευδαιμονῆσαι.

hour of peril, and by their refusal to grudge her anything they can give, even though it be their lives."[96]

I hope I have said enough to justify the contention that, to the mind of Periclean statesmanship, the spirit of Athenian polity was genuinely creative. That contention, I suggest, would hardly have been disputed even by thinkers who, like Plato, rejected the claims put forward on behalf of democracy and of the democratic man. Plato did, indeed, attack the spirit of contemporary Athens, which he identified with the spirit of disorder; but his strictures never extended to "political" life as such, any more than they did to the methods of action traditional to politics.

What Plato rather aimed at was a radical revision of conventional political values, to be realized in the light of an absolute principle, the Idea of the Good, and in this he was to be followed (with characteristic qualifications) by Aristotle, who discovered an alternative to the Platonic Good in his own somewhat mystical conception of nature. We may therefore conclude that the efforts of Plato and Aristotle to rehabilitate the *polis* were no mere eccentricity of the speculative intelligence. What these men undertook was to discover a philosophic basis for views which were generally entertained throughout the classical centuries. To accept their findings was to hold with Aristotle that, by the very constitution of his nature, man was a being whose full potentialities for orderly development were to be realized only in a political atmosphere. And that is why he declared the "political art" to be "architectonic," since it was concerned with the highest and most perfect type of human association. At the same time, he declared the *polis* to be self-sufficient, i.e., lacking in nothing of which mankind stands in need in order to "complete" the full stature of his manhood.

It is, of course, quite possible to detect traces of anti-political or, at any rate, non-political sentiment here and there in the world of classical antiquity. They are indicated, for one thing, in the occasional literary reference to the Saturnian Age, the age of primitivism before the tyrant Zeus usurped the throne of heaven. Such references reflect, no doubt, a mood of weariness with the preoccupations, cares and anxieties of "political" or civilized life. Yet it would be difficult to point to anything in the Greco-Roman classics comparable with the spirit of radical revolt manifested in so much of modern literature—the spirit which has prompted one critic to raise the curious question: Was Europe a success?[97] Apart from the vivid expression of purely personal emotion to be found in the utterances of the early Ionian lyric poets, perhaps the most extreme assertion of anti-political

---

96. Ibid., 2.43.
97. Krutch, "Was Europe a Success?," 177.

animus occurs among the Cynics. But Cynicism is significant principally as a protest of rugged individualism against the demands of the community and such a protest would have been meaningless except in relation to the political background. Much the same thing may be said of Epicureanism with its somewhat exaggerated emphasis on the values of private life. And in this connection, it is worth remembering that both Plato and Aristotle display an acute anxiety to find a legitimate and recognized place for the life of contemplation (θεωρία) within the framework of the *polis*. This anxiety reflects a commonplace of ancient controversy which had to do with the respective merits of "practical" and of "theoretic" activity. It was stimulated partly by what may be called a Spartan dislike for the life of thought as such, partly, no doubt, by a fairly widespread prejudice against philosophers as "socially useless." But it should be observed that debate on these and kindred topics would have been impossible except on the basis of certain more or less common prepossessions with respect to the fundamentals of political association.

I hope I have said enough to make it clear that the fallacy of creative politics was deeply rooted in the thought and aspirations of classical antiquity. In this connection, the special significance of Rome was precisely that she had made her own and developed to its ultimate possibilities the logic of the political idea. In saying this, I do not for a moment forget that, throughout the long centuries of her history, the Roman republic had been subject, like all historical artifacts, to an incessant process of evolution and change (monarchy, consulate, principate, dominate), a process which, on more than one critical occasion, assumed the proportions of revolution. Nor do I deny the claim, put forward on behalf of the Romans, that, in the successive reconstructions they made of their polity, they exhibited a large measure of genuinely independent political genius; and this despite the notorious fact that they appropriated freely from the techniques devised by other peoples, friend and foe alike. It may further be conceded that, in the world-wide empire of the Caesars (as, indeed, had been true within the Hellenistic cosmopolis), "political" life lacked much of the richness and color which had characterized the activities of the earlier, strictly Hellenic city-state. There is nevertheless a sense in which it remains true to say, with the Greek rhetorician Dionysius of Halicarnassus, that, outside of Hellas, Rome was "the most Hellenic" of cities. The state and empire of Rome, like that of Macedonia with which Rome had so much in common, was emphatically a "political" construction, i.e., it was a community dedicated to the achievement of essentially "political" objectives by methods which were essentially "political." And, from this standpoint, the successive revisions made throughout Roman history in the *forma rei publicae* are best to be understood merely as "transformations of power." Accordingly, there is a certain danger of exaggerating the magnitude of the revolution whereby the consulate was translated into a principate, as there is also of overemphasizing distinctions between the principate of the early Caesars and the autocracy by which that instrument of government was to be superseded at the beginning of the fourth century. For, after all, these changes were part and parcel of a process to which all political life was liable, difficult as this process might have been to comprehend and explain in terms of classical political philosophy. We may, therefore, reasonably conclude that Rome stood in the direct line of legitimate political succession; historically, the Roman experiment emerges as the last and greatest effort of creative politics to implement those ideals of liberty, security and prosperity projected by Hellenic genius into the consciousness of antiquity. And, from this standpoint, the Roman order claimed to provide a complete and final solution to the problem of power in human life. Two questions were involved. The first concerned the moral and material values to be asserted by "political" or (as we should rather say) by "civilized" man; the second, the techniques or "arts" whereby these values were to be translated into terms of practical activity. That is to say, the problem was one of ends and means; what it called for was a pattern or design for living, devised with a view to implementing the end or ends deemed proper to mankind.

It would be interesting, if time permitted, to follow Augustine in his examination of Roman polity, and to review what he has to say with respect to the positive achievements and shortcomings of the Imperial City as custodian for the values of civilization.[98] But our immediate concern is not with his criticism of the Roman order, so much as with his explanation for the eclipse of Roman power. Accordingly, I shall proceed directly to the point and, remembering that he professes to speak as a Christian realist, I shall at once put the question: Does Augustinian realism provide the basis needed for an intelligible account of the rise and fall of Rome?

In addressing himself to this question, Augustine begins (as might have been anticipated) by disposing of certain theories of secular *scientia* which evidently enjoyed wide currency in his day. "The greatness of the Roman Empire," he declares, "is not to be ascribed either to fortuity or fate—to fortuity, according to the view or opinion of those who use the word to designate an event which occurs either without causes or (at any rate) causes that present themselves in any intelligible order (*rationabili ordine venientes*); to fate, in the sense of that which is thought to happen by a kind

---

98. Augustine, *City of God*, esp. Books 2–5.

of necessary order, independent of the will of God and man."[99] This was to reject (in advance) as sheer superstition the thesis to be propounded in his day by Gibbon, viz., that the fall of Rome was "the natural and inevitable effect of immoderate greatness."[100] It was to deny that there was any essential element in the constitution of nature or the universe (*caelestis necessitas sideria fata* or Gibbon's own so-called "principle of decline") which would serve to provide a realistic explanation for the vicissitudes of the Imperial City. In short, it was to reverse the procedure of naturalism, whether ancient or modern, and, excluding every vestige of hypothesis or myth, to look for a clue to the "fortunes" of the Roman order in the outlook and aspirations of the Roman people.

From this point of view, Augustine discovers the "vice" of imperial society precisely in Roman virtue, the ideal of civic excellence of patriotism (*cupido gloriae laudis*) to which the Romans had dedicated themselves throughout their greatest centuries. "This was the vice," he declares, "for the sake of which they suppressed all other vices."[101] In that vice Augustine discerned, on the one hand, the inspiration of the arts whereby, "in keeping with the fitness of things, Rome grew."[102] On the other hand, he saw in it the true cause of those maladies by which the empire was afflicted, maladies which the pagans blasphemously imputed to Christ.[103] We may thus conclude that, to the mind of Augustine, the vice of Rome, like that of Hellas, was the vice of false doctrine, the doctrine of perfection in and through the *polis* or *civitas*. And this is the reason why, faithful to the spirit of the Evangel, he persisted in thinking of the Christian community as, in a very real sense, foreign to political or civil society; and that notwithstanding the political and social triumph achieved during the fourth century by the Constantinian and Theodosian church. This being so, the problem facing us is to determine, if we can, the precise grounds on which Augustine bases his indictment against the classical doctrine of creative politics. This we shall now attempt to do.

In a sentence charged with profound significance for politics, Aristotle had declared that "while, indeed, there is by nature (φύσει) an impulse in all men pointing to this kind of association, nevertheless he who was the first to 'construct' it was the author of immense benefit."[104] Accordingly, to say of

---

99. Ibid., 5.1.
100. Gibbon, *Decline and Fall*, 2:1219.
101. Augustine, *City of God*, 5.12–13.
102. Ibid., 3.10; *decenter Roma crevit*.
103. Ibid., 1.1.
104. Aristotle, *Politics*, 1253a29–31; ὁ δὲ πρῶτος συστήσας.

the Romans that they had carried to its ultimate limits the logic of creative politics was to assert that they had accepted a view of the relationship between "nature" and "art" which, as Augustine held, was defective or vicious. It was vicious, in the first place, because it rested on the radically false assumption that what "nature" did was to supply to man the raw materials (in Augustinian terminology a pure *possibilitas* or potentiality) for τελείωσις or *perfectio*; in the second, because it implied that the responsibility and privilege of man was, on the basis of this pure *possibilitas* or potentiality, to "complete" his nature by means of arts or techniques devised by himself. But this, according to Augustine, was to pervert or turn upside down the true and proper relationship between "nature" on the one hand, and, on the other, the "arts" of human life. It was to suppose that "nature," as such, was an area, if not of actual chaos, as Plato had been disposed to think, at any rate of imprecision and imperfection—a point of view which, as we have been at pains to argue, was wholly inconsistent with the Christian doctrine of creation as a series of absolutely free divine acts, each and every one of which was, for that very reason, thoroughly "complete." It was thus to imagine (falsely, as Augustine held) that the human capacity for autonomous self-determination was not a gift freely (*gratis*) bestowed on man by the grace of God as an essential and indestructible element of his original endowment; and to envisage freedom rather as an ideal or pattern to be realized by man himself through his own strictly human efforts of thought and activity, and accordingly, so far at least as the ideologists of classical antiquity were concerned, through some form of "political" manipulation.

As with the classical concept of freedom, so also with the classical concept of justice. It was a fundamental conviction of Christian faith that "justice," like freedom, was a constituent of human nature in the state of integrity original to it, i.e., where, as yet, the flesh did not lust against the spirit and, indeed, felt not the slightest impulse to do so. Plato, however, conceived it as a pattern of perfection which, given the picture of nature as a realm of imprecision and incompleteness, was hardly to be realized short of the Fortunate Isles. And Aristotle, while certainly much less pessimistic than Plato in his attitude to nature, was nevertheless in full agreement with him in holding that the completion of human life was to be achieved only within the *polis*, and then only by an elite capable of political excellence. Such excellence, Aristotle points out, is quite beyond the capacity of children, women and slaves. Children have it, indeed, but with them it is immature (ἀτελές); women, but in a form that naturally remains embryonic (ἄκυρον); as for slaves, since "they are *ex hypothesi* devoid of all capacity for deliberation and choice" (προαίρεσις) "they have no share in the life of virtue and felicity."[105] On the other hand, for the politically elite, the perfection of justice means the perfection of human virtue or excellence, not indeed absolutely, but in relation to one's fellow-citizens.[106] And even with these, the excellence to be realized in any particular community is, as Aristotle is forced to concede, "relative to the constitution."[107] This means that, notwithstanding its pretensions to finality, political justice is in reality merely temporal and historical. In the hiatus between "ideal" perfection and the grim realities of history we may discern one of the most baffling antinomies which confronted classical political thought. And it was quite unrealistic of classicism to take comfort in the hypothesis that the hiatus in question was to be bridged in "the perfect state." For this was to dismiss as inconsequential the strains and tensions of actual historical experience.

There was a further and not less serious difficulty inherent in the classical concept of justice which we may here note. Granted that justice was essentially political, it would follow that, for all who were not united in the bond of a single political association, there could exist no basis for relationship other than that of mere reciprocal advantage or (alternatively) of naked force. But to make this admission was, as has been well remarked, to relegate the whole sphere of inter-state relationships to the rule of the beast. In other words, it was to concede that, in this sphere, perfection was a sheer historical impossibility. This is a conclusion from which classical political theory did not shrink; and it is not without a certain grim significance, particularly in view of the tragic record of inter-state conflict that blighted the life of the independent and autonomous city-states of Hellas. Nor was the difficulty to be overcome (so far at least as the Greeks are concerned) by any of the projects of federalism and cooperation so freely proliferated by the Hellenic genius, any more than it was through either the Spartan or the Athenian schemes of empire; since all that was accomplished by these experiments was to widen the area and to complicate the issues in dispute. We shall come back to this point at a later stage of the discussion. Meanwhile we need only remember that it was against such a background of historical actuality that classical political theory envisaged its problem and its task.

Broadly speaking, the problem of the classical *nomothetes* was conceived to be that of establishing and maintaining the conditions necessary for perfection. And, in this connection, *nomothesia* was accurately defined by Aristotle as "the art and training which aims to supplement the

---

105. Aristotle, *Politics*, 1.13.
106. Aristotle, *Nicomachean Ethics*, 1129a15.
107. Aristotle, *Politics*, 3.4.

deficiencies of nature";[108] otherwise as a kind of soul-healing, the counterpart of medicine in relation to the pathology of the body.[109] This means that virtue or excellence was regarded as a completed and stable condition (ἕξις), to be realized through a regimen (δίαιτα) of political or civil discipline. Hence the task which, according to Aristotle, devolves upon the *nomothetes*, lawgiver or statesman, the task of devising a program calculated to produce, out of the raw materials (physical and human) at his disposal, the best possible result. From this point of view, "the whole of life," remarks Aristotle, "may be divided into work and leisure, war and peace, and, so far as concerns practical activity, into those pursuits on the one hand which aim at the necessary and the useful, and on the other, those which aim at the ideal good.[110] Furthermore, political discipline is designed with an eye not to necessity and utility, but (ultimately) to "freedom" and "beauty";[111] in other words, in order to ensure the possibility of a "proper employment of leisure."[112] We thus arrive at a question of crucial importance for the theory of creative politics: can virtue be imparted or taught?[113]

To this question, the answer given by Aristotle is (as might have been anticipated) a qualified affirmative, in keeping with his doctrine of the multiple soul. The task of statesmanship being to achieve a stable condition of body, spirit and mind, the statesman seeks to "complete" this state on three planes as follows:

1. Of nature, or the physical constitution (φύσις), through nourishment (τροφή) calculated to produce a well-formed and well-developed body.

2. Of habit (ἦθος), through a process of habituation (ἐθισμός), designed with a view to the formation of a specific "way of life," the practices (ἐπιτηδεύματα) conventional to civilized or political man.

3. Of reason (λόγος), through teaching or instruction (διδαχή);

    a. of the practical intelligence (φρόνησις or *prudentia*); that "part" of the reasonable mind which is thought to be organically related

---

108. Ibid., 1337a1; πᾶσα γὰρ τέχνη καὶ παιδεία τὸ προσλεῖπον βούλεται τῆς φύσεως ἀναπληροῦν.

109. Ibid., 1.13; ἡ πολιτική compared with ἡ ἰατρική, the former concerned with τὰ περὶ ψυχῆς, the latter with τὰ περὶ σῶμα.

110. Aristotle, *Politics*, 1333a30.

111. Aristotle, *Politics*, 8.3; παιδεία ... οὐχ ὡς χρησίμην παιδευτέον ... οὐδ᾽ ὡς ἀναγκαίαν ἀλλ᾽ ὡς ἐλευθέριον καὶ καλήν.

112. Aristotle, *Politics*, 8.3; πρὸς τὴν ἐν τῇ σχολῇ διαγωγήν.

113. Cf. Burnet, *The Ethics of Aristotle*, 67.

to the life of sense, emotion and appetite; the part which thus (when perfected or completed) serves to provide a principle of organization and control for what may be called the life of society.

b. Of the pure or speculative intelligence (νοῦς, διάνοια or *sapientia*). This part of the reasonable mind, though thought to require for its activation a sub-structure of physical and social health or well-being, is nevertheless held to be intrinsically separate and independent (κεχωρισμένη). Further, inasmuch as it is concerned with exalted and divine objects, it is conceived as itself less strictly human than divine.[114]

Such was the context of thought in relation to which Hellenism envisaged the task of *nomothesia* or statesmanship. Accordingly, with impeccable logic, it proceeded to describe the role of the statesman as that of "making the citizens good by rending them submissive to the laws."[115] This the statesman was required to do by bringing the elements aforesaid, the elements of "nature," "habit" and "reason," into an harmonious relationship, one with another.[116] Plato had supposed that the qualities requisite for this, the creative and salutary activity of statesmanship, were those of a divine or, at any rate, a divinely inspired being, a superman (θεῖος ἀνήρ). Less poetic in his imagination than Plato, Aristotle nevertheless agreed with him in deifying the statesman in a sense which, if somewhat different, was no less decisive. It is profoundly significant of the limitations imposed on creative statesmanship, as Aristotle saw them, that they were limitations merely of the material or physical order. It was acknowledged, in the first place, that the physical materials of political activity lay, to some extent at least, within the gift of natural necessity (ἀνάγκη) or fortune (τύχη). It was further conceded that the human material to be used by the statesman must be endowed with intelligence and spirit,[117] if he was to make anything of it. These conditions, then, were evidently beyond control. Otherwise, however, the "nature" on which he undertook to operate was regarded as almost infinitely malleable; clay, so to speak, in the hands of the potter, out of which it was his business to manufacture good men and good citizens.[118] And this, thought Aristotle, he might well be expected to do, provided the material was sufficient for his

114. Aristotle, *Nicomachean Ethics*, 10.7.

115. Ibid., 1102a9–10; βούλεται γὰρ τοὺς πολίτας ἀγαθοὺς ποιεῖν καὶ τῶν νόμων ὑπηκόους.

116. Aristotle, *Politics*, 1332b5–6; συμφωνεῖν ἀλλήλοις.

117. Ibid., 7.7.

118. Ibid., 7.7; and 7.13, τὴν μὲν τοίνυν φύσιν οἵους εἶναι δεῖ τοὺς μέλλοντας εὐχειρώτους ἔσεσθαι τῷ νομοθέτῃ.

purposes, and that he was free from outside interference in the performance of his creative task. In these notions we may discover the *fons et origo* of political doctrine to be put forward by modern exponents of the classical tradition; for example, the famous description of the state as something more than "a partnership in things subservient only to the gross animal existence of a temporary and perishable nature . . . a partnership in all sciences, a partnership in all art; in every virtue and in all perfection."[119] Or the hardly less familiar assertion that "with every step in the socialization of morals and the moralization of politics, something of Greek excellence is won back."[120] Or the dictum less well known, but almost equally outrageous, that, "What makes the State natural . . . is the fact that, however it came into existence, *it is as it stands the satisfaction of an immanent impulse in human nature towards moral perfection—an immanent impulse which drives men upwards, through various forms of society, into the final political form.*"[121]

As thus envisaged by classical theory, the *polis* was thought to make possible the perfection of human justice. To understand what was meant by this, we cannot do better than repeat the words of Aristotle, "The very existence of a *polis* depends upon proportionate requital. If men have suffered evil, they seek to return it; if not, if they cannot requite an injury, we deem their condition to be servile. And again, if men have received good, they seek to repay it; and it is by this exchange that we are bound together in society."[122]

And further, in what is perhaps an even more significant observation, "This is the reason why we set up a temple to the Graces (Χάριτες) in sight of all men, to remind them to repay that which they receive (whether good or evil); for this is the special characteristic of charity or grace. We ought to return the good offices of those who have been charitable or gracious to us, and then again to take the initiative in doing favours to them."[123]

This, declares Aristotle, is "proportionate requital," "the rule of justice that holds society together" (τῷ ἀντιποιεῖν (γὰρ) ἀνάλογον συμμένει ἡ πόλις). By contrast with what he pronounces to be the deficiency of simple requital, the repayment of equals for equals, it means, for example, that "if an officer strike a man, he ought not to be struck in return; but if a man strike an officer, he ought not merely to be struck back, but also to be punished."[124]

---

119. Burke, *Reflections on the Revolution in France*, 85.
120. Bradley, "Aristotle's Conception of the State," 241.
121. Barker, *Politics of Aristotle*, xlix; emphasis added.
122. Aristotle, *Nicomachean Ethics*, 1132b34–1133a3; cf. Cicero, *De Officiis*.
123. Ibid., 1133a4.
124. Ibid., 1132b29.

Could there have been a more vivid or impressive symbol than this Hellenic temple of the Graces of the error enshrined at the heart of a society erected on the basis of φιλαυτία, *amor sui*, or, as we should say, self-love? Or a more precise indication of just what Augustine means when he denounces such a community as an expression of secular perversity?

The perversity of secularism, as I have tried to show, rested on an initial error, the error of having misconceived the true and proper relationship between "nature" and "art." And the result of this error was, in the suggestive Augustinian metaphor, to have completely inverted or turned upside down the realities of both. Secular perversity thus uncritically assumed that, if indeed there existed some "flaw" or "fault" operating to prevent the fulfillment of the human potential, the place to look for such a fault was in "nature" (envisaged as the sphere of incompletion) when, in point of fact, the fault was not in "nature," but in the construction placed upon it by the human mind. To make this assumption was to suppose that man begins, so to speak, where nature leaves off; that the human task is to perfect the imperfection of nature's handiwork. In other words, it is idolatry in its most subtle and seductive manifestation, the worship by man of himself.

On the other hand, to reject the initial error of secular perversity was to perceive that the human mind, as such, enjoys no natural exemption from imperfection which it is entitled to deny to the sub-rational elements of human nature, merely because they are sub-rational. It was to acknowledge that the claim of the mind to supply in "right reason" (ὀρθὸς λόγος, *recta ratio*) an absolute criterion of perfection was fallacious; nothing more or less, in fact, than the classical version of secular pride. The pride in question was that of a being who, simply because he is conscious of his rationality, presumes on that account to legislate for what he fallaciously imagines to be naturally and intrinsically "incomplete" or "imperfect" viz., the life of emotion and appetite; compelling that life to defer to what he presumptuously holds up as the dictates of "right reason," but which are in fact merely the dictates of "his" reason; or, in a characteristic sophistry of politics, "forcing it to be free." And this he does with a view to "securing" the freedom of the reasonable mind which he thus fallaciously identifies with the freedom of the organism as a whole. Hence, we may infer, the whole grandiose structure of creative politics, the concept of the classical commonwealth. To see the classical commonwealth with Augustine as an expression of human pride and self-sufficiency is to understand what he means when he declares in his first preface that "the king and founder of the celestial society, in the writings of his people, has disclosed a sentence of divine law, in which it is stated: *God resists the proud, but to the humble he giveth grace.*"[125] There can be no possible doubt that, to the mind of Augustine, this divine sentence has a specific and immediate application to the pretensions of Eternal Rome.

In this connection, it may be of interest to recall the words in which, more than four centuries earlier, Vergil had formulated for his compatriots his sense of their imperial mission; words which, it will be remembered, were echoing in Augustine's ear as he set his hand to the work; if it was only to stigmatize them as evidence of the vainglory with which the human spirit is inflated when, arrogating to itself the prerogative of God, it craves to be addressed in terms of praise like these:

> *tu regere imperio populos, Romane, memento, hae tibi erunt artes, pacisque imponere morem, parcere subiectis et debellare superbos.*[126]

But, although no doubt having a special application to Rome, the divine sentence in question was (as Augustine sees it) of universal validity.

"Wherefore also," he proceeds, "I am bound to consider in general, so far as the argument requires and opportunity permits, the question of secular society of the *civitas terrena*, which while, in its pursuit of dominion, it reduces the nations to subjection, is itself dominated by the lust for domination (*libido dominandi*)."[127]

But thus describing the *hormé* or impulse of secular society as a collective will-to-power, Augustine associates himself in some degree with the most hard-headed and least sentimental of classical historians, the "atheist" Thucydides, with whose concepts of interpretation he was, of course, familiar insofar as they had been reproduced in Latin by one of his favorite sources, viz., Sallust. At the same time, he anticipates in a surprising way the position to be assumed by representative modern exponents of power-politics, notably Machiavelli and Hobbes—an aspect of his thinking which, incidentally, has occasioned no little perplexity to certain of his critics (Carlyle, Hearnshaw, Baynes, McIlwain among others) who find it hard to understand why, as a devoted Christian, he should keep such apparently strange company. For a classical formulation of the doctrine of power-politics, or rather of the assumptions with respect to human nature on which it is based, we cannot do better than turn to the words of Hobbes himself:

> By Manners, I mean not here, Decency or Behavior, as how one man should salute another, or how a man should wash his

---

125. Augustine, *City of God*, 1. Preface.
126. Vergil, *Aeneid*, 6.851–53.
127. Augustine, *City of God*, 1. Preface.

mouth, or pick his teeth before company, or such other *small Moralls*; but those qualities of Mankind, that concern their living together in Peace, and Unity. To which end we are to consider, that the Felicity of this life, consisteth not in the repose of a mind Satisfied. For there is no such *Finis Ultimus* (utmose ayme) nor *Summum Bonum* (greatest good) as is spoken of in the books of the old Morall Philosophers. Nor can a man any more live, whose Desires are at an end, than he whose Senses and Imaginations are at a stand. Felicity is a continuall progresse of the desire, from one object to another; the attaining of the former, being still but the way to the latter. The cause whereof is, that the object of man's desire, is not to Enjoy once onely, and for an instant of time, but to assure forever, the way of his future desire. And therefore, the voluntary actions, and inclinations of all men, tend not onely to the procuring, but also to the assuring, of a contented life; and differ onely in the way; which ariseth partly from the diversity of passions in divers men; and partly from the difference of the knowledge or opinion each one has of the causes, which produce the effect desired.

So that, in the first place, I put for a general inclination of all mankind, a perpetual and restless desire of Power after power, that ceaseth only in Death. And the cause of this, is not always that a man hopes for a more intensive delight, than he has already attained to; or that he cannot be content with a moderate power; but because he cannot assure the power and means to live well, which he hath present, without the acquisition of more.[128]

The Hobbesian picture of nature as a picture of permanent war, in which competing egos are represented as joined, one with another, in an incessant struggle for power, would have impressed Augustine as anything but strange or abnormal. Indeed, there is every reason to suppose that he would have accepted it as an accurate description of the world in which he himself lived. Yet we cannot too strongly insist that, in the diagnosis he offers of the human situation, Augustine adopts a position diametrically opposed to that of Hobbes. To him, the condition depicted was emphatically not one of nature in the state of physical and spiritual integrity which, he firmly believed, was original to it. On the contrary, it was one in which nature had been vitiated and corrupted by the sin of *superbia* or secular pride; in other words, it was pathological, an excellent illustration, in fact, of what he calls *perversitas saeculi*. Accordingly, it was not to be effectively remedied in the

---

128. Hobbes, *Leviathan*, 1.11.

manner proposed by Hobbes, i.e., by substituting for the multitude of conflicting individual egos (the warfare of each against all) one vast collective ego with which, he declares, "no power on earth is to be compared"; or, as Vergil in his day had put it, by "imposing a habit of peace" after the theory and practice of Eternal Rome, the effort of creative politics in terms of which he sought to justify the role of Rome in world history.

It is a common-place of Christian, and so also Augustinian, wisdom that the just man lives and walks by faith.[129] But the faith by which the Christian is justified has nothing in common with secular credulity or secular orthodoxy, the classical sense of πίστις as a blind and purely emotional impulse of confidence in flat defiance of reason; any more than it has with the personified Πειθώ, the goddess *Persuasion* whose one aim is to gain her end, whether by fair means or foul. Christian faith rests upon an unshakable conviction that, notwithstanding the efforts of secularism to rationalize and justify its pretensions, the order of nature revealed by Christ and the Scriptures is, in fact, the true order; to acknowledge which must therefore be the starting-point for all genuinely fruitful investigation into the problem of perfection. To accept that conviction is to recognize that nature, as a realm of precise and orderly motion, is wholly dependent upon the will of the Father, operating by His Word and through His Spirit to create and sustain it, and doing so in such a way that nothing whatsoever escapes His providential care. It is thus to recognize that what secular pride has done is to invert the proper relationship between "nature" and "art," thereby misconceiving the real character of both. And, in the light of this truth, Christian faith perceives that the task of mankind is emphatically not one of "creation," as secularism in its arrogance has supposed, but rather one of "construction," in humble and patient submission to the divine will. The prerequisite to this task must therefore be a complete reversal of the attitude characteristic of secularism, an acknowledgement that the *sine qua non* for genuine perfection must be a rebirth, renewal or renovation of the human spirit. That such a spiritual rebirth was historically possible had, of course, been the constant theme of the long line of Hebrew prophets, by whom it had been insistently reiterated. To the eye of faith, that possibility of history had, in the fullness of time, been translated into an historical actuality in the perfect humanity of Christ and His assurance: *He who hath seen me hath seen the Father.*[130]

In my final lecture I shall try to deal with the Christian sense of history as a progressive fulfillment of the promise of perfection, extended originally to the old Adam and freshly attested in the new. My immediate concern is, however, with the question of pride and its workings, particularly as these

129. Augustine, *City of God*, 19.4; *iustus ex fide vivit.*
130. John 14:9.

may serve to illustrate what I have ventured to call the imperfection of politics. The characteristic of pride is that it ignores or rejects the divine promise of fulfillment through historical experience, and therewith the way of life proposed by the Master to his followers for their pilgrimage through this troublous world. Repudiating the hope of Christianity and in defiance of its warnings, secular pride presumes, out of the plenitude of its own resources, the resources of strictly human excellence (intelligence and endurance) to create "of and from itself a system of right living."[131] In the presumption of secular pride that it is competent to do so we may discern a generalized version of what is familiar to students of classical antiquity as the doctrine of autarky or self-sufficiency. And, in the presumption of classical self-sufficiency, we may find the reason for Augustine's stern condemnation of political action as "a perverse attempt to emulate the creative activity of God."[132]

Christianity is in full accord with classicism in defining the criterion of perfection as "security." In this connection it is important to note that the word *securitas*, as it is used by both parties to the controversy, indicates a condition of the spirit, "freedom from care or anxiety" (*se + cura; se* being privative), in the absence of which it is agreed that genuine perfection is unthinkable. The question thus arises: how is such perfection to be attained? To this question Christian faith had, of course, its answer, an answer which was determined by its acceptance of Christ as the Messiah, and by the consequent assurance of perfect felicity in the "life to come."[133] As for this temporal life, the promise of the faith was merely that of a burden to carry and of a task to perform.[134] "What flow of eloquence," demands Augustine, "is capable of doing justice to the miseries of this life?"[135] Of these miseries not the least is a haunting consciousness of insecurity, a sense which is irrepressible in view of the changes and chances which mortal life is heir to. Consider, for example, the so-called *prima naturae*, the rudimentary goods which men desire naturally i.e. without instruction or cultivation, viz; physical pleasure and repose, or some combination of the two, together with bodily integrity, health and strength, as well as the intellectual gifts which, to a greater or less degree, are common to mankind. These goods,

131. Augustine, *City of God*, 19.4; *ipsum recte vivere nobis ex nobis*.

132. Ibid., 19.12; *superbia perverse imitatur Deum*.

133. Ibid., 19.11; *beatitudo pacis aeternae, in qua sanctis finis est, id est vera perfectio*; cf. 22.30; *ibi vacabimus et videbimus, videbimus et amabimus, ambimus et laudabimus. Face quod erit in fine sine fine.*

134. Ibid., 19.27; *tranquillitas in hac temporali vita non potest adprehendi. Pax Dei in hac vita—potius remissions peccatorum constat quam perfectione virtutum*.

135. Ibid., 19.4; cf. 22.22–23 where he almost succeeds in answering his own question.

in whatever measure man may possess them, are uncertain and, in the end, they inevitably fail him. Nor are the moral goods, the virtues which are capable of development through training, any less precarious. Temperance, for instance, is engaged in an endless conflict with vices which are not adventitious but our very own, the warfare of the members to whose rebellious impulses we give our reluctant assent. As for prudence, how can it hope to discover a principle in terms of which to discriminate accurately between truth and error, good and evil? And does not the precept of secular justice, that we should render to each man his due, demonstrate clearly that justice is a project on which to labor, rather than an end in which to find repose? Finally, what is to be thought of an ideal of fortitude which inspires men, in the stupidity of their pride (*superbiae stupor*) to destroy themselves, merely because (in the popular phrase) they cannot "take it?"[136] The plain truth is that, amid the changes and chance of life here below there is, and can be, no security even for the good, and the very saints themselves are not immune from trial and temptation.[137] "Yet in this abode of weakness and in these wicked days," concludes Augustine, "that state of anxiety is not without its use, since it stimulates men to seek with keener longing for that security which is complete and unassailable."[138]

Such are the facts of secular life as seen by Christian realism. If the picture be true, and this is hardly to be questioned, the inference must be that the quest for finality is doomed, in advance, to defeat; since to repeat Hobbes's words, "There is no such *finis ultimus* nor *summum bonum* as is spoken of in the books of the old Morall Philosophers." To this conclusion Augustine had arrived when he declared that, "Divine truth speaking through the Prophet and the Apostle, laughs to scorn the vanity of those who imagine that the ultimate goals of good and evil are to be found in this life."[139]

In repudiating the pretensions to finality implicit in secularism, Augustine, in effect, asserts that the impulse, dynamic or *hormé* by which the patterns of secular life are determined is one of insatiable desire. The desire in question is a desire for security, and it is none the less "real" because the objects in which it seeks satisfaction invariably prove, on experience, to be anything but adequate. This is as much as to say that, whatever the specific forms it may assume, the *pax terrena* (the order constituted by secular man)

---

136. Ibid., 19.4.
137. Ibid., 19.8–10.
138. Ibid., 19.10.
139. Ibid., 19.4; he quotes Ps 94:11; *Dominus novit cogitationes hominum*, and 1 Cor 3:20; *Dominus novit cogitationes sapientium, quoniam vanae sunt.*

is, in the nature of things, a *pax imperfecta*. It thus enjoys no title to finality, a finality which is, in fact, denied to any merely human artifact, whether of hand or brain. To this insight of Christian wisdom we may, I think, ascribe certain of the most distinctive aspects of Augustine's thought in relation to (a) the question of order and motion in secular history and (b) the criticism he makes of the classical doctrine of perfection through politics. I shall conclude this lecture by saying a word about each of these points in turn.

Augustine sees the driving force of secular life as a passion for security—a passion which cannot be satisfied since, as he puts it, "the good to which it aspires does not suffice either for the individual or the community, lacking, as it does, the requisite character."[140] From this point of view, secular history emerges as a process (*procursus*) to which there is no logical end or term. Nevertheless, in his yearning for ἡσυχία, *otium*, or rest from his travail, secular man is under a constant temptation to identify the goal of his pilgrimage with some mere halting place which he discovers by the way. He thus endeavors to create and maintain for himself successive forms of order, of which Augustine (no doubt with is eye on the actual course of Greek and Roman history) distinguishes three, as follows:

1. that of the household or family (*pax domestica*)
2. that of the *polis* or *civitas* (*pax civica*)
3. that of the imperial state (*pax imperiosae civitatis*)

But this he does only to discover that, despite all his efforts, despite the blood, sweat and tears which they have cost, he has not succeeded in putting an end to his misery or in advancing a single step toward genuine security.[141] The bankruptcy of his efforts is, however, revealed only in the "third grade" of human society, viz., that of the *cosmopolis*, when he finally discovers that the sum-total of his achievement is to have produced an imperfect compromise of more or less opposing wills with respect to these goods which pertain to mortal life.[142]

Envisaged against such a background, what is to be thought of the classical concept of the commonwealth (*notio rei publicae*, in Cicero's words) as an organization for the purpose of "establish[ing] and conserve[ing] a complete and finished program of life"?[143] To this question the answer given

140. Ibid., 18.1.

141. Ibid., 19.7; *sed hoc quam multis et quam grandibus bellis, quanta strage hominum, quanta effusione humani sanguinis comparatum est! Quibus transactis, non est tamen eorundum malorum finita miseria.*

142. Ibid., 19.17; *quaedam compositio voluntatum.*

143. Lindsay, *Religion, Science and Society*, 7.

by Augustine is that it is one of the most colossal, and one of the most tragic, manifestations of secular perversity, in its effort to delude itself as to the realities of human history and experience. Nor is its character, as such, in any way improved (quite the reverse) by the attempt of men like Cicero to relate the *notio rei publicae* to a purely hypothetical principle of natural reason and equity, which he thus audaciously identifies with cosmic mind (*mens summi Jovis*). Accordingly, Augustine rejects the Ciceronian definition of the state in order to redefine it in terms of Christian realism as "a multitude of rational beings, united together by the bond of desires which they hold in common."[144] The redefinition thus proposed is not, as certain of the commentators would have us believe, either fortuitous or anomalous. On the contrary, it is quite deliberately put forward by Augustine as a necessary implication of his Christian faith. And its effect is to give rise to a wholly new theory by which the state is envisaged in terms of legitimacy, that is, of a concept which does not claim, on the face of it, to be unhistorical.

There could hardly be a better illustration of secular perversity, as Augustine sees it, than is to be found in the celebrated dictum of Aristotle that "he who by nature and not accidentally is without a *polis* is either below humanity or above it, either a beast or a god."[145] To accept this dictum was to ascribe to the *polis* the character of an absolute, in relation to which the values normal to the life of men as social beings, were resolved into terms of pure functionalism. This meant for example that the problem of conduct was envisaged pragmatically as a question of "my station and its duties." It meant that education, the discipline of *bonae* or *liberalis artes*, was conceived, not as an instrument to equip its possessor with the tools for life, but rather as a means towards advancement, in the official hierarchy of the existing imperial order, this is, purely and simply from the standpoint of its economic utility. Finally, it meant that the slightest deviation from the conventional standards of "political" or "civilized" order was regarded as subversive. On the other hand, to accept those standards was to commit oneself, in practice, to a hopeless battle of reaction against the forces of development and change; like the Emperor Julian, for instance, whose public profession was a hatred of innovation in every form, and who was thus content to live and die as a martyr to the faded gospel which he dignified by the name of Hellenism.

To Augustine the position in which Julian and others like him found themselves was the direct and inevitable consequence of an attitude to historical experience which, as he held, was radically vicious. The attitude in

---

144. Augustine, *City of God*, 2.20–21; 4.4; 19.22–23.
145. Aristotle, *Politics*, 1253a1.

question was that of classical pride, and, as we have seen, it rested upon a tacit assumption that the human mind, by reason of its own intrinsic powers, had access to a reservoir of ultimate truth which was, so to speak, beyond experience and beyond history. In that assumption Augustine detected the root cause of classical error, an error which could have but one result viz., that of vitiating and perverting the judgment with respect to all the great issues of human life. One characteristic expression of that error, as he saw it, was to suppose that the perfection of nature, and, therewith, peace and freedom, was to be achieved through the subjugation of the life of sense and emotion to the demands of a reason which claimed to be unhistorical, in what was euphemistically described as "the commonwealth of reasonable men." Another and not less deadly fallacy was to imagine that there was simply no alternative between the order thus prescribed by classical reason and, on the other hand, intellectual and moral chaos.

It was in this context that Augustine undertook the task of convincing his pagan opponents that, if they persisted in addressing themselves to the issues of the day in this quite unhistorical and unrealistic spirit, they were doomed to utter and irrevocable defeat; and of making them understand that the one hope of salvaging what was of more than merely temporary worth in the achievement of the classical past depended upon a radical revision of their attitude toward the potential values of a barbarian and Christian future. I shall deal further with this question in my next lecture.

Personality and History[146]

The issue of nature and grace were debated by Augustine and his opponents in the most general terms and with hardly the slightest reference (so far as I can recall) to the momentous historical developments currently taking place within the Greco-Roman world. But this does not mean that they were without relevance to those developments. On the contrary, they underlay and determined the interpretation to be placed upon them by Augustine in his account of the two societies, the *civitas terrena* and the *civitas caelestis*. The suggestion has recently been made that the doctrine of the two societies was not original with Augustine, but that he purloined it from an obscure Christian sophist named Tyconius.[147] It is hard to be patient with this type of criticism. In a purely formal sense there may, indeed, be something to the notion. Yet, in this instance as always, the critical problem is not so

---

146. [Charles Norris Cochrane, "Personality and History," Charles Norris Cochrane Fonds. University of Toronto Archives, B2003-0011/006 (19).]

147. Laistner, Review of *Christianity and Classical Culture*, 314–15.

much one of derivation as of the use to which they are put. And, from this standpoint, the question of entitlement can hardly be a matter for dispute.

If any doubt existed on this point, it could be settled simply by reference to the first preface of the *De Civitate Dei*, a carefully considered and highly elaborated statement in which Augustine records his sense of the issue to be discussed and the lines on which he proposes to discuss it: "In this work, addressed to you, my dear son Marcellinus, in discharge of my promise, I have undertaken to defend the most glorious society of God against those who prefer their own deities to its founder, both here in this world of time, where it subsists, and also in that solid estate of eternity, which it now awaits with endurance, until the final consummation of divine justice, when, by reason of its excellence, it will in due course achieve a final victory and a perfect peace."[148]

Augustine was fully alive to the magnitude and difficulty of his enterprise; it was, as he puts it, *magnum opus et arduum*: "I know," he declares, "how hard it is to convince the proud of the virtue of humility, through which it becomes possible to attain to heights far surpassing the loftiest pinnacles of all transitory and mundane achievement, heights which are unassailable to human pride but are made accessible by divine grace."[149]

In my last lecture I sought to illustrate the result of applying the Augustinian concepts of understanding to certain of the traditional questions of classical ethics, by showing how the procedure made possible a drastic revision in terms of Christian realism of the conventional "political" values cherished by classical antiquity. In this, the fourth and final lecture of the course, I shall venture upon a still more ambitious undertaking, and try to demonstrate their applicability to the interpretation of history. And I shall begin by referring briefly to the difficulty which Augustine declares he experienced in preparing his thesis in support of the divine society; since this difficulty was, in my opinion, a real one, and since it was intimately related to his special problem as a propagandist for the faith.

It need hardly be remarked that, for the ordinary reader, even though he were familiar with the Latin language, the *De Civitate Dei* could hardly be classed as an easy or an attractive book. In saying this, I am not so much thinking of the peculiarities of the Latinity, formidable as these undoubtedly are, with its long and involved periodic sentence-structure, the endless and not always agreeable efforts to achieve assonance and alliteration, the highly elaborated and (occasionally) far-fetched antitheses, and other stylistic devices characteristic of the time when it was written. Nor yet of the

---

148. Augustine, *City of God*, 1. Preface.
149. Ibid.

fact that the work of composition was prolonged over a period of not less than thirteen years, and that it was subject to the manifold interruptions which fell to the lot of a busy ecclesiastic and tireless controversialist. The difficulty confronting Augustine was of a much more serious and disturbing character. And it is peculiarly significant that this difficulty, as Augustine himself sees it, was not so much intellectual as it was moral, or rather, that it was the one because it was, at the same time and in an even deeper sense, the other. The audience to whom Augustine addressed himself was not an audience of common men, the man on the street of Carthage, of Rome, or of Alexandria. It was made up of the intellectual and official aristocracy of the declining empire, persons like Ausonius, Aurmianus Marcellinus and Symmachus Prefect of the City; that is to say of men who, whatever their nominal religious affiliations—Christian or pagan—had all been so effectively schooled in the ancient classical discipline of liberal arts that their minds were, in consequence, largely closed to anything other than classical modes of thought. To such an audience the argumentation of Augustine must have appeared strangely remote and meaningless, even on the strictly intellectual plane.

But the intellectual difficulty, as Augustine realized, was merely one aspect of a greater difficulty, viz., that of combating *superbia* or secular pride. Accordingly, to state his position in the way he does was to recognize that what it involved was a problem of personality or will; in other words, that it was fundamental and went to the very heart of the issue which divided Christianity from secularism. And this not merely because it struck at the vested interests which had been created through the *entente cordiale* established between Church and Empire under the renovationist princes of the fourth century.[150] For actually what Augustine had to say in the De Civitate Dei was so far-reaching as to threaten the very foundations of organized society itself, so far at least as these were determined by "classical" political principles; and it was, no doubt, his perception of this truth which prompted the bitter comment of Edward Gibbon to which I earlier referred.[151] Its publication was thus, quite naturally, to be interpreted as a challenge to all the material and spiritual values for which civilized man had struggled throughout the millennium or more which had elapsed since the "springtime of classical song" on the Ionian coastland. And, from this point of view, it is not hard to understand and (in a way) to sympathize with the antipathy it must inevitably have excited among those whose position and prospects were bound up with the survival of the empire and were destined

---

150. See Cochrane, *Christianity and Classical Culture*, 195.
151. See "Augustinian Prognostic," above.

to be shattered by its fall. The plain truth is that Augustine's message was, as it was blindly felt to be, profoundly subversive of the established order; and in no respect more so than its implications for history. Indeed, it is not too much to suggest that, in the views Augustine put forward about history, we may discern the crux of the whole work.

It is a common observation that classical historiography, at any rate from the time of Polybius, had been in general "pragmatic" and moralistic; that is to say, it treated the past as a laboratory from which to select *exempla* or patterns of behavior, virtuous and vicious, which it aimed to record with a view to their supposedly practical value as models to be imitated or avoided in the future. The earlier Greek historians, Herodotus and Thucydides, had indeed attempted to make something more than this out of the material at their disposal. Herodotus, for instance, had undertaken to turn history into a search for causes,[152] by applying to it the methods of investigation (ἱστορία) originally devised for their own purposes by the physical scientists of Ionia, especially, perhaps, by Heracleitus.[153] And Thucydides, while feeling bound in the name of scientific humanism to reject what he calls "the general hypothesis" of Herodotus, and therefore confining his attention to the actual λόγοι and ἔργα of history, "the things men say and the things they do," was obviously no less concerned than his predecessor with the possibility of reducing his material to terms of general law. In Herodotus, the pragmatic interest had been overlaid (a) by the sense of history as cosmic drama and (b) by the desire of the historian to celebrate the epic achievements and failures of the human actors on the stage. But, with Thucydides, the pragmatic interest comes into the immediate foreground, and history presents itself as a textbook of power politics, designed for the information and instruction of those who were desirous of learning how politicians and generals would, in all human probability (κατὰ τὸ ἀνθρώπειον, κατὰ τὸ εἰκός) respond when subjected to physical and moral shocks such as were occasioned in Hellas during the twenty-seven years of intermittent conflict we know as the great Peloponnesian War. And it was as just such a textbook of power politics that the author confidently pronounced his work to be "a possession forever"; not without good reason, as posterity was (somewhat grudgingly) to attest. Certainly among his successors in Greco-Roman times, there was none who approached Thucydides in the skill with which he marshaled and presented his evidence. And, even by comparison with the most notable of the moderns, he easily holds his own as a master in the craft of "scientific" historiography.

---

152. Herodotus, *Histories*, 1.1
153. See Cochrane, *Christianity and Classical Culture*, 503–09.

Envisaged against the background of classical achievement, the approach of Augustine to history was strikingly original; so complete, indeed, was his departure from Greco-Roman models that the very language hardly existed into which he could effectively cast the ideas which flowed from the white-hot crucible of his thought. But if we consider attentively what Augustine had in view, it will, I think, become evident that this was nothing less than to formulate the elements of a dialectic of human history designed to be of universal validity and application. No enterprise such as this had ever before been undertaken in the Greek and Latin world, except possibly by Herodotus nearly nine hundred years before. But the elements (στοιχεῖα, *elementa*) which had gone to constitute the Herodotean dialectic were confessedly "mythical" or "hypothetical" in character; they were, in fact, nothing but abstractions of the conceptualizing imagination. The result was a panorama of historical action which, however majestic in its scope and grandeur, failed nevertheless to do justice to the facts of historical life; notably, to that of human freedom. In the Herodotean pattern, human beings emerged as the helpless puppets of divine and cosmic energy (τὸ θεῖον), an impulse or urge (ὁρμή) which was conceived to operate as relentlessly and remorselessly as, for example, the mechanism of an earthquake or the movement of the tides. Accordingly, the only "moral" to be derived from the world-picture of Herodotus was what the pious author arbitrarily chose to read into it in his doctrine of natural retribution or compensation (νέμεσις); and its value could only be as a warning to the credulous of the perils entailed in all "excessive" human effort. For this reason, both the method and the findings of the Father of History were rejected by the deliberate judgment of his successor and, after Thucydides, the tendency of classical historiography was to remain on a "safe," pragmatic level. This meant, *inter alia*, that it was intensely conservative in spirit; in no sense qualified to provide a radical criticism of classical achievement and classical shortcomings.

To understand the deficiencies of classical historiography, we need only remember that the effort of the representative classical historians, like that of the classical poets, had been to "compose" a picture in which (to paraphrase Butcher) the "sequence of events was not the empirical sequence of fact, but the logical and conceivable sequence of ideas";[154] a picture "from which the element of chance had (so far as possible) been eliminated," in order to exhibit "the unity and significance of characters and events" for the edification and guidance of the reader. And the image or likeness (ὁμοίωμα) of historical reality thus put together by the art of the historian was, with typical secular perversity, actually pronounced to be superior to its original,

---

154. Butcher, *Aristotle's Theory*, 398.

precisely because it excluded what secularism in its arrogance presumed to "eliminate" as "the lawless, the fantastic, the impossible."[155] But secularism ignored the truth that, in thus mutilating its material, it was destroying the veritable and authentic substance of history and resolving it into a kind of myth, inferior in value to poetry and philosophy.

Augustinian realism, on the other hand, laid the foundation for a new view of history as a subject of investigation wholly independent of poetry and philosophy, and governed by laws peculiar to itself. And for this the point of departure was a full and frank recognition of the essentially empirical character of historical fact. For to recognize that historical fact is, by its very nature, empirical was, after all, merely to recognize that, in the providence of God, events "happen" or "occur" as, if and when they do and not otherwise; in other words, it was to acknowledge them as "objective." And to acknowledge the objectivity of historical fact was to declare that, as fact, it carries with it its own credentials; in other words, that it is theoretically impossible to determine its authenticity *a priori* or in advance. In short, it was to perceive that the one valid test or criterion of historical fact is to be found in experience.

In this insight of Augustinian realism there were concealed implications of the utmost importance for historiography. For if it be true that experience is the one valid criterion of historical fact, the conclusion follows that no fact whatsoever, provided it be sufficiently attested by experience, can properly be ignored by the historian, however disagreeable or disconcerting he may find it. Accordingly, the historian enjoys no right to prefer any one fact to any other merely because it appears to suit his particular pragmatic purpose (didactic or otherwise), or merely because it is thought to conform to the standard of a preconceived and arbitrary "logical" pattern. To suppose otherwise is to be guilty of the presumption of assuming that, from any merely human vantage-point in history, it is possible to envisage history as a whole and to comprehend its meaning, as the saying is, *sub specie aeternitatis*. Accordingly, Christian historiography repudiates *in toto* this disastrous error of secular pride. It recognizes that the prime duty of the historian, as historian, is to show himself hospitable to "new" fact, as this emerges empirically or by "chance" in human experience; never forgetting that what one age and one culture dismisses as incredible ("the lawless, the fantastic, the impossible") may for another prove to be the sheerest commonplace. It further acknowledges that another and not less vital part of the historian's duty is to respect as sacred the fact which is thus authenticated by experience, and to realize that, as fact, it is not to be tampered with in the

---

155. Ibid., 184.

interests of any pragmatic purpose, whether economic or social or political. For, unlike the poet and the philosopher, the historian, as Christian historiography perceives, does not "make" his own fact, by the process of abstraction or otherwise. His is the humbler but not less exacting task of accepting fact as he finds it, and of seeking to explore its meaning in the light of divine and cosmic truth. And, from this standpoint, even the most enigmatic and outrageous of historical events (such, for instance, as the crucifixion of the Master) may well turn out to possess the utmost value and significance, if only its meaning be properly understood. Finally, Christian realism insists that, in order to comprehend that meaning, the historian must envisage his facts, the so-called "events" of history, not in abstraction, or as the manifestation of "vast impersonal forces," but for what they really are, viz., as the outward and visible expression of personality or, to use the term employed by Augustine, of *voluntas* or will.

At this point a warning may, perhaps, be timely. By the word *voluntas* Augustine does not mean some "natural," "physical" urge or impulse, an impulse which is non-rational or even anti-rational in character. Such as would seem to have been implied by the word as used by William James in his famous essay on the *Will to Believe*. To suppose that Augustine was tainted with "voluntarism" in the modern sense of the term is utterly to misconceive him; it is to miss the whole point of his polemic against "secular perversity," a perversity which dogmatically ascribes to what I have called the abstractions of the conceptualizing imagination a reality which it denies to the actual human beings who "construct" such abstractions as a regular and, indeed, essential, part of the normal processes of human thought. It is thus to commit the fallacy of supposing that ideas make men, whereas the truth is that men make ideas, and these ideas, if indeed they may be said to "live" at all, do so only in the consciousness of those who invent and those who accept them; otherwise, the "types," "patterns" or "forms" proliferated by the conceptualizing imagination are still-born. Augustine, therefore, quite deliberately rejects this particular brand of secular perversity in order to insist that history, in the only real and intelligible sense of the word, is the history of wills or (as we should perhaps say) of personalities; i.e., of human beings, as they think, feel, and wish, and as they act. And, from this point of view, the truly significant historical event, whenever it occurs in human experience, is what has recently been called the "dynamic assessment" which precedes and determines the moment of action.[156]

To see "will" in this light is to recognize it, not as an abstraction, some hypothetical faculty or power operating *in vacuo*, but, in Augustinian

---

156. See MacIver, *Social Causation*, 238.

terminology, as a determination of the "total man," i.e., of man in his being, his reason or intelligence, his desire or affection; in other words, of man conceived as "made in the image of the Trinity," the creative and moving principle in nature and in human life. Christian anthropology holds that these three elements of personality or will are all equally original to human nature; the third is not to be derived, by any neo-platonic theory of emanation, from the second, nor the second from the first. Further, they are all three equally involved in the moment of dynamic assessment and action, i.e., of "action" in the proper sense of the term. From this standpoint, "action" is quite precisely described as the consequence and expression of voluntary motion or the motion of the will and so, in its essential character, "free." Furthermore, the freedom which is thus believed to be original to mankind by virtue of his nature and constitution as a will or personality cannot conceivably be lost; although, indeed, the capacity of man to exercise his freedom may well be and, in fact, is so impaired and enfeebled as to be partially or wholly ineffective, a truth to which universal experience only too painfully attests.

What I have just said needs, perhaps, some further clarification. In asserting that man, by the constitution of his nature, enjoys a capacity for free self-determination which, however, he had lost the power to implement, Christian anthropology does not mean to suggest that this capacity is in any way naturally independent of the situations and relationships which are normal to his life as an embodied spirit and from which he cannot hope to escape; since to do so, even if that were possible, would be to deny his specific character as a human being; and, as Augustine points out, "we know by the witness of nature herself that a union of body and soul is essential to the fulfillment and completeness of our being."[157] Accordingly, although fully agreeing with the secular proposition that while "man is born free, he is everywhere in chains,"[158] Christianity rejects the conclusion that the chains in question are those of situations and relationships, to break which is the way to peace and freedom. What Christianity means by the statement that man is "naturally" free is, then, merely that by his nature he is capable of more than a purely physical reaction to physical stimuli; in other words, that he is free to assert himself as will. And, further, that in order to operate as factors in voluntary motion, the physical stimuli to which he is subjected have to be translated into terms of volition, with its characteristic ingredients of sense-perception, appetition or aversion, and idea. Viewed in this light, the response a man makes to any situation with which he is confronted de-

---

157. Augustine, *City of God*, 10.29.
158. Rousseau, *Social Contract*, 1.1.

pends upon how he assesses its significance in relation to his interests and purposes, and any such assessment requires the assent of the will in order that he may be moved to action. In this sense, all significant human "action" has its counterpart in "passion," all "doing" in "suffering." But "passion" or "suffering" is not on that account to be explained as "irresistible physical impulse"; since, if that were indeed its character, there would be no appreciable difference between the motion of a human being and that of a stone. On the other hand, it is equally illegitimate from the standpoint of Christian anthropology to resolve the motion of the human will into terms of pure "ideas"; in other words, to think of the "idea," "form" or "pattern" as in itself a principle of motion. And this for the simple reason that, taken by itself and out of relation to will, sense-perception, appetite and judgment, the elements of the dynamic assessment, the idea is a mere abstraction and has no legs on which to march. But to say this is to assert that all truly significant human situations and relationships are relationships of personality or will. Thus, if it be, in any sense, proper to speak of life as self-realization or the realization of personality, then this is to be accomplished in and through the relationships in question and any attempt to escape from or to transcend those relationships is self-defeating; it is to mutilate the very texture of human experience.

The problem of personality is further complicated by reason of the fact that, in literally every situation which a man encounters in the course of his life and in every relationship or contact which he seeks to establish, there is contained an element of genuine novelty. For this indubitable truth of human experience, classical naturalism had sought an explanation and, faithful to its principles of interpretation, it had looked for this explanation in one of two places, viz. in "nature" or in "opinion." Thus Heraclitus, looking for it in nature, discovered it in the "law" he formulated as the doctrine of the flux. The Eleatics, on the other hand, denounced the whole idea of natural motion (and, consequently, of novelty) as a mere illusion of opinion and formally denied that there was anything in the world of genuine being or reality to which such illusory opinion might correspond. Plato, whose concern (as I have earlier remarked) was to find a *via media* between the absolute fluidity of Heracleitian, and the absolutely static character of Parmenidean naturalism, asserted the substantial existence of natural order as a hierarchy of patterns or forms emanating from the form of the Good, but in such a way as to leave room for a certain unspecified element of natural motion, the motion of matter or the indeterminate, thereby recognizing in "nature" a degree of metaphysical indeterminism or contingency which presented itself, alike to God or man, as τύχη, chance or luck.[159]

From these and all such ambiguities of speculative naturalism, Christian anthropology was, as I have elsewhere argued, delivered by faith; a faith which exhibited nature as a consequence of the free and deliberate creative activity of God, a Creator who, in Augustine's words, "has made what has been made purely and simply because of his bounty (*sola bonitate*), in utter independence both of any necessity of nature beyond Himself or of any want He had to satisfy within Himself;[160] a creator who is thus Himself the one and only absolutely necessary being or existence, "in whom we live and move and are."[161] To acknowledge God in this sense is, then, the first demand of Christian faith; the point of divergence between Christian humility and secular pride.

I have already alluded to the view of natural order (*ordo naturalis*) which follows as a logical consequence from the acceptance of this fundamental proposition of Christian faith and humility—an order which is variously referred to by Augustine as *pax universitatis* and *pax Dei*,[162] and which, you may remember, I tried to describe in his language as an order at once determined and free, since each and every specific nature which goes to constitute the universe as a whole is permitted by divine justice to enjoy and exercise its own appropriate motion. To this I need now only add by way of reminder that the picture of nature thus presented is no mere blueprint or pattern, such as it had appeared, for example, to Plato; but it is the picture of a concrete and substantial order, "complete" alike in its whole and in its parts; not dead but living, in the sense that the order and movement it embodies are both alike and in precisely the same degree manifestations and (in a way though not in any Platonic or pantheistic sense) expressions of, that substantial order and substantial movement which inhere as persons in the essence of the God-head, envisaged as a Trinity of substance, order and movement. It goes without saying that in such a universe, all created beings without exception experience the "peace" to which they are determined by the will of the Creator, a peace which consists in the unimpeded satisfaction of such needs as are specific to their respective natures and which is thus at once "order" and "freedom."

---

159. See above, "Natural Necessity and Human Freedom."

160. Augustine, *City of God*, 11.24; *nulla necessitate, nulla suae cuiascuam utilitatis indigentia*.

161. Acts 17:25.

162. Augustine, *City of God*, 19.13–14.

To assert, in this context, that man is a being created in the image of the Trinity is to assert that, by the constitution of his nature, man is predestined to freedom but in a somewhat peculiar sense, a sense analogous to that whereby freedom and power are ascribed to God Himself as the creative and moving principle. For the freedom and power to which mankind is thus predestined are the freedom and power of voluntary motion, i.e. of self-determination through a principle of inner control; and in this fact is to be discovered all that is peculiar to and distinctive of human experience and human history. For the fact that mankind is endowed with a capacity for autonomous self-determination through the motion of his will means that, by comparison with other living creatures, his status in the universe is, to all intents and purposes, unique; since he and he alone enjoys the capacity of responding as a will or personality to the deliverances of experience, as these are presented to his consciousness through the normal channels of perception, viz., ideas and impressions of sense. Connected with and, in a very real sense, dependent upon his possession of this capacity, there is the further fact that man and man alone is in a position to minister to the necessary demands of the appetites which are congenital to his nature and which are thus to be satisfied with justice and expediency to the life of the "total man," as his experience may determine. But to say that mankind is capable of experience in the sense I have indicated is to say that he alone is capable of history. It is, moreover, to say that human history, as the history of conscious and deliberate activity based on developing experience, is also unique; in no sense to be thought of, according to the concepts of Aristotelian naturalism, as merely a variant, with certain peculiar and specific characteristics due to the rationality of the human animal, of a more general and comprehensive *historia animalium*. For, as I have just suggested, it is the very essence of experience that it should "develop," i.e., that it should be cumulative, though not in any merely mechanical sense; and to this development of human experience, intelligence, memory and imagination, not to speak of appetite and emotion all contribute inasmuch as they each and all enter as factors into the successive determinations of the will to action, whether for good or evil. So true is this that, as Heraclitus in his day observed, a man cannot possibly experience the same event twice, since the very fact that it is for the second time suffices to constitute it, for him, a different experience. This is not to deny the obvious truth that human life tends to fall into patterns, that these patterns correspond in general to the more permanent and less ephemeral demands of human nature. Yet it should never be forgotten that the patterns in question are in general patterns not of "nature," but rather of "art" and "habit," as Aristotle, with his customary discernment, observes. Furthermore, (at any rate so far as concerns civilized or political man, and there is no reason to suppose that, in this respect, the life of the savage is essentially different), these patterns are normally the result of a conscious and deliberate effort to relate the remembered past and the anticipated future to the demands, real or supposed, of the living present. Yet it should be observed that, if Christian thinking is right in what it has to say about the empirical character of all historical experience, then in the nature of things neither the traditions of the past nor the habits and institutions of the present can by themselves possibly afford adequate guidance and direction as to the needs of a constantly evolving and always problematical future. In this sense there is not and cannot be any finality to human history, no city of refuge in which historical man may rediscover the security of his lost Eden and protect himself from the impact of change and novelty; but the life of historical man is in truth a *peregrinatio*, pilgrimage or trek through the wilderness, a trek which must inevitably continue until, as Christianity puts it, the consummation of all things. To such an experience and such a history mankind is committed by the law of his being as a free agent. By the selfsame law of his human freedom he is, indeed, in a position to reject his destiny, but, in so doing, he merely stultifies himself and his humanity, and deliberately paves the way for his own destruction. That is to say, he is guilty of mortal sin. And the sin which thus makes inevitable the disintegration and death of personality is, as Christian realism sees it, the sin of pride. Accordingly, in the life of history, secular pride emerges as the antithesis of Christian humility; and on the interplay of these two antithetic principles, both of which are real because they are the expression of real though opposing wills, depends what at the beginning I ventured to call the Augustinian dialectic of history.

In order to elucidate the character and operation of this dialectic, Augustinian realism takes as its point of departure the perfection of human nature in what Christian thinking describes as the state of original justice; i.e., when the elements of personality or will are in the fullest and most complete accord and the demands of personality as a whole are satisfied without the slightest evidence of impediment or hindrance, whether from within or without, because they remain within the bounds fixed by the Creator as the norm or standard for human nature and because these bounds are understood and accepted by man himself, so far at least as such understanding and such acceptance is possible to a being who, as yet, is innocent of the temptation to violate them in any way. And, in this connection, it is to be noted that the state of original justice and primitive innocence thus depicted by Christian thought is put forward, not as a utopia, but as an actuality, "in the beginning"; and no alternative assumption is consistent with faith in God as an omnipotent and beneficent creator, whose works are in consequence both "complete" and "good." That such a state did, in fact, actually exist "in the beginning" is, of course, not attested by what Augustine calls *historica cognitio*, the evidence of historical observation, for, as he acutely remarks: "where was Moses, the author of the Pentateuch, when it existed?" It is, however, amply attested in history, Christian faith asserts (1) by the authority of Scripture and (2) by the deliverances of experience; the fact that, even in the state of intellectual, moral and physical disintegration brought about through secular perversity, man still confesses to the reality of a shattered wholeness original to his nature whenever, with reference to that nature or to any element of it, he uses the pronoun "I."

The state of original justice and primitive innocence thus accepted by Christian thinking as the point of departure for the historical dialectic is described as a state or condition of good will (*bona voluntas*). It is so described because it is conceived as embodying a harmony of the whole and the parts (συμφωνεῖν ἀλλήλοις), a harmony which is thus regarded as a gift of God to man and not, as classicism had supposed, an ethical "ideal" to be achieved empirically by economic and political action. This natural harmony is thought of, in the words of Augustine, as having comprehended "perfect physical well-being, and utter mental tranquility."[163] It therefore involved a *posse non peccare* which manifested itself as spontaneous power (*spontanea potestas*). Furthermore, the state or condition of complete and perfect harmony, when the will is said to be good because it is fully integrated, is envisaged as a state to which there was no necessary end or term, so long as the will continued to operate naturally in accordance with the inner and autonomous law of its life or being; since manifestly it contained no essential element which, by working within it, might serve to bring it to a natural end.[164]

But if this be indeed the state of original justice and integrity, how are we to understand and account for the evident failure which, in point of fact, has taken place in what was, presumably, intended by God to be the fairest and noblest expression of His creative activity? For the actual situation, as everywhere attested in history and experience, is precisely the reverse of the situation just described. The actual situation is that human life is everywhere vitiated and corrupted; it is marked by tension and malaise, as a consequence of which the freedom and power of action characteristic of the fully-integrated will is, in effect, lost, or at any rate drastically impaired. And, with the impairment of its natural freedom, the will or personality suffers frustration, and there occurs a progressive disintegration which culminates inevitably in

---

163. Augustine, *City of God*, 16.36.
164. Ibid., 12.22; cf. Augustine, *Retractations*, 1.10.3.

death, the final dissolution of the integral relationship which "in the beginning," existed between body and soul—a point of view from which, it should be noted, death is conceived, not as a "necessity of nature" (*lex naturae perire*), but as a penalty for vice or sin, the sin of a bad or imperfectly integrated will.

The question arises: what is the true character and operation of the ἁμαρτία, *vitium* or fault which thus appears to stultify the promise of human life? And further, is the situation, in fact, irreparable; the final verdict on human life that it is nothing but a tragic farce:

> . . . a tale
> Told by an idiot, full of sound and fury,
> Signifying nothing?

Or, on the other hand, is there any practicable means whereby mankind may hope to recover the power and freedom of action which, as every instinct of his consciousness insists, is natural to his being?

To this problem Christian realism proposed its own distinctive solution, the clue to which it found in the notion of original sin (*peccatum originale*). Original sin was thus put forward as a final answer to the problem of evil, the real explanation of that fault or flaw of which secularism so idly prattled, but to the true character of which it was so willfully and persistently blind. Yet, in seeking to formulate what it had to say on this vitally important point of doctrine, Christian teaching experienced considerable difficulty; a difficulty to which Augustine himself bears witness when he confesses that, while nothing could be more notorious as a fact of common experience, yet there is nothing more difficult to understand.[165] The problem of explanation was, I suggest, anything but accidental; it arose from the circumstance that, in this as in other fundamentals of its teaching, Christian realism was under the necessity of breaking absolutely fresh ground. And, with respect to original sin, the difficulty was particularly acute, since on this element of Christian doctrine depended all that was unique to Christianity as an historical religion; the aspect under which it was to be presented, especially perhaps by Augustine. This fact becomes obvious the moment one considers the Augustinian doctrine of original sin in relation to the background of contemporary discussion against which it was developed, viz., the Manichean and Pelagian controversies.

In this connection, it must be borne in mind that the fundamental truth to which Augustine clung so tenaciously throughout the storms of controversy was that of moral freedom and responsibility, otherwise of personality expressing itself through the autonomous self-determination of

---

165. Augustine, "On the Way of Life of the Catholic Church," 1.22.

the will.¹⁶⁶ And from this standpoint the error of Manichaeism was that it annihilated personality by resolving the human impulse to sin into terms of an irresistible physical or physiological necessity from which there was thus not the remotest possibility of escape. On the other hand, as against the Pelagians, Augustine argued with equal insistence that their particular version of secular error, although superficially opposed to that of the Manicheans, was equally fatal to the Christian concept of personality. For Pelagius contended that vice was nothing but an error of judgment, and this implied that it was purely "personal" or individual, since only individuals enjoy the capacity of forming judgments, whether right or wrong. In this characteristically Pelagian thesis, Augustine detected the source of fatal heresies.

The first such heresy had to do with the question of selfhood or personality, considered by itself and quite apart from the situations and relationships into which persons naturally enter in the course of human life. And it was of the gravest character, both as regards the diagnosis of the situation, and the remedy to be applied. For, by identifying vice with a mere error of judgment, Pelagius in effect denied that it even touched the core of selfhood; as the self finds expression in what I have called the dynamic assessment; the determination of the will to action. In other words, he supposed that "willing" was a *naturalis possibilitas*, a simple question of preference, on strictly rational or utilitarian grounds, between alternative possibilities of good and evil, advantage and disadvantage, pleasure and pain, alternatives which in theory always remained open. But this was to admit that "experience" or "history" as such is utterly devoid of meaning in relation to the "essential" self and its development.¹⁶⁷ It was thus to reduce the strains and tensions actually experienced in historical life to quite insignificant proportions; for example, by representing lust *(concupiscentia, πλεονεξία)* merely as a *vigor naturae*, a natural potency which, in certain circumstances, might well become excessive. And, should this occur, the remedy, Pelagius argued, lay entirely within the power of the individual so affected; and it was to be achieved quite simply, by the mere assertion of a preference for good works rather than bad; although in exceptional cases, as, for example, where the excesses of avarice and ambition had become inveterate through long-continued imitation and the force of custom or habit *(vis consuetudinis)*, there might arise the necessity of countering the strength of bad example by good. And it was precisely for this reason that, according to Pelagius, Christ appeared on the stage of history at a time when normal and social evil had become rampant, in order (as Augustine puts it) "to incite or stimulate men to sanctity and to overcome the example of vice

---

166. See above, "Natural Necessity and Human Freedom."
167. See Augustine, "On the Grace of Christ and Original Sin," 18.19 and 20.2.

by that of virtue."[168] So far was Pelagius from perceiving any necessity on the part of men for a new birth (*regeneratio*) as the preface to a radical renovation of spirit (*renovatio animae*); or from understanding the mission of Christ as one of redemption through divine power and grace, and through the gift of the Holy Spirit, apart from which the salvation of man must have remained a sheer historical impossibility.

Deficient as a system of individual psychology and ethics, Pelagianism was no less faulty in its implications for social relationships. For if, as Pelagius contended, the sin of Adam was purely individual,[169] then the only possible significance it could have for individuals other than Adam himself was that it was "primeval"; and it was thus because it occurred at the dawn of history, that its consequences were felt in widespread and inveterate ignorance, reinforced by habit. From this standpoint, the problem confronting the Pelagian Christ was two-fold. It was (1) to illuminate by his teaching the darkness in which men lived and (2) to overcome the evil habits and practices to which they were enslaved, by exhibiting to them the model of a genuinely virtuous life. In this conception of the Savior, Pelagius in effect put forward a pseudo-Christian variant of the ancient Platonic notion of the philosopher-king, a king who differed from his classical prototype only in the fact that he was lacking in everything but the prestige of intellectual and moral authority to enforce his sovereign will for good.

Manicheism and Pelagianism represented the last frantic efforts of speculative naturalism to solve the problem of τελείωσις or *perfectio* launched centuries before in the great classical schools. Thus, by defeating the opposition from both quarters, Augustine closed one epoch and opened another in the spiritual history of the West. This he did by finding a way of escape from what I earlier described as the dilemma of classicism, a dilemma whereby human imperfection was imputed either (subjectively) to "opinion" or (objectively) to "nature." To resolve this dilemma and the consequent antinomy of thought, Augustine invoked the Pauline doctrine of original sin,[170] and developed its implications for the theory of perfection. By so doing he laid the foundation for a realistic philosophy of history.

To deny that the root-cause of human imperfection is to be found either in "opinion" or in "nature" is to assert that it originates in experience or history; and the sin that is thus identified as original to history or experience is, quite properly, described as a sin of our fallen nature, since, of all animate beings, it is the nature of man, and of man alone, to have an experience or a

168. Augustine, "On the Grace of Christ and Original Sin," 2.11.
169. Ibid.
170. Rom 3:22; 5:12; 8:18–22, etc.

history.[171] The question thus arises: what is the precise character of this sin, and how does it operate to thwart the fulfillment of the human promise? To this the answer must be that, as sin, *peccatum originale* is unique and not to be in any way confused with actual sin, the sin of *concupiscence* or lust (*concupiscentia, libido*). The unique character of original sin lies in the fact that it is a sin of disposition or attitude (*habitus*); the attitude which makes actual sin, the lusting of the flesh against the spirit, both possible and inevitable.[172] This attitude is that of the bad or imperfectly integrated will (*mala voluntas*), otherwise of *superbia* or pride. The sin of pride is that, while admitting (as, indeed, it must) the existence of positive evil in human life, it refuses to acknowledge that this evil has its source and origin, not in the deliverances of experience as such (e.g., the sense of pleasure or pain), but rather in the attitude with which the bad will addresses itself to experience and in the construction it seeks to put upon it. In other words, the sin of pride is that it is blind to its own deficiencies: its characteristic assumptions are those of φιλαυτία, *amor sui* or (as we should say) self-righteousness. Pride thus leads inevitably to error, the error of identifying "evil" with what it fallaciously supposes to be some defect in "nature" or "opinion," in any case with something conceived as extraneous or adventitious to what it holds to be its own essential being. Accordingly, it undertakes to eliminate or suppress this hypothetically defective element by legislative action or "by law." But, in so doing, it is guilty of the presumption of supposing that to "construct" is to "create," i.e., the presumption of "creative politics," perhaps the most subtle and seductive of all forms of self-idolatry. It is guilty of the same presumption when it claims for the "law" which it thus invents the status and authority, the universality and finality peculiar to the authentic law of nature, the truth being that, if this man-made law enjoys any degree of objectivity, it is merely that of history.

We have seen that, according to Christian thinking, original sin, the sin of pride, is described as mortal sin, i.e., as the sin which (quite literally) brought death into the world, and all our woe. To understand this, perhaps the most startling of all Christian paradoxes, we must remember that secular pride rejects the major premise of the faith, viz., that God created the universe and that the work of creation is thorough and complete. By rejecting this proposition, and by claiming the right to perfect what it conceives to be the imperfection of nature's handiwork, pride arrogates to itself the status and prerogative of a god. But it does not thereby alter the facts of natural life;

---

171. Augustine, "Unfinished Work in Answer to Julian," esp. Book 6.

172. Augustine, *Homilies on the Gospel of John*, 25.16; *caput omnium morborum superbia est, quia caput omnium peccatorum superbia*.

it merely sees them in terms of its own inverted and distorted perspective. In other words, it deliberately cuts itself off from the authentic source of being, truth and goodness and condemns itself to a life of subjectivity. Thus, as Augustine puts it, while seeking a principle of order and value within itself, it succeeds merely in distracting and disintegrating itself; the result being a progressive vitiation and corruption of life. The corruption of life is, in the first instance, a corruption of love (sense and emotion), the love which, in our first parents, found expression "in an undisturbed attraction for God and for each other, in the pure and faithful association of their union—a love which was thus the source of boundless satisfaction (*grande gaudium*), since its object was always theirs to enjoy."[173] The corruption of love is, at the same time, the corruption of reason, when, as he adds, reason decides not to please God, but to please itself,[174] i.e., when it allows the shadow of *amor sui* to come between itself and the truth. Finally, the corruption of love and reason is the corruption of life itself, or rather of the being which finds expression therein. In other words, it is death.[175] But the sentence of death thus passed on human life is not unconditional. For divine justice, unlike the justice of man, is good order tempered with good feeling. Accordingly, it does not itself take life, although it can hardly prevent the life which is created free from taking itself, since its power to do so is, after all, a function of its very freedom.[176]

Original sin, the sin of pride, is regarded by Christian thinking as universal in human experience and human history. It is thus ascribed, in the first instance, to Adam, the first man; from which it is thought to have been transmitted, as though by a kind of spiritual contagion, to all his descendants.[177] Viewed in this light, it presents itself, not merely as a *damnosa hereditas*, a legacy of obligation imposed upon reluctant heirs by the rash act of a remote ancestor, but also as an attitude or disposition of mind and heart which reasserts itself in successive generations, to find expression in precisely the same way and with precisely the same fatal consequences, so far as concerns the integrity of personality or will.[178] And it is just because he is so acutely aware of these consequences that man seeks, in every possible way, to fortify himself against them. Accordingly, his passion for freedom

---

173. Augustine, *City of God*, 14.7.

174. Ibid., 14.13.

175. Ibid., 13.3.

176. Augustine, "Contra Julian," 3.18.35; *bonus est deus, iustus est deus; potest aliquos sine bonis meritis liberare quia bonus est; non potest quemquam sine malis meritis damnare, quia iustus est.*

177. Augustine, *City of God*, 13.1; Cf. *In Adam peccaverunt omnes non imitatione tantum sed contagione*. Elsewhere, the term used is *propagatione*, "by propagation."

178. Rom 5:12.

and security manifests itself in an unquenchable thirst for power. From this standpoint, the human quest for power is seen for what, in fact, it is, viz., the real *hormé* or dynamic of all secular endeavor, the impulse which serves to explain the most splendid and impressive achievements, as well as the most abject failures of the race. Thus envisaged, the problem of power emerges as the crucial problem of human history. Thus also, for Christian wisdom, the meaning of universal history is epitomized in the figures of two historical personalities, the old Adam and the new, the bad will and the good.

In undertaking to assess the significance of Christ as an historical figure, Christian wisdom started with the proposition that He was, *inter alia*, perfect man. And (we need hardly add) the perfection thus attributed to Christ's human nature, in contradistinction to the nature of the first Adam, was conceived to be that of a good or fully integrated will, i.e., of a will which, in its determinations to action, exercised the power proper to it in the state of original integrity, before it was vitiated and corrupted by the sin of pride. Christian wisdom further asserted that the source of this power and goodness lay not in any man-made program of *ascesis* or discipline, but in the peculiarly intimate relationship which existed between the Son and the Father. To begin with, this relationship was regarded as one of nature; Christ was held to have been, quite literally, born of the Spirit and so an authentic, full and final embodiment of divine order and divine power. In the second place, it was held to be one of attitude, disposition or spirit, a spirit of complete and utter dependence upon the divine will, the humility of Christ. And in this two-fold relationship of nature and spirit Christianity discovered the basis for the power and grace manifested by Christ. In the same relationship it discovered His title to authority, the authority with which He uttered the precept: *Be ye perfect*, as well as the injunction: *I am the way; follow me*.[179]

By thus inviting and even demanding allegiance, the Christ of St. Paul and St. Augustine presented himself, not as any mere exemplar of Platonic or Pelagian virtue, the θεῖος ἀνήρ or "divine man" dreamed of by secular pride as a cloak for secular misgivings, but as a genuine Savior with an efficacious program of fulfillment to offer to mankind. The first aspect of that program consisted of a demonstration, provided in the life of the Master Himself, of the power of the good or fully integrated will; and it sufficed to prove that, however tenacious the grip of sin, it has ultimately no power to hold mankind in bondage; that, in fact, the perfection to which mankind aspires is not an historical impossibility, but, on the contrary, the goal of history itself. Over and above this demonstration of divine and human power, however, Christ came to men with a gift, "The gift of the Spirit by which they

---

179. Matt 5:48; John 14:6; Matt 4:19.

are sanctified."[180] To accept that gift on the authority of the Master was thus to be assured of illumination and power analogous to His own; and, therewith, of all that was necessary for the recovery of that freedom of action lost to the human race at the beginning of time.[181] In that assurance the believer was already "set free" in anticipation and "by hope," if not altogether in fact; discovering the possibility of a final termination of the warfare in his members which had thus far prevented him from realizing the promise of his humanity by doing the good that he would.

We have at last reached the point at which it becomes possible to assemble the elements of the Augustinian dialectic and to consider how it operates. That dialectic is realistic, because the factors that enter into it are not mythical or hypothetical, but the real wills of real persons, as these are determined to thought and action, whether for good or evil. But, whatever their specific determinations, they are one and all subject to an impulse which is genuinely universal, viz., an impulse which drives them to pursue that perfection, in the realization of which is alone to be found the peace and order for which their nature yearns.[182]

The question then resolves itself into one of the arts or techniques by which this impulse to perfection may be satisfied. And it is at this point that, according to Augustine, the paths of secular pride and Christian humility diverge. Each seeks a principle of integration, on the basis of which it undertakes to erect an enduring house for the spirit. The one finds this principle in *amor sui*, the other in *amor Dei*, which are thus put forward respectively as principles of association for the *civitas terrena* and the *civitas caelestis*.[183] In the conflict and interplay of these two societies, from their beginnings to their appointed ends, Augustine discovers the concrete logos or pattern which governs and determines the dialectical movement of history. In the world of history the two societies are, indeed, intermingled (*civitates permixtae*); but they are none the less opposed at bottom as the bad will to the good. And, in the very nature of this opposition, Augustine finds ground for assurance that it must ultimately be resolved by the victory of the good will over the bad. To this victory he thus looks forward as to the term and goal of the long and wearisome pilgrimage, the consummation of historical process; and, therewith, the achievement of a perfect peace.

180. Augustine, "Unfinished Work in Answer to Julian," 3.146; cf. Augustine, "On Nature and Grace," ch. 23.

181. Augustine, "On the Spirit and the Letter," 30.52.

182. Augustine, *City of God*, 19.14; *pax animae rationalis, ut mente aliquid contempletur et secundum hoc aliquid agat, ut sit ei ordinate cognitionis actionisque consensio, quam pacem rationalis animae dixeramus*. Cf. Augustine, "Unfinished Work in Answer to Julian," 6.11.

183. Augustine, *City of God*, 11.33.

2

The Latin Spirit in Literature[1]

FACED WITH THE PROBLEM of depicting the spirit of Rome, the question may well be asked, to begin with: who were the Roman people? The mists that obscure the dawn of Roman history rise to disclose the city of the Seven Hills. But is there any connection, apart from the name which they held in common, between the spear-bearing populace of the Servian city and the citizens of an empire which, nine centuries later, "comprehended the fairest part of the earth and the most civilized portion of mankind?" And who, moreover, of all the names that appear in Roman history, are to be taken as most typically Roman? Are they the Valerii, the Camilli, the Decii, those colorless heroes of the primitive commonwealth, rather than, for example, the Catos, the Scipios and the Gracchi of the second century BC, or, again, the Caesars and Pompeys of the last days of the republic? What connection, in turn, may be discerned between the senatorial aristocracy whose very names were extinguished in the agony of the republic, and that of imperial times when the provinces of Spain, Gaul and Africa gave not merely senators but emperors to Rome; or between these latter and men like Diocletian, Constantine and Theodosius? The long gallery of Roman statesmen contains figures of the most diverse origin and character. The same is true of the writers whose labors created Latin literature and indirectly, through it, the various literatures of modern Europe—Sallust, Cicero and Caesar, Lucretius and Vergil, Livy and Tacitus, Tertullian, Lactantius, Jerome, Ambrose, Augustine and Boethius—to name no more. The list is far from exhaustive; but it will serve to recall a fact which no student can

1. [Orginally published as Charles Norris Cochrane, "The Latin Spirit in Literature." *University of Toronto Quarterly* 2.3 (1932–33) 315–38.]

afford to neglect, viz., that provincials as well as Italians, and Christians no less than pagans, made their contribution to Latin letters. There are, indeed, good grounds for asserting that even Cicero and Vergil should not be regarded as final exponents and interpreters of the Roman spirit, their true role being rather that of pioneers, in precisely the same sense in which the Eternal City was but the prototype and model of the city of God. For it was the function, especially, of Latin Christianity to point out how and why the empire of Rome fell short of that ideal of permanence and universality to which she aspired, while endeavoring, at the same time, to do justice to her solid and substantial achievements as the mother of civilization in the West. And it is unjust to stop short of these last models of Latinity in any attempt to estimate the significance of Latin letters, whether from the standpoint of sincerity, originality and power, or from that of their influence upon the thought and imagination of posterity.

Not that at any time, perhaps, did Roman literature afford the fullest and most adequate expression of the national genius. For nearly seven centuries, indeed, the Latin muse was dumb and, except for rustic farces, annalistic chronicles, and certain adaptations of Greek comedy made by Plautus and Terence, the Romans were practically illiterate. Even in the days of Sallust, a man felt that some apology was needed for putting pen to paper. Sallust's explanation of the backward state of Latin letters, that all the most intelligent people were engaged in business[2] reveals the fact that literature was hardly less foreign to the contemporary society of statesmen, landlords and financiers than it had been to the nation of intelligent peasants which constituted the early commonwealth. Nevertheless, if Mommsen is to be trusted, it was in the century which preceded the outbreak of the First Punic War that the moral and political vitality of the Roman people reached its *apogée*; and, at least throughout republican and early imperial times, no one would deny them either boldness and originality in the conception, or resolution and endurance in the execution of their designs.

If these qualities are somewhat imperfectly reflected in Latin literature, the reasons are partly inherent in the Roman temperament, partly the result of historical accident. The artistic spirit in Rome had to contend against peculiar handicaps—the stubborn fundamentalism of a Cato, expressing itself in a mingled contempt for and fear of ideas—the national quality of *gravitas* (a congenital disinclination to let oneself go) well illustrated by the remark of Cicero: nobody dances except fools and drunken men. Coupled with these was a rooted distrust of mere aestheticism, which the Romans persistently refused to recognize as an adequate substitute for character. It

---

2. Sallust, *Bellum Catilinae*, 8.5; *prudentissimus quisque maxime negotiosus*.

was not so much because he was considered a bad emperor as because he considered himself a good fiddler that Nero was stripped of the purple. That the Romans should have confused such aestheticism with the true spirit of creative art is not surprising; it is still less surprising that Roman Puritanism should have revolted against it as the most serious possible menace to the national morale. For it must be remembered that Hellenism was stale and weary when it invaded Rome; and the Alexandrians, despite their original and vital work in science, were on the literary side organized to preserve a culture exhibiting all the marks of decadence and already moribund. It was, therefore, a tainted source from which the Romans had to draw their inspiration, while their own powers of discrimination were as yet immature.

Nevertheless, with the reception of Greek letters in certain aristocratic circles of the second century BC, the Romans proceeded to lay the foundation of the first great bilingual culture of Europe, and old Cato himself could not long refuse to breathe the intoxicating atmosphere. Literature was cultivated at first with a somewhat indiscriminate enthusiasm and a certain degree of affectation; the earliest Roman efforts at composition were characteristically enough in Greek, and even Cicero wrote a Greek history of his consulship of which he was inordinately proud. Yet the revolutionary character of the movement began to be manifest when Latin presently took its place beside the tongue of Homer as a literary medium; and the precise nature of the impact of Greece on Rome is nowhere better illustrated than by its effect on the language itself.

When the movement began, Latin was but the dialect of a race of intelligent peasants, revealing little more than a capacity for homely wit and wisdom, strongly reminiscent of the Spanish or Italian proverb; and the language which, in its maturity, constituted an admirable vehicle for terse and pithy expression, remained at all times somewhat bald and metallic, incapable of conveying the finer and more delicate shades of meaning possessed, for example, by the Greek. Its poverty, however, was enriched by the inventive genius of men like Lucretius and Cicero, whose services in perfecting the instrument of expression were not the least important part of their work as men of letters. Through these men, Latin was not merely provided with an adequate vocabulary, much of which English speech has in its turn appropriated; but they also initiated the study of rhetoric, which was one of the best and worst of the legacies of Greece to Rome. The structural possibilities of the language were fully explored, and resulted on the one hand in the evolution of the Ciceronian or Livian period, on the other in the development of that aphoristic form of expression, in which for many, the real genius of Latin may be thought to reside. What other language has the capacity for expressing such a wealth of meaning in two or three words?

caveat emptor.
princeps legibus solutus.
summum ius, summa iniuria.

But whichever style was adopted by Latin writers, it may be affirmed that their work was invariably the product of the most meticulous attention, and *curiosa felicitas* was by no means a monopoly of Horace. It may be added that while, no doubt, careless spontaneity has its charms, study of the art of expression becomes a vice only when men are so preoccupied with how they are to say it that they do not pause to consider what they have to say. But since when has it become a crime to entertain as well as to instruct?

This is to make no apology for the cult of rhetoric at its worst. The magic of the spoken or written word seems to have fascinated the society of the empire, as it had that of the old Greek cities, and the growth of the spirit of pure *belles lettres* became more pronounced as the end approached. Painting and sculpture the imperial aristocrats left to slaves and subjects, satisfied themselves to possess and enjoy after the fashion of American millionaires; but the cult of rhetoric they cherished from the days of the free commonwealth, though its life survived all possible meaning. The spectacle of a Sidonius, blandly composing Vergilian hexameters on his Gallic estate, or addressing letters in the vein of Cicero and Pliny, ostensibly to his friends, in reality to a more than dubious posterity, at a moment when civilization itself was crashing about his head, affords few parallels for frivolity in any age.

The somewhat undue emphasis on rhetoric in Latin literature was no doubt occasioned largely by the fact that the Romans felt themselves always as custodians rather than creators, their function being to appropriate and diffuse the elements of a culture, the unique excellence of which they were sensible enough to recognize; and if this feeling tended to promote an inferiority complex from which they were never quite able to shake themselves free (*excudent alii*), it at least implied the virtue of modesty, a quality not altogether to be despised. At the same time, without in the least pretending to be original, they succeeded in infusing a typically Roman spirit into all their work—their initial inhibitions themselves, perhaps, coming to their assistance in this respect. Their outlook remained at all times somewhat narrow and their attitude rigid, never wholly that of the artist or the seer. But their work was characterized by an element of high seriousness, inspired no doubt by the strong sense of social purpose with which they addressed themselves to their task, and thus they achieved effects which, at their best, are almost if not quite Miltonic.

These qualities may be illustrated by almost every phase of their literary work. They are obvious in the satire, which the Romans claimed as the only branch of literature distinctively their own, from the Horatian criticism of human life and human foibles, none the less severe because it is gentle, to the blazing wrath of a Juvenal, denouncing with prophetic fervor the follies and iniquities of mankind. Historiography, emerging under the inspiration of Greek models from the state of mere annals, developed in Roman hands along distinctively Roman lines. The speculative and scientific spirit of an Herodotus or a Thucydides is almost entirely missing; so also is the spirit of all-embracing *curiositas* which produced those compilations of world-history so characteristic of the Hellenistic *cosmopolis*. Roman historians are one and all intensely propagandist. In their hands history is made to serve a moral and political purpose, and that this should be done the more effectively, all the tricks of rhetoric are summoned into play. Thus, in the guise of a Thucydidean analysis of the revolutionary spirit, Sallust comes to the rescue of a discredited Roman radicalism, while Caesar employs the aid of history in presenting his case in the controversies excited by the Gallic and Civil Wars. Of a piece with these are Livy's paean of triumphant republicanism and the moral superiority of the republican spirit, which were to wake an echo more than a thousand years later in the heart of Machiavelli; together with Tacitus's hardly veiled attack on the despotism of the Caesars, the effectiveness of which may be gauged by the fact that, until the memory of Julius was vindicated by Mommsen in our own day, public opinion was almost unanimous in condemning him as a second Catiline—only worse than Catiline because he succeeded while the latter failed.

It is important to notice that Roman satire and Roman history are both concerned with persons; and that what they afford is really an analysis and criticism of the psychology of rugged individualism—the spirit of individual and collective self-assertion on which depended at once the strength and weakness of Rome. The Romans, if they do not represent the origin, at least typify the essence of the acquisitive and conservative spirit in modern civilization. It was Marcus Aurelius who described his fellow-countrymen as hard-boiled; and they were in truth a tough-fibred, materially-minded people if there ever was one, almost devoid of the sensibility of races to whom even physical pain must have been a torment inconceivable to this race of coarser grain. Thus, while to the Greeks life was an art, for the Romans it was a business. While therefore, the rich Hellenic genius exhausted itself in the effort of speculation, and in the cultivation of various forms of artistic expression, the Romans, with infinitely fewer spiritual resources, devoted themselves to the acquisition and conservation of material power, and this aim they pursued with narrow concentration and undeviating consistency for as long as they deserved their name. The Greeks shrank in terror from excess; the Romans found nothing excessive which was possible, and their measure of the possible was based on a "will to live," cherished by them to a degree almost unique among the peoples of antiquity.

The roots of the Roman system go deep into human nature and experience. Its ultimate basis lay, no doubt, in the family right characteristic of the pre-political form of association in Italy. This right, destined though it was to slow attrition in the civic order, nevertheless resisted the process to such a degree that the *patria potestas* could still be described by Gaius (two centuries after Christ) as "our peculiar institution." *Patria potestas*, indeed, lasted in principle throughout the whole classical period, and it was only under the Lower Empire, when its religious basis was undermined, its moral and social value impugned, that it finally disappeared.

This family right, centering about the conception of property, reflects the mentality of the peasant proprietor who thereby asserts his unequivocal claim to use and consume (*uti abutique*) his own. The Roman was thus the original "man of property"; and the notion of *dominium*, carried over from the pre-political to the political stage of development, was made the cornerstone in the Roman fabric of the state. It was not John Locke but Cicero who (in a little noticed passage) first asserted that the state exists to protect property.[3]

This notion survived in full vigor until late in imperial times, and its general acceptance served as an effective check upon tendencies toward administrative autocracy throughout the period of the principate. It was, indeed, destined to perish only under the dominate, when political absolutism combined with Christian social philosophy to effect its overthrow.

Moreover, the scope of the idea was much more comprehensive than the mere tenure of land and goods. *Potestas, manus, dominatio* are aspects of a right which expressed itself in the family discipline, an "order" of the most far-reaching character, religious, moral, and penal. In Roman law, the moral subjection of wife and child was tantamount to actual slavery. The position of the slave himself was developed with a vigorous logic which knew no mercy. And, in the laws of *nexum* and *addictio*, by which the claims of the creditor were asserted against those of the debtor, the conception of right can go no further. The myth of Shylock probably had an actual counterpart in the primitive republican law which equated not merely liberty, but life itself, with solvency; and for centuries the law continued to bear heavily upon liberty, even after it had reached the point of sparing life. Against the

---

3. Cicero, *On Obligations*, 2.73; *in primis videndum erit ei qui rempublicm administrabit ut suum quisque teneat neque de bonis privatorum publice dominutio fiat . . . Hanc enim ob causam maxime ut sua tenerent res publicas civitates constitutae sunt. Nam, etsi duce natura congregabantur homines, tamen spe custodiae rerum suarum urbium praesidia quaerebant.*

solid rock of *dominium*, the waves of radical agitation pounded in vain. The first effective bankruptcy act in Rome dates from Julius Caesar, and even it registers the fact that the greatest of demagogues and revolutionaries was forced to make his peace with property as the price of power. Throughout the whole period of classical jurisprudence, *suum cuique reddere* and *caveat emptor* remained the stern maxims of the law.

Patria potestas non in atrocitate visa, declares the humane jurist of the third century. It is vain to attempt to throw a veil of sentiment over this conception, which made it possible for a father, as late as the time of Cicero, to condemn and execute his son, just as it had made a hero out of Brutus for slaying his offspring in the first days of the republic. Nevertheless, the family discipline, harsh and brutal as it was, was perhaps the source of that ingrained passion for social order which pervaded all departments of Roman life, and continued to manifest vitality through all the changes which came about in the long evolution of Roman society. It was, no doubt, the seed-bed of many of those qualities which have been recognized as peculiarly or distinctively Roman—the sense of *pietas, gravitas, dignitas*, as well as the intense conservatism of the *mos maiorum*. But its chief significance was that it gave material content to that conception of empirical personality which was to find expression in the law. It was what the Romans meant when they spoke of liberty.

Accordingly, they stand for all time as the type of a practical people whose objectives are realizable because they are clear, and clear because they are limited to what the eye may see and the hand may grasp. It is no accident that the spear was for them the symbol of ownership, or that the process of conveying property (land, slaves, horses, cattle) continued for centuries to be marked by the ritual of the copper and scales. They struggled for rights rather than right, they recognized duties rather than duty; both rights and duties they defined with a formal precision for which the lucid and exact phraseology of Roman law constituted the perfect instrument. Classical jurisprudence reveals the most meticulous definition of the rights of the juristic person in relation to other persons and things, as well as of obligations, whether arising from contract or delict, and the precise modes by which such obligations might be extinguished. The history of Rome reflects the same essential legal-mindedness, not merely in the picture which it reveals of the evolution of Roman public life, but also in the way by which the Roman people faced and solved the problems of their imperial and foreign relations. It was this spirit which largely exhausted, if it did not entirely obliterate, any sense of fairness or chivalry in their dealings with friend and enemy, thus giving color to the oft-repeated charge of Roman bad faith; as when, for example, in repudiating an agreement made by a general in the field, the Roman people handed to the embarrassed enemy the unfortunate diplomat, bound and naked, as if that were adequate compensation. Concrete rights, clear and definite obligations, such were the elements which constituted that status of which the Romans were so proud, and which they cherished rather than abstract conceptions of liberty, equality and fraternity, or any of the various forms of democratic control.

Amor sui, in the sense of individual self-assertion, was however but one aspect of the Roman spirit. Throughout the whole course of Roman history, it was counterbalanced and held in leash by the assertion of a collective egoism no less intense and no less characteristic. And, as the one found expression in *dominium*, so the other manifested itself in *imperium*, public authority and the discipline of the city. These two conceptions were, of course, never wholly in accord. The Romans were, indeed, to discover that no final reconciliation between them was possible; though this was the task to which they addressed themselves from the beginning and it constitutes the main theme of Roman history, the main preoccupation of Roman historians. "Nerva was the first to reconcile the two formerly contradictory principles of liberty and authority." Thus Tacitus, when the ship of state appeared once more to have reached calm waters and sunny skies, after the storm and stress of revolution and tyranny lasting over a period of two hundred years, his enthusiasm for the Antonine peace with its slogans of prosperity and humanity tempered perhaps by doubts and fears born of his reading of human nature and human history. For this was not the first time at which it appeared that the Romans had solved the baffling question of social peace, only to discover that the foundations were no less insecure than those which had crumbled in former convulsions, mocking the efforts of earlier architects and confuting the testimony of those who endorsed their plans. Disillusionment and cynicism were, therefore, the lot of those, like him who lived at a time when the classical world was sinking into the lethargy of old age; and they were inclined to question the value of the over-ripe fruits of a culture which had been purchased at the cost of so much bloodshed and so many tears. *Solitudinem faciunt pacem appallant.* With this stinging comment, Tacitus brands Roman imperialism as though the expansion of the empire had been marked by nothing but heaps of skulls; while elsewhere he flings down the challenge of barbarous innocence to cultured decadence and, in unmistakable accents voices the theory that civilization is a disease. For him, as for Juvenal, the miasma had invaded and poisoned every department of life, but its manifestations were nowhere more clearly evidenced than by the corruption of public affairs of which Caesarism was at once the cause and the leading symptom. Hence, with mingled sarcasm and invective, he depicts the spectacle of a Tiberius, a Nero, or a Domitian, cowering in the palace whose very existence constituted a flagrant insult to the monuments of the free republic over which it towered; and from thence, with the sinister backing of slaves and mercenaries, exercising a domination over the former Lords of the World intolerable even to cringing Orientals; while, through the *Lex Maiestatis*, they mocked the majesty of the people by turning the very bulwark of their freedom into the instrument by which they were remorselessly destroyed.

Corruptio optimi pessima. The scathing criticisms of a Tacitus are directed against the perversion of an idea to which, in keeping with the best Roman traditions, he gave his ultimate if not unqualified adherence. They are, in fact, an inverted defense of republicanism. For while it may be true that "the state has no finality and can have no perfected form," this fact did not deter the Romans from their efforts to construct an enduring political fabric. Committed from the dawn of their history to a solution of the problem of material justice, the Romans, like the Greeks, found it in the idea of the commonwealth, and to this idea they made a distinctive contribution which is not less impressive or less instructive than that of any other people. It is impossible to understand the Romans without some appreciation of their conception of the state.

This state, with its peculiar social and political discipline, was the outgrowth of settlements by kindred stocks on neighboring spurs of the Seven Hills. The labors of Roman historians, ancient and modern, have made familiar the process by which, through the constant pressure of foreign wars, and a memorable series of incorporations, the city of Romulus and Numa grew till it came in almost literal fact to comprehend the world. Our concern, however, is not with the history of the city, but with the nature of the civic bond as it was apprehended by the Romans.

To the Romans, the state was sacred but not divine. For them, as for the Greek cosmologist, the world was full of gods; but these gods were never revealed in the manner palpable to the senses and within the range of human sympathy, subsisting merely as mysterious and awful natural forces with location but no shape, and quite devoid of the human impulses and passions, the vices and the virtues which, although in transcendent form, characterized the denizens of Olympus. Accordingly, there are no Roman legends of supermen or nobles sprung from the gods. Mythologies and theogonies, statues and idols, represent merely the accretions which gathered about the religion of Numa, as the imperial destiny of Rome brought her in contact with Greeks and Orientals. But this religion itself remained in essence a singularly pure if somewhat unusual form of naturalism, from the standpoint of which all supernaturalism was either superstition or atheism.

While, therefore, the Romans described themselves as the most religious of mortals, what they meant by religion was nothing more than the sanctification of the material means of life; and this they effected by means of rites and ceremonies purely formal and external, as was appropriate to a people who employed them merely to secure material claims upon a material providence. Accordingly, the religious impulse exhibited itself in a scrupulous attention to those observances by which malignant forces were averted and those which were friendly propitiated; and the impulse was satisfied by the correct interpretation of the divine will as revealed in extraordinary natural phenomena, and by the series of offerings, supplications, prayers and purifications which marked the religious year. Roman religion was, therefore, merely the expression of an attitude which was determined to be at home in this mysterious world, and to discover pragmatically the means of doing so. The establishment of the *pax deorum* was thus but the first step in the establishment of the *pax Romana*, and Symmachus was true to the spirit of his ancestors when, in the last expiring hour of Roman paganism, he defined religion as "the soul of a people."

How much of this spirit may be detected in Latin literature, the student of Vergil and Ovid may judge. Paradoxically enough, it is strongly reflected even in Lucretius, who preaches the Greek gospel of liberation through enlightenment with conscientiousness possible only to a Roman, inspired with a fervor and earnestness engendered not by Greek atheism, but by the Latin sense of a power working in nature, the mysterious force of *natura naturans*. It is this force which sanctifies the labors of men's hands; by it and through it Aeneas, the minister of fate, was sustained in all the trials, dangers and temptations which attended his painful migration to Italy:

> *dum conderet urben*
> *Inferretque deos Latio, genus unde Latinum*
> *Albanique patres atque altae moenia Romae.*

Thus Vergil to a generation which, in its mad and suicidal competition for place and power, had forgotten that Nature exacts a price from those who frustrate her purposes, and that the price she exacts is national extinction.

The intention of Vergil is clearly to remind his countrymen of the solid foundations upon which the Eternal City had been laid and upon which they must continue to build if Rome was to realize the full significance of her imperial destiny. The argument is developed with artistic power in keeping with the grandeur of the motive; an artistry so rich and splendid, indeed, as almost to obscure attention to the theme. His work is thus in a large sense, like that of Lucretius, didactic, and the real subject in both cases is not god or nature but man. Otherwise, the difference between them is as wide as the difference between Greece and Rome. The one preaches a gospel of salvation through knowledge; the other that of salvation through will. The one holds up an ideal of repose and refined sensual enjoyment; the other, one of restless effort and activity. Lucretius urges the recognition that men are limited as the dust; that the pursuit of their aspirations is as vain and futile as are the impulses of religion, pride, ambition which ceaselessly urge them on. The purpose of Vergil is to vindicate those obscure forces within the self by which mankind is impelled to material achievement and inhibited from destroying the work of his own hands. Thus, while he may address his friend in the fine compliment: *Felix qui potuit rerum cognoscere causas*; it is clear that, in his heart, he condemns the shallow Hellenic intellectualism no less than the conclusions to which it leads, and summons Romans to renewed faith in the secular meaning of what their ancestors had accomplished in the past, and what they themselves might hope to accomplish in the future. It is this difference which makes the distinction between the melancholy resignation of Lucretius and the resigned melancholy of Vergil; the one characteristic of a man who accepts the intellectual assurance of futility, the other the mark of one who, like all enlightened men, is beset by the problem of finding a reasonable ground for his faith. It is this difference that makes the distinction between the epic of civilized materialism and that of material civilization.

For, as Vergil sees it, civilization does not evolve of itself; it is not the ultimate but unforeseen result of a fortuitous collocation of atoms. It must be constructed, and Vergil envisages his countrymen above all else as builders. Properly to understand Aeneas, it is necessary to think of him in the role of immigrant and pioneer. Man against a background of nature which he seeks to subdue to his purpose; concentration of all the powers of heart, head, and hand in the steady pursuit of an end kept in view to the exclusion of all else; the will to work, the will to fight; boldness of innovation combined with intense desire to conserve accumulated gains; that passionate affection for what one has made by blood and sweat, tears and misery, which men call patriotism, a sentiment even for us akin to religion, for the Romans religion itself—these are the elements of the picture which Vergil unfolds in measured stanzas which themselves deserve the immortality due to their theme.

If, however, the *Aeneid* has in addition the character of a national epic, this is because Vergil perceives that to build a civilization requires something more than effort, and that is organization. The magnificent demonstration of disciplined obedience which characterized the Roman state in all the greatest periods of her history is also reflected in her greatest literary monument—leadership at once "pious" and prudent (this, by the way, is the answer to the Christian charge that Aeneas had not the courage of a dog); subordination based on that iron law of inequality which seems to mark all the relationships of the natural man; cooperation, arising from the sense of a common purpose, shared by leader and led, in the task of constructing an impregnable fortress for the *palladium*, the guarantee and pledge of the national fare—a political religion, a political morality, Machiavellism two thousand years before Machiavelli; technocracy, the cold and objective measurement of forces which, whether material or psychological, must be controlled in the interests of national and imperial utility, for the realization of an empirical freedom of action which is never achieved except at the expense of others; the essence of this "objectivity," which lies in undivided attention[4] to the problem at issue, to the exclusion of hatred or love, anger or sentiment, the passions which blind (*officiunt*) men to their true interest.

Thus does Vergil seek to justify that urge to practical activity, the spirit of which we shall best understand if we think of the Romans as having achieved in the Old World precisely that to which men of our own race have set their hands in the New. The state and empire of Rome depend fundamentally on *will*: virtue is not knowledge, it is character; and its fruits are seen in activity, rather than in repose or contemplation. Aeneas is thus the pilgrim father of antiquity; his followers the Mayflower company of the Ancient World; while the organized society of the empire is the ancient version of the New England Kingdom of the Saints; subject, it may be added, to the same limitations and threatened by the same dangers as confront all societies in which *amor sui* disguises itself as the love of God.

Accordingly, Vergil gives authentic expression not merely to the Latin temperament, but in considerable degree to that of Western civilization as a whole. In so doing, he touches a high-water mark of achievement in Latin letters, never to be surpassed except by Augustine. In him alone, you see them all. For he makes us understand the real basis of that principle of concord or agreement which underlies the Roman philosophy of the state—shallow intellectual assent or social compact but, as the Latin word itself implies, "a union of hearts"—as is clear from the realistic definitions of the *civitas* or *respublica* which are found everywhere in Latin literature.[5]

Those who called themselves Romans, no matter what their race or origin, well knew on what they could agree. They set out to make the world safe for property. On this principle depend two of the most characteristic phenomena of Roman history: (1) expansion, by which the provinces, the

---

4. Sallust, *Bellum Catilinae*, 51; *ubi intenderis ingenium, ibi valet*.

5. Cicero, *De Republica*, 1.39; *multitudo hominum in quoddam vinculum redacta concordiae*; Augustine, *City of God*, 19.24; *coetus multitudinis rationalis rerum quas diligit concordi communione sociatus*.

praedia populi Romani, as even Cicero unblushingly calls them, were extended from the British wall to the Euphrates, and from the Rhine-Danube frontier to the Sahara desert: (2) incorporation: the assimilation of fresh factors of strength wherever they were to be found, on the theory elucidated by Claudius: *quod usquam egregium, huc transferre*. It is this principle which accounts for the element of "universality" which the commentators find in Rome. But it will always be a limited and bogus universality for those who refuse to admit that, in property, the human personality finds adequate and complete expression.

That Vergil did not occupy the solitary eminence in Latin literature to which he was entitled is a curious fact, demanding explanation, even if to explain it is to throw a somewhat lurid beam of light upon the Roman spirit. It is the fate of naturalism to devour its own gods, and to this fate the Romans were peculiarly exposed because of their singularly narrow and pragmatic temper. The effort of Vergil to rehabilitate the national ethos was, therefore, nothing but a splendid failure; and the noblest prophet of the religion of civilization shared the fate of Horace who was merely its exponent. Vergil became a text for schoolboys. The pedants set themselves to rend the massive fabric of his verse to illustrate their subtle points of grammar and style, while they isolated his most stirring episodes to make them themes for infantile debate—in this way following the practice of barbarians who have always and everywhere despoiled the noblest monuments of antiquity. Paradoxically enough, almost the only people to take Vergil seriously were the Christians, who approached him with fascination as they recoiled from him in terror, for the very simple reason that they regarded him as a man who had something to say. Thus, in the estimation of posterity, Vergil came merely to occupy a place alongside Cicero, whose name bulked equally large with his in the republic of Latin letters.

This fact might seem to indicate the necessity of saying something about Cicero and the Ciceronian humanism which makes such an appeal, for example, to Professor Babbitt,—that doctrine which represents all that is left to the emancipated Puritan who has shed everything but his prejudices and wonders what to do with them; and who therefore battles with a sword of bronze against the powerful forces of a materialism with which his practical sense urges him to compromise at the most vital points. But this would serve merely to emphasize the sufficiently obvious truth that, while naturalism devours its own gods, it never succeeds in replacing them with others more impregnable to the assaults of time and circumstance. In other words, it would serve merely to illustrate the spiritual bewilderment which infected all enlightened Romans—a bewilderment which was, perhaps, the most characteristic blight on the Imperial Community of Culture.

From this bewilderment the Romans succeeded in shaking themselves free only with the second birth of Latin letters which came about under the powerful stimulus and inspiration of Christianity; and once again they were to show themselves the faithful custodians and interpreters of a tradition which they did not create. It would be absurd, of course, to attempt in a few words any real characterization of Latin Christianity; and we are here concerned merely to exhibit, if possible, the fundamental unity which underlay the Latin spirit, despite the vast chasm which divided *Romanitas* from the Christians who seceded from the system.

The Romans began as builders; as builders they ended. It has been shown that the native Roman genius was rooted in the soil; the iron masterfulness which made the Romans Lords of the World depended upon the character they possessed as pioneers. But, with the conquest of Greece, the Romans were for a time swept off their feet by the spirit of Hellas, and they imbibed the doctrines of disintegration from a people who, try as they might to diagnose the mortal malady from which they suffered, were unable to effect a cure, largely because of the intellectualist formulae which they employed. This tidal wave of Hellenic influence reached the light water mark in Rome just about the time of the fall of the republic; to which catastrophe it contributed by disrupting the traditionalist moral principles, based on the obsolete primitivism of the early commonwealth, upon which the society of a vast and cosmopolitan world empire still sought to live; but which were clearly too feeble to withstand the strain. Witness the spectacle of a Catullus or a Clodius or any other of the spineless aesthetes whom Cicero furiously denounced as spiritual affinities of the Catilinarian crowd. But presently the innate steadiness of the Roman character began to assert itself, as intelligent men suddenly perceived the chasm which yawned at their feet, if the empire should (as seemed almost inevitable) collapse. Many of them, though with fear and hesitation, threw their weight behind Caesarism, as the only possible hope. And out of the mouth of one of the worst of the devil's disciples (in a suggested program of reconstruction addressed to the dictator) came, strangely enough, the first blast of the wind of true doctrine. Why, asks Sallust, go to the Greeks for moral precepts, for a practical philosophy of life, to men who suppose, for example, that the road to heaven is paved with mathematics? If the history and experience of Romans does not suggest to them the true basis of a working system, then God help them, for Aristotle cannot.

It was in this spirit, that Vergil, as we have sought to show, attempted to depict the true foundations of the city, as a warning no less than a guide to the public to whom it was addressed. But what Vergil succeeded in revealing to his contemporaries was merely a vision of the empirical personality, with its basis, as we have said, in will. Romans still found it necessary to go to the Greeks for an answer to the question: what is to be the intellectual content of life, now that we have built the city, and it is no longer necessary to extend the frontiers? That the end of life is contemplation was a doctrine which made no appeal to this people with its thoroughly practical temper; Stoicism, with its activist implications, thus proved to be the philosophy which bid most successfully for Roman allegiance, and made the widest appeal. But its obvious defects and limitations still left the field open to Christianity.

Of all the grounds on which Christianity might appeal to the Latins, undoubtedly the greatest was because of the light it threw on human personality, and the guidance it offered for the practical conduct of life. Thus, to the theory of personality which was slowly developing in Roman hands, the Latin fathers put the coping stone. As Sallust and Vergil had discovered the empirical, so Augustine discovered the transcendental will. This, in turn, he made the basis of that Communion of Saints which was the Christian alternative to Vergil's city of men. And, through the doctrines of sin, grace, and redemption, by which the human pilgrim was to attain at last the eternal peace of the Divine City, he achieved that philosophy of progress for which the classical world had waited in vain for two thousand years; and which, even through its perversions, has been one of the chief sources of inspiration to the mind of modern man.

Thus, the function of Latin Christianity was to widen and deepen the spiritual foundations of a material life which it refused either to repudiate or deny; to assert a spiritual peace as the basis of material (or social) peace. In this way the Latin fathers supplied an antidote to the pessimism of classical antiquity by stripping life of all vague idealism and sentimentalism and representing it as something to be remade by a radical remaking of character; thus summoning men from the classical ideals of repose or enjoyment to a life of effort through which their spiritual significance would be realized.

Latin Christianity culminated in Augustine, who may justly be described as, at once, the last of all the Romans and the first citizen of the world. For he gathered up the whole vision of antiquity (Hebrew, Greek and Latin) into a mighty synthesis which only a member of the world wide empire, living at the conclusion of her cycle of history, could have achieved, and at the same time, he delivered it to posterity in accents which, though perhaps fainter in our day than for previous generations, are still intelligible to the modern man. Not satisfied like the Hebrew to weep by the waters of Babylon, nor yet, like the Greek, merely to envisage the pattern of a city laid up in heaven, but true to the native genius of the children of Romulus, he traced the outlines of an ecclesiastical polity which, if its battlements soared above the clouds, nevertheless had its foundations solidly embedded in the living rock of empirical fact. Leaving it to others to pursue millennialist dreams of a New Jerusalem, he erected the last but not the least impressive or significant monument to the spirit of Ancient Rome.

3

The Classical Idea of the Commonwealth[1]

ANY ATTEMPT TO DEPICT the character of an age or a culture involves an element of hardihood of which the writer must be at all times painfully conscious. To generalize about humanity is to run the risk of neglecting the idiosyncrasies of individual human beings on which depend the color and flavor, if not the ultimate meaning, of life. It is also to overlook the factor of time and to forget, perhaps, that the temper and disposition of communities, like that of individuals, is subject to continuous modification as they seek to adjust themselves to the demands of changing experience and to bring their present and their future into some sort of coherent relationship with their past.

These considerations apply with special force precisely to those peoples whose history is most worth study. The vain and bombastic chronicles of Oriental potentates may well constitute a sufficient record of the life of countless myriads who were content to merge their personality in that of the sovereign and to live and die in the reflection of the regal glory. The bald and insipid annals of a primitive folk may likewise be an adequate vehicle for the expression of an existence which has not yet attained self-consciousness. But with the beginning of history, in the sense of life measured no longer by eons but by the richness and fullness of the experience therein disclosed, the task of the interpreter becomes increasingly difficult. He must seek to disengage the inner principles which give this life its meaning and direction,

1. [Charles Norris Cochrane, "The Classical Idea of the Commonwealth," Charles Norris Cochrane Fonds. University of Toronto Archives, B2003-0011/004 (13).]

without, however, exhibiting them as mere abstractions, divorced from the agent and out of relation to the material setting in which they exert their vitalizing power. By these standards, it is well-nigh impossible to do justice to the many-sided genius of the Greeks, and to estimate their contribution to the human heritage in art and literature, in law, politics and philosophy. The difficulty is hardly less acute in the case of the people of Rome.

Nevertheless, beneath the manifold of Greek and Roman experience, behind the contacts and conflicts by which these peoples made and marred their fate, it is possible to discern the operation of a principle which constitutes the motive of their history and gives a fundamental unity to the theme. This was the consciousness existing among them that they had embarked upon a novel experiment in human history, and that they were working for common objects by methods which were at bottom analogous. It was this consciousness which gave to classical antiquity its peculiar tone and quality. Moreover, the distinctively classical spirit survived the extinction of the classical peoples themselves to enter into and leaven the modern spirit, not merely in Europe but in the greater Europe that has grown up overseas. It is this fact which gives perennial fascination and value to studies which would otherwise possess merely an antiquarian interest.

The spiritual affinity, which in some degree constituted a bond of union for all the Mediterranean peoples, was most pronounced in the case of the Greeks and Romans; and, no sooner had the one people come into contact with the other, then it was spontaneously recognized by both. On the part of the Romans, it served to evoke that peculiar tenderness and respect for Greek culture which was later to inspire the poet to proclaim the victory of the conquered over her fierce conqueror—a sentiment all the more remarkable because of the difficulties inherent in the political relationship. This attitude was, perhaps, more generously and ungrudgingly expressed at the beginning, when Flamininus announced the liberation of Hellas; and it was destiny, in some degree, to be impaired by the inevitable frictions of the protectorate. Nevertheless, it subsisted throughout the period of the Empire, and the last of the Roman emperors to profess loyalty to the classical heritage was proud to call himself a Hellenist. Philhellenism, indeed, may be illustrated from almost any page of Roman history, as, for example, in the famous phrase by which the dictator Caesar pardoned the Athenians who had fought against him at Pharsalus: How long will the virtues of your ancestors save you! While he thus paid characteristic tribute to the mother of civic freedom and the home of thought, his preservation of the Massiliots—despite intense and repeated provocation—was due not so much to their past as to the hope which he entertained of their future as a civilizing influence in the newly annexed provinces of Gaul. It may be added that, in thus forecasting the historic role of Marseilles, Caesar was not mistaken. Roman Marseilles, like Roman Athens, was a university rather than a city. In the West and in the East, these communities continued to diffuse their light, until the barbarian invasions destroyed the one and Justinian, by closing the schools of the other, brought the cycle of classical culture to an end.

Evidence of this kind is, indeed, so common that to recall it is almost gratuitous. The Roman annalists attempted to conceal the fact of Etruscan domination and of the extent to which the imperial city owed its beginnings to Etruria. Early Greek influence (of which there is ample archeological evidence) they generously acknowledged. It is to be seen, for instance, in the legends that the Tarquins, who gave Rome the form of the *civitas* or πολιτεία, were the descendants of an immigrant Corinthian Demaretus and that, in the political crisis of 450 BC, the Romans sought and found material for the Twelve Tables from Hellas, especially in the Code of Solon. The same attitude was subsequently manifested in the growth of the Trojan myth. To have had ancestors who fought at Troy was, for the peoples of the ancient world, the conventional badge of gentility. It was on this score that Procopius, sixteen hundred years after the fall of Ilium, admitted the right of the Goths to a share in the Greco-Roman heritage. The legend was used in this sense long before it was adopted to support the peculiar claims of the Julian house, and its value for the latter purpose attests its effectiveness for the former.

On the other hand, the Greeks were equally ready to recognize as their peers the community of embattled Italian peasants which had rescued them from the clutches of Macedonian tyranny. They admitted the Romans as they had admitted the Macedonians to participation in the national games; in this way distinguishing them both from the more remote northern barbarians and from the Orientals whom they regarded as "natural slaves," and for whom they hardly overcame their ingrained contempt even in the days of their decadence.

In this connection, there is no more important witness than Polybius, who lived for years as a hostage in intimate association with Scipio Aemilianus, one of the earliest Romans to exhibit philhellenism to any marked degree. Polybius was thus in a position to observe many of the most remarkable triumphs of Roman arms and diplomacy in the wonderful fifty years of conquest and expansion during which the imperial city laid the whole Mediterranean world at her feet. In particular, he was present at the final siege and destruction of Carthage. For centuries Carthage had been the successful rival of Hellas for control of the West until, in an hour pregnant with fate, the Romans challenged and overthrew her monopoly of sea-power. Their subsequent achievements throughout the length and breadth of the

Mediterranean were not lost on Polybius. He set the seal of Greek approval upon Roman expansion when he pronounced the growth of the empire to be the result, not of chance, but of manifest destiny working through the agency of her chosen people; and, in characteristically Greek fashion, he declared that the success of the Romans was due to the "excellence of their constitution," which embodied the advantages of the "mixed form," at that time fashionable in Greek political philosophy.

It was doubtless, also, to the ingenuity of Greek *literati* that we owe the detailed development of the Trojan legend which, despite its advantages, involved, of course, the serious drawback of representing the Romans as descendants of the "national enemy" of the Homeric epic. It remained for a Greek, by an interesting and instructive use of the methods of critical historiography recognized as valid in Alexandrian "science," to correct this lamentable mistake. In the last days of the republic, Dionysius of Halicarnassus, after examining the surviving records of early constitutional life, made that startling and comforting discovery that the Romans were after all not Trojan but Greek: One or the other, it mattered little. The record of a people in history is, after all, the record of its culture; and, culturally, the Greeks and Romans had already by Cicero's time grown to be, if they were not originally, a single people. The ideas for which they stood had come to dominate the world, and were to sustain and nourish the life of men in an empire of unprecedented dimensions over a period of centuries. They were the spiritual foundations of eternal Rome. Between them, the Greeks and Romans projected into the consciousness of mankind the classical idea of the commonwealth.

Any serious consideration of the history of classical antiquity must, therefore, involve an attempt to understand this idea, together with its implications for human life. It was the expression of faith in the existence of an order of social or political "justice" which it was within the capacity of man to apprehend. Thus it appeared to imply the possibility of human beings combining in a society in which they might realize the fullest potentialities of their nature; in other words, the notion of citizenship as opposed to the external and internal despotisms which had hitherto frustrated the development of mankind. From this standpoint, the very wealth and variety of classical experience become themselves significant. They testify to the insight with which these peoples explored, the vigor and energy with which they pursued the idea through its manifold developments.

In this great spiritual adventure, this pioneer voyage of discovery into the meaning and purpose of human life, we are confronted with something more than merely repetitive cycles. The trails of Greek and Roman, and Semite as well, crossed and re-crossed throughout Mediterranean history, as each pursued his chosen path, and the result was a constant enlargement of the map of human experience. Moreover, as the path of the pioneer is never clear or obvious, these trails frequently led to *culs-de-sac*, from which men had to extricate themselves or perish, and this experience also was not without significance. Thus, for example, Greek imperialism was quite different from Roman both in its character and development. As Thucydides noted, it emerged relatively late by land, on which its growth was retarded by physical conditions. It therefore involved the subjection of self-conscious city-state units, hitherto autonomous, and so was confronted with the insoluble problem of reconciling the liberty of the individual communities with the authority of the central power. Whether Roman imperialism, which succeeded through the federal principle in achieving what the Greeks had failed to accomplish, is on that account to be regarded as more "typical" of what has been called the "pattern of empire," is a question which is at least open to discussion.

Greeks and Romans, in their spiritual development, were, indeed, the complement, rather than the counterpart, of each other. Each people achieved a development somewhat one-sided. The Roman could not carve like Pheidias nor write like Sophocles, but he worked out a political or civic order which the Greek with his individualism failed to attain. He did this by surrendering his personal will, as in the family, so in the state, for the sake of collective freedom. Thus he manifested a patriotism to which the Greek remained a stranger, thereby achieving a unity which at last placed the whole world in his hands. In so doing, he awakened the notion of a world-empire in the spiritual realm, which was to fructify in the mediaeval project of a world-church and in the modern dream of a world-commonwealth.

These facts suggest still another consideration: viz., that the cycle of classical culture, even if it be taken as a unit, must not be regarded as "closed." To assume that such is the case is to overlook the survival of Byzantinism which, for a thousand years after the last of the Western emperors had cast away the empty trappings of his vanished majesty, continued to bear witness to the power and grandeur of antiquity, which the West knew only by its ruins. It is to overlook the vestiges of town-life and of the villa system which remained throughout the barbarized provinces. It is to overlook the *palingenesis* of the Latin language and literature, and especially of the law which the Germanic sovereigns endeavored to adapt to the purpose of government for their mixed and heterogeneous subjects. Above all, it is to overlook the vitality of the church, which had developed the outlines of an ecclesiastical polity of world-wide scope, and which bore many traces of its origin. These are considerations which vitiate the arguments of those who, reasoning from purely "materialistic" grounds, argue that because the

Colosseum lay in ruins, and the Roman roads were grass-grown tracks, the empire of the eternal city was at an end.

That empire was, in fact, more than anything else an empire of the spirit. The dominant characteristics of what we shall describe as the community of culture were the result not so much of the subjugation of the world as of the fusion of the various elements (especially that of Hellenism) brought together through the conquest into the vast unity for which the Christian critic Tertullian invented the name of *Romanitas*. Within the body of *Romanitas*, the narrower barriers of race, religion and culture fell down or were easily surmounted, and the world subjected itself to the deliberate discipline of civilization, (which is the life of the citizen), to which the earlier and more primitive cultures had each in varying degree made their contribution. In studying this civilization, we do not therefore pit one people against another, but gratefully acknowledge a common obligation to them both. Nevertheless, it is part of our purpose, if possible, to throw into somewhat clearer relief the specifically Latin ingredients in the classical idea of the commonwealth. This is a necessary task, because the more spectacular character of Greek achievement has served to obscure the work of the Romans, who, at the very least, must be credited with the material setting in which Hellenism could fruitfully germinate.

Into the melting-pot, of course, had gone other ingredients, by-products alike of Greek and Roman imperialism. How much these people found in the cultures with which they came in contact, and how much of this they made their own, will never be fully appreciated, although the work of archaeology may help us to envisage the truth. There is, for example, the standing puzzle of Etruscan influence. Despite all efforts to discover the truth, the Etruscans remain one of the unsolved mysteries of history. Yet, with their artistic and administrative talents, their advanced techniques of industry, commerce and war, above all, with their impressive religious system, this people undoubtedly contributed in days past to the making of Servian Rome, as the Roman legends themselves grudgingly attest.

Of still greater significance, perhaps, was the influence of the various Semitic races, both in the east and the west of the Mediterranean. It is beyond the scope of this essay to discuss the Cadmeian theory of Greek letters or the alleged fertilization of Theban culture by Phoenician traders. Still less can we concern ourselves with the influence of the Semites upon the cultures of Mesopotamia and Egypt with which the Greeks came in contact and which produced such an impression upon the mind, e.g. of Herodotus. Great or little, they made their contribution which was not lost on the acquisitive Greek mind. In the West, Punic influence was more direct and less ephemeral. Until at least 264 BC, Carthage dominated the seas from Sicily to far beyond the pillars of Hercules. In his review of model constitutions, Aristotle includes that of Carthage among those worth study, thus testifying to the fact that he regarded her as a civilized state. Carthaginian influence on Rome was on the whole mainly by way of conflict; but, as the war for Sicily served to impress upon the Imperial City the truth that the Mediterranean Sea must be her sea if Italy was not to be a mere appendage to an alien system of domination; so also the Hannibalic invasion drove home the lesson that, even when deprived of control of the sea, the economic imperialism of the African metropolis was still a menace to the freedom and autonomy of Italy. For that, if for no other reason, Carthaginian competition forced Rome to develop her provincial system by taking over the Punic dominions in the Islands, Spain and Africa. Thus the Romans fell heir to the legacy of what Polybius described as the wealthiest city in the world, the "London of antiquity," the very type of economic and political plutocracy. This was the beginning of their education in that peculiar form of predatory imperialism which was to enjoy its heyday during the two centuries prior to Augustus; as well as of problems confronting the Roman administration for which Roman experience as a purely continental power afforded no precedent or guide. In particular, it raised the question of how a commonwealth can govern others and at the same time preserve its own freedom. From the moment when, after acquiring Sicily, the Romans, in their stolid fashion, adopted the obvious solution of disarming the natives and themselves undertaking the defense of the island, retaining the existing Carthaginian system of tithes and customs, Rome, in Mommsen's words, put on the Nessus shirt, the fatal gift of the vanquished to her conqueror. The political innovation was of a piece with the famous translation of Mago's work on scientific agriculture and the adoption of the system of *Latifundia*, by which the Romans proceeded to exploit their enlarged domains in a fashion calculated to subvert the foundations of the peasant state in Italy itself.

Of all the Semitic people, none was perhaps in the last analysis to exercise a more profound influence upon *Romanitas* than the Hebrews, whose "wisdom" was ultimately to overthrow the "scientific" attitude to life. The full extent of this influence, however, was felt only at a relatively late date in imperial history; for, although the children of Israel had glimpsed the reality of an order transcending the limitations of naturalism and humanism, they themselves "rejected the message," refusing to see its universal implications and seeking merely to utilize it as the basis for a wider nationalism. Accordingly, they blundered into those fatal conflicts with the empire which were to culminate in the fall of the holy city and subsequent wars of extermination: and thus they came to occupy that peculiar position in relation to European culture which has since been their fate: their traditions and their sacred books having become the property of those who, in the name of *Juppiter Optimus Maximus*, overthrew the temple of Jehovah, and laid the foundations for the spiritual empire of Rome.

In the present sentimental reaction against all forms of imperialism, it has become fashionable to denounce the Roman Empire as an instrument of mere destruction which, like a gigantic steamroller, crushed out the promising nascent civilizations of Spain, Africa and Gaul, and imposed in their stead nothing but a dead uniformity, thus making a desert and calling it peace.[2] Such a view is based simply in fanciful speculation. It ignores not merely the fact that victory perched for centuries on the Roman banners, but the more significant truth that the Spaniards, Africans, and the Gauls who survived the conquest more or less cheerfully accepted their fate, discovering in the culture which they received from Rome a medium through which the national spirit was ultimately to find and express itself in a form utterly impossible for the ephemeral and local tribal cultures which it supplanted. Rome, indeed, *made* Spain, Africa and Gaul, as she had made Italy, which prior to the creation of the Italian confederacy, hardly deserved the name; thereby demonstrating the fact that imperialisms serve to generate nationality as much as to destroy it. Thus, while it may be permissible to lament the fate of the vanquished, there are no good grounds for extending to them indefinite credits upon the strength of an entirely problematical future; and history certainly cannot concern herself with such might-have-beens.

This is to hold no brief for imperialism. The truth is, however, that current nationalistic criticism, which is based on purely emotional or prudential considerations, has not a leg to stand upon. For nature concedes nothing to the merely primitive which she denies to the advanced society. Both in breadth and depth, the empire made possible a fuller development of human potentialities than the barbarians were in fact likely to achieve through their suicidal tribal wars. Nor is it possible to escape from the iron law of natural inequality by taking refuge in an equalitarianism which is itself based merely on sentiment. For this reason, it is insufficient to condemn Rome merely as the greatest of slave-states, slavery as such being regarded as the nemesis of nations. Aristotle's argument for the exploitation of human beings as if they were mere things is doubtless weak on the positive side; but at least it disposes of the notion that the relationship of master and slave is wrong merely because it violates some presumptive "natural" right to liberty. Thus countless thousands of nameless barbarians served their turn in making possible the evolution of Greco-Roman economic techniques; and this was their significance in the system of *Romanitas*. For others a better

---

2. See for example, Chapot, *The Roman World*.

fate was in store; they constituted the potential material of Roman citizenship itself. They were the heirs to the legacy of Greece and Rome.

But, while *Romanitas* may have owed much to these contacts with Etruscans, Semites and barbarians, the informing principles of the system were unquestionably native; it was the Greeks and Romans themselves who created the world-wide partnership of law and culture to which Tertullian gave the name. This they accomplished by joint effort, displaying a generous spirit of cooperation as remarkable as it is rare in history. No account of the ingredients of *Romanitas* would, therefore, be worthwhile if it neglected the element of Hellenism, the contribution of that gifted people which started out of gallantly to develop the art of life, only to end by treating life as a mere art. The Greeks, indeed, launched into the world the classical idea of the commonwealth. The first exponents of scientific humanism, they were the first to fall victim to the scientific attitude of life, and the fruits of their labor were to be garnered by other hands. For this reason, they must be counted surely among the forerunners and pioneers.

So rich and fertile was the Greek genius, that it is almost impossible to say anything of Hellenism which does not appear to involve the most flagrant contradictions; and to judge the Greeks from the evidence of their art alone would certainly give a very false picture of the Hellenic temperament. Statuary, exhibiting repose even in vigorous movement, architecture revealing the perfection of form and grace, devoid of the mysterious sense of the undiscovered and undiscoverable so characteristic of the Gothic, a literature notable for lucidity and precision of expression, the quality for which Horace's *curiosa felicitas* is perhaps the only possible description—these are the merest commonplaces of literary and artistic criticism when applied to Greek achievement. We cite them simply to emphasize the melancholy truth that the Greeks did not attain in life the "finality" which they attained in art. Indeed, these very characteristics of their art indicate a sense of their failure to achieve in practice anything beyond mere process—the restless movement and change which marks the world of "becoming," and gives their history that curious kaleidoscopic effect which makes it so difficult for the historian to keep the threads together. This must have constituted a torture to the Hellenic spirit. In the Hellenic Tartarus, the victims do not scorch in unquenchable flames; but one forever grasps at the elusive apple, another vainly rolls the stone, or endlessly fills the bottomless water-jar. On the other hand, Greeks of whatever temperament join in applauding the rest that crowns either mental or physical toil, the stability which in social and political relations stands impregnable against the corroding acid of change. In philosophy, they pursue the λόyos or principle which constitutes the explanation of the ἔργα or facts and is, therefore, the end of inquiry; and in their art they register a passionate longing for the perfection which they missed in practice.

To this endless process, however, the Greeks were condemned by the logic of their genius; their temperament and outlook fated them to a career of restless adventure. This was the result of their insatiable *curiositas*, the passion to understand, which they regarded as the highest function of the human animal and which was, indeed, the mainspring of their science and philosophy. This was the spirit typified by Odysseus, the man of many devices or, better still, by Prometheus, whose story (as we have it) registers an insoluble puzzle of Greek theology. Why should the discovery and transmission to mankind of the arts, or rather of that art which makes civilization possible, seem to be branded by a curse which must be expiated by such cruel and ceaseless torment?

But if the crucifixion of Hellas was prefigured in that of Prometheus, the history of the Greeks as a whole was forecasted by their vision of the Olympian gods—the dazzling picture of the immortals outlined against the somber background of those earlier and wilder deities of pre-Hellenic origin, one at least of whom—the Zeus of Ithome—continued into historic times to manifest a thirst for human blood. These barbarous gods were far from extinct; they were destined, indeed, to have their own renaissance as the Hellenic spirit began to wilt and fade in the glare of its own noon-day. But, as the mists rise to disclose the bright morning of Greek history, it is clear that they were driven under cover by the gods of Homer, a civilized and civilizing Valhalla. The Olympians were no less unique for their strength and beauty than for the unperturbed serenity of their existence. They were, indeed, imperishable or immortal because they were enshrined in an *ideal* world, created by the conceptualizing imagination and thus exempt from the corruption of decaying matter (the world of *genesis* and *phthora*).

Thus primitive Greek religion already forecast two significant elements of the Greek spirit—the naturalistic humanism which yielded an anthropomorphic conception of the gods, and the idealism which depicted them as free from all the defects and weaknesses of mere mortality. Such was the religion of Hellenism as Herodotus already perceived when he remarked that if the Ethiopians were to create an Olympus of their own, they would give its denizens snub noses and woolly hair. Modern research, working on this clue, has succeeded in recovering from the debris of cults and cult-epithets, a picture of the complex ramifications of the Greek faith, which thus exhibits in a remarkable way a hitherto neglected aspect of the many-sided Hellenic genius.

But if Greek religion prefigured, it also predetermined the cycle of Greek experience, the triumphs of which were chiefly in the realm of the spirit and the results (successful or otherwise and conspicuously both) due to the intense inquisitiveness of the Hellene. This spirit of curiosity found an outlet in that torrent of invention, of speculation and of criticism which was the essence of his attitude to life, and of which his art, literature and philosophy was the logical (and pathological) reflection. We are here concerned, however, not so much with the reflection as with the actuality of the life which sought above all things to come to grips with "the really real" and to make it the basis for a rule of conduct; as well as the methods whereby the Greek hoped to attain that end.

Here, also, the finality aimed at was in sharp contrast with the results achieved—the rapid evolution of the living societies from the stage of the patriarchal village community through the innumerable forms of the *polis*, and from the *polis*, racked by internal strife and bled white by external feuds, toward those short-lived experiments in federalism whereby the Greeks sought in vain to overcome their domestic troubles and, at the same time, to erect a dyke against the threatening flood of barbarism. Such were the results of the constant urge to a richer and fuller, as well as to a more secure life, which, as often as it was defeated, sought to repair the disaster by the adoption of alternative schemes.

It was this urge which suggested the need, as the inventiveness of the Greeks suggested the form, of their most characteristic political discovery, the city-state. In its essence the city-state represents the project of a planned social and economic order, impregnable to assaults from without and, at the same time, immune from the tendency toward division inevitable in societies of the patriarchal or tribal type, as well as from the curse of fatal blood-feud. It was the supreme contribution of the Greeks to the classical idea of the commonwealth; and the path of Hellenism was strewn with the wreckage of hundreds of working (if defective) models in which the Greeks sought to embody this idea, to serve as an inspiration and a warning to posterity.

As perhaps the most characteristic expression of the Greek genius, the *polis* deserves a much more adequate treatment than is here possible; and we must be content with a few random suggestions to indicate its more striking features as they were apprehended by the Greek mind. To begin with, the Greek view of the state was profoundly unhistorical. As a planned social and economic order, the counterpart among men of the rational and intelligible order of the universe, it was envisaged in terms of the self-conscious ego and of ends to be achieved. It was the necessary means of "self-realization" as conceived by a hypothetical founder who, by force or guile, laid down fundamental principles to dominate the life of the community for all time to come, thus emancipating it from the sway of chance or circumstance.

From this curiously static view of society, the direct reflection of Greek rationalism, few, if any, Greeks escaped; and Aristotle, despite his supposed empiricism, was no exception. It presupposed the possibility of realizing in the community an ideal of absolute justice; betraying no sense that this goal may well be unattainable or, that if it is to be attained, this is possible only through the long and tedious process of historical evolution. Yet Aristotle, with characteristic Greek complacency, observes that, "Justice is the bond of men in states, and the administration of justice, which is the determination of what is just is the principle of order in society"; as in the *Nichomachean Ethics* he had boldly embarked on the task of working out, by a sort of mathematical calculus, the principles of "distributive justice." This, despite the pessimistic warning already given by the more far-sighted Plato, for whom the pattern of the ideal city was laid up only in heaven.

Yet such was the fascination of the political idea that it largely determined the constitution of Hellenic society, and the actual course of Greek history. Thus, through the division of labor for the development of natural resources, the typical Greek community sought to achieve a measure of security which would make possible the "good life"; justifying in this way the exploitation of forced labor (δώματα οἰκετικά, ὄργανα ἔμψυχα) to yield a precarious economic and social equilibrium. This equilibrium the Greeks sought to reinforce by maintaining a principle of autarchy as a basis for the moral self-sufficiency in the interests of which the economic order was established;[3] undertaking "the socialization of morals and the moralization of politics" whereby the excellence of human character was to be achieved. Herein also they discovered the role of creative politics "the adjustment of function to capacity and instruments to both"; the notion of laws something more than merely regulative thus passing into the notion of education for the manufacture of character as the ultimate purpose of organized society; as well as the idea that the proper use of leisure is the end of existence for civilized man.

But even the partial realization of these ideals could not be achieved without giving rise to grave problems, the inevitable by-products of the planned economy. These were to some extent the result of weaknesses in the social systems which they evolved; but to some extent they pointed to defects in the ideal itself. Of the former, perhaps the most obvious was the creation of a landless class consequent upon the recognition of private property in land. This involved the control of population by emigration or by the extermination of the unwanted or unfit. Another conceivable outlet was the

---

3. Aristotle, *Politics*, 7.9–10; γῆ παντόφορος, Χδφαλεία καὶ εὐπορία τῶν ἀναγκαίων.

development of economic imperialism (foreign trade and depots), but this would have been to imperil the moral ideal by erecting a counter ideal of power. The same danger was concealed in the elaboration of techniques for which the Greeks were thoroughly competent, and which they might have achieved had they not realized the menace of the machine; though Aristotle, in an interesting aside, remarks that if the day should come when shuttles could weave of themselves, slaves would no longer be needed.

From the adoption of such expedients, however, the Greeks were deterred by their dread of opening the door to innovation, their congenital terror of the great god *Whirl;* Pericles alone, in the Funeral Speech, speaks of innovation in the modern sense, as if it might imply the idea of progress.[4] Otherwise, Greek statesmanship thought entirely in terms of protection— how best to maintain the *status quo.* Hence the limitations of Greek political speculation, which devoted itself to such questions as the classification of constitutions according to the valuation placed on personality and the ends to be realized through different types of association; the nature of the political decision and how best it might be obtained; the question of education as an ingredient of the social environment. This last was by every count the most important of all questions envisaged by social philosophy; for, as Plato in the *Laws* observed, few peoples, if any, were spontaneously good.[5] Normally, therefore, goodness must be the result of cultivation and training, which thus became the supreme problem of statesmanship. Thus the Greeks, aiming at absolute justice, achieved a kind of Sinn Fein. In this way alone could they be sure of maintaining the identification of the individual citizen with the corporate life. And this was in the last analysis just as true of Greek democracy as it was of any other of their political forms. In Athens no less than Sparta, "virtue was relative to the constitution"; and the only way to deal with incongruous elements which could not be assimilated to the life of the community was to expel them from the body politic. Such were the limits of classical "liberalism."

Through law and education the Greeks hoped to impose controls especially upon the acquisitive instinct and to inculcate that morality of self-restraint so assiduously preached by the Delphian Apollo, preeminently the city-state god; and the fruits realized at first were so rich as to justify that intense feeling of superiority which they felt in the presence of all barbarians; it made possible "self-realization" in a sense incomprehensible alike to the half-starved Scythian nomad and the cringing Oriental slave. Recognizing the autonomous character of the various natural dispositions, it sought

---

4. Cochrane, *Thucydides,* 20–21.
5. Plato, *Laws,* 642C.

to blend them into a harmony by a "compromise" or agreement not unlike that which governed the commonwealth itself. The city, as Plato said, was merely the individual writ large.

Thus the Delphian ethic was in a curious fashion the counterpart of city-state politics. Like it, it was the product of a rational view of things, appealing to the head rather than the heart; and it possessed the defects of its qualities. It was said of the Spartans, for instance, that when withdrawn from the atmosphere of the city, they flung to the winds the restraints imposed by the social environment, obeying the laws neither of God or man. The Athenians, also, experienced no little difficulty in asserting the claims of the state upon the devotion and self-sacrifice of her sons, whether on grounds of reason or emotion.

It was hard, indeed, for the community which set before its members the ideal of self-realization to curb that disposition when manifested against itself. It was difficult also for the citizens to realize that they must hang together lest they hang separately; that their common welfare was dependent upon sticking together to dominate the less fortunate, the Spartan helots, the Thessalian Penestae; or, in Athens, the subjects of Themistoclean and Periclean imperialism. Thus the city-state was constantly threatened with *stasis;* against the menace of which even Periclean democracy proved in the end to be an inadequate safeguard. It was in vain that the Greeks sought to close their ears to the slogans of the revolution.

The various endeavors to combat this chronic evil are set forth in the *Politics* of Aristotle, in which we learn of all sorts of radical proposals, such as that of economic equality or the limitation of property. Aristotle himself rejected all doctrinaire schemes to advocate his ideal of a Jeffersonian democracy of small holders; but, "conservative" as he was, the limitations which he imposed on private property would shock all but the most advanced of modern socialists. Plato could see no cure short of the communization of the governing class. Thus he consecrated the system of exploitation in the very effort to remove its sting. Finally, it should be noted that both Plato and Aristotle abandoned the project of the planned society except on a scale so tiny and insignificant that it could not hope to survive the more massive organizations of power which were possible for those who were content to think in cruder terms and who were satisfied to throw overboard the chimerical ideal of social justice. But to say this is to admit failure; to pass to other hands the torch of political experiment. It registers the transition of Hellenism from the first to the second phase of its activity—the great revolution from *polis* to *cosmopolis*. With this transition, the allegiance of the Greeks was diverted from the gods of civilization and devoted to the gods of power.

Thus, with the final collapse of Greek hopes at Chaeronea, it was the fate of Hellenism to be swallowed up in the first of those massive agglomerations of power which were to characterize the next phase of Mediterranean culture. Doomed to the loss of all but a precarious independence, and destined to serve as pawns in the game played by the great Hellenistic succession states, the Greeks were compensated by a vastly enlarged opportunity to exploit the barbarian world, and this they proceeded to do with a refined technique for which the crude Oriental monarchies afforded no parallel. But the Greek spirit in expansion, while it gained in power, lost in depth and concentration. The Hellenistic *cosmopolis* never overcame its hybrid character; the territorial and feudal principle continued to exist side by side with the transplanted *political* life of Alexander's civic foundations. Thus, the Hellenistic sovereignties exhibited even harsher contrasts and bitterer anomalies than had characterized the autonomous city-states. So far from repairing the inner unity of life which had been dissolved by Greek rationalism, they were satisfied with a merely formal and external unity which expressed itself in emperor worship—submission to incarnated force. In keeping with this, Greek thought was now devoted to the *externalia* of life. This was the period of applied science and the development of techniques, such for example as that of warfare. Yet, through the mere ascendancy of the Hellenized Macedonians, the East received a veneer of Greek culture. The language of Homer became the *lingua franca* of the dominant classes from the Nile to the Euphrates and from the Danube to the Persian Gulf. Within this area, the cumbersome succession kingdoms endeavored to maintain an uncertain balance of power, till, one after the other, they succumbed to the might of Rome.

Meanwhile, for old Greece, the rise of a new champion excited the wildest hopes of a renaissance of freedom. These hopes were destined to evaporate under the protectorate until, with the destruction of Corinth in 146 BC the Hellenes entered upon a captivity which, unlike that of the children of Israel, was destined to be endless—its bitterness mitigated only by the contempt of their conquerors for their present weakness mingled with a genuine admiration for the glories of their past and by a sense that their services were needed to Hellenize or civilize the West.

4

Pax Romana[1]

THE ROMAN SPIRIT FOUND characteristic expression in Roman achievement. Phoenicians and Greeks had between them explored the fringes of the Mediterranean from beyond the Pillars of Hercules to the Land of the Golden Fleece: and the pages of Herodotus bear witness to the keenness and vigor with which they prosecuted their schemes of competitive imperialism in both East and West. Yet in both cases their enterprises were circumscribed by the limitations of their character and outlook. They were, as Plato says of his countrymen, mere frogs around a mill-pond. Even when they founded depots and colonies, their settlements rarely extended to any distance from the coast. And, while each people sought to exploit the interior lands by the establishment of trading monopolies maintained at the expense of the other, neither was able to generate sufficient striking power to drive its rival permanently from the field; the Greeks condemned to ineffectiveness by the national passion for economic and moral self-sufficiency which repeatedly ruined their experiments in inter-state cooperation, the Pheonicians doomed the ultimate failure by the narrowly mercantile outlook of the capitalistic society which passes through civilization to decadence without ceasing to be barbarous.[2]

It was otherwise with the Romans. Their destiny was to subdue the continental hinterlands themselves and to open up their rich lands for settlement and exploitation. It was to bind together their domains by a network of highways, radiating in all directions from the golden milestone in the

---

1. [Charles Norris Cochrane, "Pax Romana," Charles Norris Cochrane Fonds. University of Toronto Archives, B2003-0011/004 (12).]

2. See Mommsen, *History of Rome*, vol. 3, "Carthage."

Forum and extending to the very limits of the empire. On that vast empire they were to impose a common legal and administrative system, as they were to give it a common system of defense. Within its bounds they were to set up the original mixing-bowl of races, neutralizing the fierce radical and religious sentiments of Gaul, Spaniard and Moor by the solvent of the Greek culture of which they made themselves the missionaries, and reducing the savage tribesmen to a common type of civilization, as to some extent they brought about their assimilation in blood. The Romans maintained and developed their *pax* or order for a period unprecedented in the records of Western history. From the Gallic raid under Brennus to the sack of Rome by Alaric the Goth was a period of exactly eight hundred years, and in all that time Hannibal was the one foreign enemy to approach even within sight of the Imperial City. From the traditional date for the foundation of the city to the so-called fall of the Western Empire, there elapsed more than twelve centuries. Throughout that time, the tough threads of communal life held firm, frayed and worn though they were as the end approached. *Romanitas* perished in the West as an organized system of life toward the close of the fifth century, but the memory of the *Pax Romana* survived to haunt the imagination of Europe long after the reality of the Roman order had gone down in a welter of blood and confusion. Thus, if the Romans devoted themselves to the things of this world beyond doubt they received their reward. They laid the foundations of an earthly city which with some show of right might claim to be eternal.

The spiritual basis of the order, as revealed by its most characteristic exponents in Latin literature, will be found to lie in the urge to individual and collective self-assertion, expressing itself in *libertas* and *imperium*, private right and public authority. It is impossible to exaggerate the importance of these conceptions and of the distinction between them. Together, in fact, they constitute the specific Roman contribution to the idea of the commonwealth. Through them the Romans were enabled to work out empirically that peculiar ordering of social relationships for which they also invented the name. They were the twin pillars of the republic. *Imperium*, in contradistinction from *dominium*, the principle of Roman liberty was non-hereditary and it conferred no property right. It is perhaps true that the community usurped certain of the prerogatives belonging to the *pater familias*. Whether, for instance, the Roman censorship should be traced originally to the right of the father, or to the needs of the public military and fiscal regime, is a nice question. Yet from the very first the public order was felt to be different in character from the *domestica disciplina*, the order which governed private relations, and, for the Romans, the state was never merely the family writ large. Neither kings, consuls, nor emperors were ever, except in a purely metaphorical sense, the fathers of their people.

On this point, the traditions are clear and unanimous. It was the failure of the last Tarquin to respect the independence of the subject, his attempt to translate his *imperium* into a *dominatio*, that constituted tyranny and provoked the revolution. The Tarquin tried to make himself a master; but ancestral custom, reinforced by the practice of self-help, sufficed to stem his encroachments on freedom and to vindicate republican commonwealth liberty. On the other hand, Roman radicalism, typified by the mythical figure of Spurius Cassius, might propose the measurement of the public lands and their distribution among the poor. And the menacing specter of Cassius might rise again and again from the tomb to haunt the possessing classes with visions of the *tyrannis*. Nevertheless, the solidarity of economic interest among the "householders" was sufficient to break one revolutionary after another. The Caesars themselves consolidated their victory over the aristocracy only by accepting, in its fundamentals, the republican idea. Thus, while the Romans were ready enough to recognize the claims of a public interest corresponding to the private interests asserted in the form of *patria potestas*, they were unwilling to permit the former to swallow up the latter. Such, indeed, was the respect accorded to property that, as late as the days of Marcus Aurelius, the state refrained from exercising a right of expropriation against land-owners, even when the interest to be served was as important as the provision of a water-supply for the imperial capital. Despite all subsequent invasions of private right by public authority, one has to wait till the days of Diocletian and Constantine for the effective assertion of omnicompetency and dynasticism and, even then, the name *republic* survived to remind the sovereign (as it occasionally did) of the *de facto* limitations of his power.

In this sense, the Greeks, for example, possessed neither the name nor the idea of the state. Envisaging the commonwealth as "one big family," they never succeeded in putting a construction upon the nature of συνομιεμός which could save them from absurdities and extremes of communism and anarchy. The political question was, indeed, merely the reflection of the deeper philosophical problem of individuality, and the solution of the former was impossible so long as the latter remained to constitute a stumbling-block to Greek thought.

From the perplexing difficulties of Greek speculation, the Romans were, so to speak, delivered in advance; for them, indeed, the questions that troubled Hellenism hardly arose until after they had laid a sound basis in practice for a workable scheme of social relations. It was the destiny of the Romans to produce a living exemplar of that bourgeois society which Aristotle had sketched in theory. Herein consists the high originality of Roman political achievement and of the intention by which it was inspired and directed—unless, indeed, it be supposed that the Romans created the republic in a trance (Pollock, Marriott, etc.) Their thought, however, is hardly to be discovered in formal treatises, such, for example, as the moral and political essays of Cicero, where the genuinely native elements, significant as they are, are somewhat overlaid by notions derived from Greek philosophy. It must be gathered from other sources—historians and the poets, the orators and the jurists, above all, the extant fragments of the law.

From these sources, it becomes possible to reconstruct the peculiarly Latin version of the idea of the commonwealth, by which citizenship is envisaged as a sharing of burdens made possible by a union of hearts, in respect to objects of common desire, "rational" in the sense that life and experience dictate to men the imperative necessity of an order which they fail to apprehend at their peril. The definition is of course that of Cicero as recorded by Augustine, it fully expresses the characteristically Roman attitude to the commonwealth, the spirit in which the Romans combined to erect the republic.

The Roman definition of the commonwealth as *res publica* made possible for them distinctions of the utmost importance to which the Greeks, for example, were notoriously blind. Unlike the Hellenic *polis*, "an all-in partnership," the *res publica* was definitely limited in scope, and the term itself could hardly be used without a suggestion of its counterpart and counterpoise, the *res privata*. In other words, the state was merely the expression of the "common interest" as opposed to the interest which remained "private." But what was this common interest as the Roman saw it? We shall find the answer in the formula *res publica res populi*. The state was the work of human hands, embodying the element of deliberate and rational purpose, so that if "nature," or animal impulse, helped to create it, in doing so she played the part of step-mother.[3] The myth of the asylum embodies the first crude statement of the doctrine of social utility. Accordingly for the Romans, to vindicate the majesty of the state was to vindicate the majesty of the people, *maiestas populi Romani*, which they felt might be injured no less by its representatives than by any other enemy, secret or avowed. Finally, there was implicit in the Roman order the principle *Salus populi suprema lex*, and thus, as will be seen, the Roman peace exhibited a gradually unfolding plan of substantial right, at once progressive and conservative, and both because it was the expression of life and experience.

The basis of political association among the Romans was the recognition of common purposes, supported and sustained by a common will,

---

3. Cicero, *De Republica*, 3.2.

which may thus be defined as effective desire controlled and guided by a sense of common interest. This common will came to be represented mystically by the deified *Concordia*, and the interests which they envisaged were quite concrete, the solid advantages of security and well-being as these were conceived by the Romans; so that (up to a point at least) every extension of the public interest implied an extension of right to those who made it possible. Thus, for example, in the case of the original burgesses, the soldier-householders, the development of the *ius commercii* and its liberation from primitive formalism gave them increasing scope and freedom of action during their life-time, as the concession of a right of testamentary bequest implied the projection of their personalization even beyond the grave.

Civitas, like the Greek πόλίτις, is simply an abstract, collective noun, and it points to the *civis* as the unit of political association. In a sense, therefore, citizenship, like the state itself, is artificial, for here also nature is a stepmother, by herself creating neither the one nor the other. To be a citizen, then, is to achieve a distinctively human purpose, and to assert civic rights is to assert a principle which is essentially qualitative, as the Romans put it, *status* or *dignitas*. On this principle it is false to say that Roman democracy "was cankered in the bud"; for, in truth, the notion of democracy, regarded as mass domination, or the government of the poor, was utterly repugnant to the republican idea, and the state was never a democracy except in the sense of a Jeffersonian community of small proprietors. It was, however, "individualistic," because individuals alone enjoyed a position which they were able and willing to vindicate by the process of regulated self-help sanctioned under the law, and only individuals could represent or "carry the person" of those who by reason of natural disability such as age, sex, or origin, were incapable of asserting the claims or assuming the burdens of citizenship.

The union of those associated in this way constituted the *populous*, and thus in Rome there was never any question as to the seat of ultimate sovereignty. Sovereignty lay with the body of burgesses who exercised their prerogatives because they had the will and power to maintain them. Moreover, because they conceived of these as a bundle of *iura*, capable of being extended in whole or in part to suitable persons, the way was opened for that monumental series of incorporations, by which the state was to receive fresh recruitments of strength, and the world was ultimately transformed into a city, or the city into a world. Such incorporations, however, were always made on a qualitative rather than a quantitative basis, *quod usquam egregium, huc transferre*, and this was equally true of Attus Clausus and his Sabine mountaineers, of the plebeians, the Latins and the Italians, of those who received citizenship or the Latin right as the reward of military service, and of the free *municipales* in the subject provinces of the empire.

The achievement of the common interest designated as *res publica* was thought to involve the articulation of functions within the body politic, to use a term which the Romans themselves employed in the famous story of Menenius Agrippa at the time of the first secession of the plebs. In particular, it involved the development of the three organs of government more or less common to the city state, although the Romans infused a peculiar meaning into these organs in accordance with their unique point of view. This was preeminently the case with the magistracy which, so long as it functioned "legitimately," whether in its executive, judicial or legislative capacity, was never regarded as infringing but always as augmenting the liberties of the people.[4] Like the *pater familias* in the household of which he bore the person, the holder of the *imperium* was truly representative. During his tenure of office, he supported the majesty of the people by the power of coercion with which he was vested, and republicanism knew no way to neutralize his authority except by forcing him to act within the restrictions of the annual and collegiate principle, or by subjecting him to the dangers of trial and condemnation after he had "abdicated" his office. Of the Senate, the great Council of State, little need be said except that it typified, both in its constitution and functions, the Roman mentality. It was natural that this people should have laid great stress on consultation and deliberation and that they should have entrusted these duties to a body which, whether composed of *patres* or *patres et conscripti,* clearly embraced the wisdom and experience of the community. It was equally natural that the advisory function, committed to such hands, should have grown as it did with the growth of the republic, till the Senate could properly be described a parliament of kings. On the other hand, *Comitia,* plural in number and representing the people meeting either in the form of the Servian army (*centuriata*) or as landowners and taxpayers (*tribute*), exercised such functions as were appropriate to the representatives of the ultimate sovereign. These were judicial, as when they were required to deprive a citizen of his *caput,* or to impose lesser penalties upon him; and legislative, as when they were asked to endorse proposals presented by the executive, by and with the approval of the Senate or (perhaps occasionally) without its consent. But no account of the *populous* would be complete without reference to that curious body, the "council of the plebs," and to the sacrosanct representatives of the plebeian order—an anti-assembly and an anti-magistracy which nevertheless came to stand for the people, as its plebiscites gradually took the place of law. This was the strangest anomaly of the Roman constitution and at the same

---

4. Sallust, Bellum Catilinae, 6; *Regium imperium . . . conservandae libertatis atque augendae reipublicae fuerat.*

time perhaps its most distinctive feature. It was anomalous in the sense that it acquired, with the growth of *tribunicia potestas*, the character of a state within a state. It was distinctively Roman, for it was based on that idea of *vindication* by coercive measures, upon which citizenship itself rested, and because it reflected a concord or agreement of the lower orders analogous to that which in the first instance had created the burgess body itself; so that, when the plebeian organization had once blasted its way to recognition, it acquired the legitimacy which characterized all Roman institutions and, indeed, the sacrosanctity of the tribunes came to be regarded as the corner stone of political freedom itself.

The evolution of the Roman order depended on time and circumstance, as Cicero, speaking as orator and statesman, rather than as philosopher, apprehends.[5] The Roman order thus admitted of growth, adaptation and adjustment, at the same time as it clung tenaciously to its own past. In crises, for example, it permitted the appointment of a dictator, a step which was tantamount to the temporary abolition of all constitutional guarantees, and the placing of the whole community under martial law. That this and other provisions for emergency government (such as the promagistracy in the first instance) were not more freely and more frequently abused was due to nothing but the operation of public opinion, with its strong sanctions in religion and custom; including a prescriptive "right" to resist despotism, which the Romans exercised on more than one momentous occasion, when legal and constitutional means of redress seemed to have failed.

Thus to the question: what things are Caesar's? Roman experience provided no final answer. This and similar questions were left to history, to the march of events by which alone such problems can be resolved. Nevertheless, Roman history affords a clue to the answer which might be expected from a people who thought, as the Romans did, in terms of legitimacy rather than of abstract justice; or with whom justice was regarded as the expression of substantial right, substantial right in turn depending upon the two conceptions of good faith and equity. To Plato, the tyrant is one who flouts all justice, human and divine. To the Romans, authority becomes despotic when it passes the bounds of law; and legitimacy is that which is well understood and accepted (by practice or statute), and that which can be enforced.

It was this sense of "legitimacy" which gave a character of objectivity to the Roman order, an objectivity which the Hellenic systems aiming at "absolute" standards, obviously failed to achieve. Thus might and right flew apart in Greek jurisprudence, and it required more than the arguments of

---

5. Cicero, *Oratio de Lege Manilia*, 20.60; *Non dicam hoc loco maiores nostros semper in pace consuetudini, in bello utilitati paruisse, semper ad novos casus temporum novorum consiliorum rationes accommodasse.*

an Aristotle to bring them into some sort of intelligible relationship; but for the Romans right was never out of association with the capacity to vindicate or enforce it. The fact, however, that Romans regarded law neither as "written reason" nor the voice of God ensured the possibility of free growth for the law, making for progress in fact if not in theory, and in this respect constituting both the strength and the weakness of the Roman order.

This analysis reveals the underlying principles of the Roman order, as it expressed itself in a progressively unfolding plan of substantial or material right, based on the formula, "render to each man his due." Historically, the original sanction of this order lay in *fas*, religious conformity or "good form," with its concomitant, the penalty of excommunication, which continued for centuries to be valid within a limited field of application. The sanction of *fas*, however, was supplemented and gradually overlaid by another sanction, namely, that of *ius*, or positive law, and the growth of *ius* at the expense of *fas* marked the secularization of the state. The stages of this process were traditionally distinguished as: (1) the Etruscan monarchy, through which the plebeians were probably recognized as landowners and admitted to membership in the citizen body; (2) the revolution of 509 BC, whereby the civil character of society was definitely established and all danger of theocracy removed; (3) the recognition of the plebeian corporation and the growth of plebeian influence in the early commonwealth, which resulted in the XII Tables, *fons et origo omnis publici et privati iuris*, and still more significantly, in the Valerio-Horatian legislation of 449, reinstating the old constitution of checks and balances (consuls and tribunes) which had been superseded two year before by the Joint Commission of Ten, but now, owing no doubt to the importance of the plebs, "men without family and without religion," on a definitely legal and penal basis; (4) the growth of the Italian confederacy and, along with it, of a body of law which, though Roman, was yet free from the formalism of "civic" law, namely the *ius honorarium* or the law uttered by the praetor or magistrate and enforced by his *imperium*. It was the development of these tendencies rather than any scheme of mere domination which constituted the essence of the *Pax Romana* in Italy.

It is indeed, true that the Roman peace applied only to citizens and allies, and that it was jealously guarded as a privilege. For those beyond the pale, the ancient prescription of law quoted by Cicero from the XII Tables doubtless applied, *adversus hostem aeterna auctoritas*. The whole world of *hostes* was theoretically an open field for Roman expansion. Against the *Uitlander* the Romans in their collective capacity might exercise unlimited freedom of action, thus expressing a self-assertive spirit analogous to that by which, as individuals, they vindicated their status and claims within the body politic. This accounts for the element of Machiavellism which

Machiavelli saw in Rome. It helps also to explain the militant temper of the Romans, which manifested itself in the endless series of conflicts whereby the whole world was brought to their feet. During the earlier period at least, it is hardly an exaggeration to say that warfare was the national industry of Rome, so that, in the words of the Samnite rebel, the Capitoline wolf fittingly symbolized the character of those wolves who issued from their lair to devour the people of Italy—fighting which stimulated and perhaps helped to fix that disposition towards brutality which was subsequently to find expression in the bloody spectacles of the arena.

In view of the need for *securitas* against the constant menace of attack by their neighbors, the Romans were compelled to stand together or perish; and thus they came to develop and maintain a military machine destined to be the most formidable in antiquity. The harsh and stringent measures of military discipline, including its stern penalties for evasion of service and the autocratic powers which it conceded to the general in the field, survive as warnings of the price which a people must be prepared to pay for collective freedom and empire. Likewise, the willingness of the Romans to submit at critical moments to the institution of the dictatorship, which involved the complete (though temporary) suspension of all constitutional liberties, showed a recognition of Cicero's claim that amid the clash of arms the laws are silent.

Yet, with all their fighting, the Romans never exhibited themselves merely as homicidal maniacs; and, despite the slogan *vae victis*, their history was marked by an astonishing mitigation of the ancient rules of war. This showed itself in the subordination of the military to the civic spirit. Thus, at least until the days of Marius, the army was simply the embattled people, and warfare the ultimate instrument of diplomacy. Diplomacy, in turn, was dominated by the notion of public interest, however narrowly conceived. The Romans fought to win; but their notion of victory lay in the concrete advantages of security, land and booty to be acquired. Consequently, their wars were never prolonged beyond the point necessary to impose favorable terms upon the enemy, and peace beyond the frontiers was felt to be an extension of that civic peace which it was their constant effort to maintain.

Thus they carefully distinguished between brigandage (*latrocinium*) and warfare which is *iustum piumque*, because conducted according to principle.[6] Finally, as Roman arms advanced, the conquered peoples were either incorporated into the citizen body or left as "allies and friends" with no duty save that of cooperation in the general defense and with at least

---

6. The imagination of the Romans was too obtuse to see that their enemies did not always understand their rules.

the possibility of future citizenship—a departure from recognized city-state ideals and practice so great as to be almost incomprehensible to the modern mind. Moreover, the graduated system which presently arose, of Roman and Latin colonies, municipalities, and allied states, although indeed an application of the Roman maxim "divide and rule," was none the less an attempt to impart to the conquered the gifts which the Romans themselves held most precious, namely, law and order.

The principles which inspired and underlay the development of Roman militarism were doubtless mixed, and the spirit of aggression soon developed to reinforce the original motive of self-defense. These in turn were supported and supplemented by the love of glory (*amor gloriae, la gloire*) endorsed universally by Romans and indispensable to any administration which aimed to capture the popular imagination. It was these qualities which made up that body of *splendida vitia* to which the Romans owed their mastery of the world.

Vices or shortcoming as they were from a more exalted standpoint, they nevertheless gave birth to that ideal of patriotic devotion so characteristic of Rome, and enshrined in countless legends such as those of the Decii; they led also to the growing sense of an Italian mission (*sociis prodesse magis quam praeesse*) which culminated in the federalization and nationalization of the peninsula. It was these again which, in a fateful moment, gave the Romans courage to challenge the might of Carthage, thus saving the West from Semitic domination, as they subsequently became champions of Hellenism in the East. The tenderness and respect for Greek culture exhibited by Flamininus never quite evaporated among his countrymen, despite their contempt for the *Graeculi* as individuals, or for the decadence of surviving Greek communities.

If all this was imperialism, it was imperialism of a kind new and strange to the ancient world. So long, indeed, as the peasant state survived, Roman expansion meant little more than the acquisition of additional land to satisfy the needs of a growing population, and exploitation was directed primarily upon that land in the fashion of the intelligent peasant always and everywhere. Yet it should be emphasized that this system contained within it germs of the predatory imperialism of later days. The steady operation of social and economic evil was evidenced by the prolonged struggle focusing about the laws of debt; from the impasse created by which the policy of land grabbing in Italy offered relief in a manner acceptable to poor and rich alike. In reality, however, expansion merely postponed the trouble, which came to a head about the time of the Licinian bills, as it served also to conceal the failure of these measures. For the Licinian bills actually promoted the new social alignment based on the solidarity of the patricio-plebeian nobility of land and office, the final triumph of which was to be registered by the Hortensian law of 287 BC.

But the full fruits of the Roman system were to be manifest only with the conquest of the Mediterranean, which transformed the community of embattled farmers into a great cosmopolitan society at the same time as it transformed their empire, formerly a model of right and beneficence, into an intolerably oppressive instrument of oppression.[7] It was, of course, unthinkable that the Italian federal system should be indefinitely extended to alien peoples overseas. In the provinces, therefore, the Romans adopted the expedient of disarmament, taxation, and defense by standing armies of occupation. This, however, involved the liberation of the overseas "*imperium*" from the restrictions applicable to its exercise within the peninsula. It involved also the adoption of the Sicilian system of tithes and customs so well described as the "Nessus shirt," the fatal gift of the victim to his conqueror; for this system made possible that vast extension of public contracting which gave rise to the money-power. These concessions, coupled with a system of protected finance and guaranteed credit, operating almost invariably to the prejudice of provincials, provoked a rising tide of resentment against the empire throughout the Mediterranean world. For the Romans were adept in mastering and applying the technique of exploitation as it existed in Carthage and the Hellenized East. Indeed, they were usually able to improve upon the numerous and excellent examples of it which they found; as when they embraced the Punic system of plantations. It is probable also that the Romans invented the notion of systematic war-indemnities and reparations, that form of slow strangulation which they applied with such success to Carthage, Macedonia and Syria.

Typical of the new imperialism was the ruthless destruction of Carthage and Corinth, and the mock heroics and false sentiment of Scipio before the doomed city of Hannibal do not serve to conceal the fact that he made himself the agent of a brutal and savage crime. The Romans exterminated the Samnites as an organized people and the same fate was meted out to many of the most gallant and resolute of the Spanish tribes. Slave raids in Dalmatia conducted by Aemilius Paulus resulted in more than 100,000 human beings being flung on the market at a single stroke. Similar raids at Sempronius Gracchus in Sardinia resulted in the rounding-up of so many captives as to give rise to the phrase "cheap as a Sardinian." Even Julius Caesar, unique perhaps among his countrymen for clemency, on at least one occasion callously slaughtered myriads of Gauls. When one remembers that

---

7. Sallust, *Bellum Catilinae* 10.6; *Civitas immutate, imperium ex iustissimo atque optumo crudele intolerandumque factum.*

the fate of the surviving victims of this predatory warfare was to be chained like cattle in the work-houses of the great Roman landlords, or to be selected and trained for service as gladiators in the arena, one ceases to wonder at the familiar characterization of Roman imperialism, "they make a desert and they call it peace."

The new imperial society was one of vastly widened intellectual and spiritual horizons; nevertheless, within it harsh social distinctions, founded on social and political position but tending strongly to become hereditary, emphasized the widening gulf between the new millionaire and the new pauper—a vast chasm which nothing could bridge. As Mommsen writes:

> Riches and misery in close league drove the Italians out of Italy, and filled the peninsula partly with swarms of slaves, partly with awful silence. It is a terrible picture, but not one peculiar to Italy; wherever the government of capitalists in a slave-state has fully developed itself, it has desolated God's fair world in the same way ... The all-powerful rule of capital ruined the middle-class, raised trade and estate-farming to the highest prosperity, and ultimately led to the hypocritically whitewashed moral and political corruption of the nation.[8]

Consciousness of the full meaning of the new imperialism dawned slowly on the Romans. The beginnings may perhaps be traced to the final stage of the first Punic war, when successive fleets having been vanquished or wrecked, a "number of sagacious and high-spirited men" determined to save the state by equipping a squadron through private subscription and presenting it to the government. That act has been hailed as an example of patriotic devotion "perhaps unparalleled in the annals of history."[9] It was rather the last desperate gamble of the newly-created financial class to salvage what they could of their past acquisitions, and to make good in a contest which held so much of promise for them in the future. For who, in the twenty-third year of an exhausting struggle could have provided the funds required, except the group of money-magnates (the so called *equites*) who were later to reap the fruits of empire, even if in so doing "they made the name of Rome stink in the nostrils of the provincials?" Again, after Pydna, the booty which was poured into the city and the promise of inexhaustible future plunder made it possible to relieve the Romans from direct taxation for all time to come. The grand gesture of Paulus was, indeed, merely a sop to quiet a nervous public opinion, flung by that bloc of office-holders and

---

8. Mommsen, *History of Rome*, 5:395–96. The chapter as a whole contains a brilliant description and analysis of the phenomena.

9. Mommsen, *History of Rome*, 3:194.

financiers who were determined to profit by the occasion of this and future wars.

That certain sections of Roman opinion were already disturbed and frightened is clear from the strong opposition which arose to further expansion, especially in the East. Roman hesitancy, however, was due not so much to any conviction of the inherent evils of imperialism, as to the fear of its consequences—a fear which more than a century later was to prevent for so long the plundering of Egypt. This is clear from the act that it was old Cato, author of the famous sentiment *Carthage delenda est,* who made himself its mouthpiece.

Well, indeed, might the Romans sigh with Alexander for more worlds to conquer, or with Cato for an impossible return to the simple and unsophisticated past! The acquisition of empire brought its own speedy nemesis and, already in the second century, BC the symptoms were evident in the creeping paralysis which overcame hope, personal initiative and manly independence. The Roman ethos, apparently fixed by the narrow and intense discipline of the primitive commonwealth, was for that very reason in flux. Cato might bleat about the perils of enlightenment; and he was right in so far as morale, grounded merely on tradition and practical sagacity, afforded no protection against the seductions of Greek rationalism. The real danger, however, was otherwise. Roman training contained no ingredient sufficiently powerful to counter the natural predisposition to avarice, ambition, or both; while enlightenment served merely to remove traditional inhibitions and reveal the means to gratification. Thus Catonian obscurantism was useless even if it had been possible, and there was set for the Romans a new problem of the individual and the community for which experience afforded no precedent. With the removal of their last dangerous foreign enemies, and faced with the temptation to plunder a prostrate world, there were released among them the forces of individual self-assertion which had been submerged but not eliminated by the collective egoism of the civic ideal. For the spirit which had created the republic and empire contained no internal principle by which it might guard against its own excess. Accordingly, it revealed itself as self-contradictory and self-destructive when, now that all the barriers were down, *contentio* or competition degenerated into that fierce scramble for *dominationes et potentiae* which marked the last century of the republic, and culminated in the utter collapse of the economic, social and political order.

It was, indeed, evident, as observers presently perceived, that in the struggles which succeeded the affair of the Gracchi, Rome was confronted with the disease of which Greek history had shown so many fatal examples. Men might study its symptoms and its course in the history of Thucydides[10] or, with Plato and Aristotle, they might seek to penetrate to its inner logic and trace the process of social revolution and decay, reading their own future in the Hellenic past. On the other hand, men might attempt to recover something of their own history and its meaning for their generation, as they did with Sallust and Livy, for whom no doubt this, rather than any vain theory of art for art's sake, was the impelling motive to historical research.

The question was pressing and likely to become acute: how should the republic meet the threat to its existence and the future of civilization? In the words of a later observer, "If this empire perishes either from disease or fate, who can doubt that there will arise world-wide devastation, warfare and bloodshed."[11] The peril was realized by everyone except perhaps the die-hard reactionaries of the Senate and the ragged and half-starved proletariat of the forum. For the sole aim of the governing classes being to exploit the provinces, in order to secure their power they pandered to the mob, and the mob, while growing conscious of its might, was satisfied with the tribute by which its votes were purchased. Thus justice was poisoned at its source; so that nothing could prevent the spirit of political compromise giving way in due course to that of internecine faction. Indeed, the public concord, which appeared to cement the state, was already menaced even when the historian Polybius put on his philosophic blue spectacles and declared that in the Roman constitution there had been realized the stability of that "mixed form" which fashionable Greek speculation regarded as the last word in political wisdom. He made this pronouncement at a moment when the empire was bursting with explosive forces soon to pass beyond control.

---

10. See Cochrane, *Thucydides and the Science of History*.

11. Sallust, *Duae epistolae de republica ordinanda* (accepted by Edward Meyer as genuine and written from Africa in the summer of 46 BC); *Quippe si morbo iam aut fato huic imperio secus accidat, cui dubium est quin per orbem terrarum vastitas, bella, caedes oriantur?*

5

Revolution: Caesarism[1]

THE ROMAN REVOLUTION BEGAN when Tiberius Gracchus launched his tremendous assault on wealth and privilege during his tribunate, 133 BC. The movement thus initiated was to pass through many and various phases, to be concluded more than one hundred years later, when, at the historic meeting of the Senate on January 1, 27 BC, the Emperor Augustus cancelled all the irregular and arbitrary *acta* of the triumvirate, and formally transferred the republic from his control to the authority of the Senate and people. The program of Tiberius Gracchus was very simple and, indeed, naive—a back-to-the-land movement by which he hoped, in the face of economic tendencies, to restore the peasant state, and thus to revive the Roman morale. But he was soon to discover what wise men like Laelius had already perceived, that a publicly- assisted and controlled scheme of land-settlement, based on inalienable lease-holds, infringed the sacred right of free contract; so that the movement could not be sustained without an elaboration of state action utterly foreign to the spirit of the republic which he sought to save. Moreover, the Gracchan settlers could be protected in their holdings only by heavy public subsidies, which involved the organized plundering of the provinces (in this case the newly acquired province of Asia) in the interests of the poor, thus making them parties to the profitable game already discovered by the rich. Aristocratic opposition, expressed in the Senate and through the tribunician veto, served merely to drive Tiberius into violent courses. He asserted the principle of the "recall" which meant in fact the sovereignty of the urban proletariat, and that of "reelection" which trans-

1. [Charles Norris Cochrane, "Revolution: Caesarism," Charles Norris Cochrane Fonds. University of Toronto Archives, B2003-0011/004 (11).]

formed the tribunate from a quasi-magistracy into a popular "ministry" with a mandate and a program. Likewise, Gracchus's project of a standing agrarian commission, having control of vast patronage and semi-judicial authority was an innovation of the most fundamental character. In reality, it set up a sort of "first triumvirate" with sweeping powers for the administration of Rome and Italy. Accordingly, while the die-hards united to crush Tiberius, moderate men stood aloof. For they could not forget that, desirable and salutary as might be his program of social legislation, it involved new and far-reaching claims regarding the function of the state.

These claims were to be re-asserted on a gigantic scale in the program of the younger Gracchus a decade later. Gaius initiated his tribunate by an attempt to democratize the obsolescent plutocratic assembly of the centuries, and by an attack on the validity of the *Senatus Consultum Ultimum* through which his brother had been done to death. By virtue of this resolution the Senate had advanced a claim, to declare the existence of a crisis, empowering the magistrates to proceed against domestic agitators as if they were public enemies, and thus depriving Roman citizens of the protection of the courts in a matter involving their highest interests, inasmuch as it over-rode the ancient rule of law whereby no citizen might be deprived of his *caput* except by conviction before the Roman people. The *Senatus Consultum Ultimum* was, therefore, tantamount to the declaration of a state of siege and, although in certain circumstances justifiable, as Julius Caesar himself admitted,[2] it was obviously capable of the utmost abuse—a deadly blow in fact at the integrity of the republic.

The program of Gaius represented a revival of his brother's radical measures, with the addition of fresh ingredients calculated to disrupt the serried ranks of privilege, by the creation of a faction based on the consolidation of the impoverished masses with the money-power. Gaius's hope of the knights as a revolutionary force depended upon their interest in public order and mercantile credit, and he could hardly have anticipated the fatal limitations of their narrowly financial point of view whether on the jury-bench or in public policy. As for the masses, he faced the impossible task of uniting the demoralized city rabble with the proletarian workers (*opifices*). Hence the ambiguity of his program—organized relief destined to develop into the bread and circuses of imperial times, combined with the promise of land-grants in the provinces and, especially, the restoration of Carthage as a Roman colony. This latter plan gave fresh imperial significance to the revolutionary movement, and had its inevitable repercussion in the development of Numidian nationalism. The Gracchan law of military service,

---

2. Caesar, *Civil War*, 1.7.

which showed a disposition to interfere directly with senatorial control over the army, was hardly needed to reveal his program as a full-fledged scheme of personal government—a Roman version of the Greek *tyrannis*. It led directly to the formation of a faction of the right, with a program so seductive as to break Gracchus and shatter the domestic reform movement for nearly a generation; while his adherents were prosecuted by the machinery of a special court in a fashion now becoming conventional, but nevertheless involving the prostitution of law to political purposes.

On the other hand, the acquittal of the consul Opimius, who had executed the terms of the *Senatus Consultum Ultimum* directed against Gaius, marked the triumph of a reaction which lasted until the corruption and incompetence of the oligarchy provoked a revival of democratic agitation fourteen years later in the field of imperial affairs. This had two aspects, illustrated respectively by the attempt to create more effective machinery of popular control over senatorial officers (the *lex maiestatis*)[3] and by the direct assumption on the part of the democracy of responsibility for imperial defense. To this program the powerful financial interests heartily subscribed; the rise of Marius would have been impossible without the support of this moneyed class. The response of Marius was to initiate a vigorous and popular imperial policy in both Africa and Gaul; in the course of which he contributed a fatal element to the struggle for political power by creating the proletarian army and depriving the Senate of control over the armed forces of the state. He thus made possible the future ascendancy of the great proconsuls and brought the empire as a whole into the arena of party strife. But the attempt of land-assignations and cheap grain with the new democratic imperialism of Marius drove the financiers once more into the arms of the Senate and disrupted the forces of progress so effectively that the consulship of Marius (100 BC) seemed likely to be his last.

The revival of the popular cause in the form of "Troy democracy" by the younger Drusus, while perhaps more seductive than earlier movements, was hardly less subversive. To the old program of colonization to which the radicals stubbornly reverted—a back-to-the-land movement when the real problem was to make Italian agriculture pay—Drusus added the platform of "soft-money," by a modest law of inflation designed not merely to ease the position of debtors, but also perhaps to provide additional much-needed funds for purposes of social legislation.[4] He proposed also to settle the vexed question of land-tenure in Italy and, at this same time, to widen the basis of citizenship by extending the Roman franchise to the Italians. But

---

3. Cf. the *lex perduellionis* of earlier times.
4. Pliny, *Natural History*, 33.4.46; *Octavam partem aeris argento miscuit.*

the forces of reaction were too powerful. Despite his attempt at healing and settling by a restoration of senatorial control over the courts, at the same time as he opened the curia to a limited number of equestrians, the agitation for a wider franchise took on the complexion of a conspiracy. His supporters flocked to Rome, in a fashion calculated to intimidate the oligarchy. But his laws were invalidated by a senatorial decree which declared them to be contrary to the auspices; Drusus himself was mysteriously murdered, and his followers were hunted down by a judicial commission. These events were enough to blow the long-smoldering embers of Italian discontent into the flames of the Social War.

In the meantime, while the hands of Rome were tied by the greatest military and political crisis of her history, at the same time as the administration was confronted also by a violent financial disturbance, a pressing imperial problem developed in the East as a result of the militant pan-Hellenism of Mithridates. The nomination by the Senate of the Consul Sulla to command of the Asiatic war seemed to afford to his old senior and rival, Marius, the opportunity of a "come-back," such as had not presented itself since the fatal year of Saturninus's tribunate. An attractive program of laws was offered to the plebs by the tribune Sulpicius, which included the replacement of Sulla by the old hero of the *populares*. But Sulla settled the question of the disputed command by a march on Rome which, for the first time, brought the new army directly into politics. At the same time he endeavored to make binding arrangements for the control of imperial administration in his absence. His departure for the East, however, was the signal for a violent popular reaction which delivered the capital into the hands of Marius and Cinna. These envenomed leaders of the downtrodden and dispossessed masses proceeded to set up what amounted to a genuine dictatorship of the proletariat, marked by a savage massacre of their opponents and by the continued re-nomination of themselves and their henchmen to magisterial office, without the faintest pretense of popular election, for a period of five years. This was sufficient to display the utter futility of their program, the most striking feature of which was a measure of repudiation carried by the Consul Flaccus in 86 BC. This law abolished three quarters of all indebtedness by providing for the liquidation in bronze of all debts contracted in silver, at that time the standard medium of exchange. It occasioned violent fluctuations, which conferences could do nothing to check, because, as Cicero later remarked, no man knew what he had or what he owed. The administration also repudiated Sulla, denouncing him as a public enemy, and sending out a general to replace him, while they made gigantic military preparations against his inevitable return. This program was accepted willy-nilly by decent democrats such as Sertorius, who nevertheless endeavored to keep their hands clear of blood. It was the climax of fifty years of agitation and civil strife.

Opposition to the revolution had throughout centered mainly in the ranks of the senators—that parliament of kings now become a block of landowning and office holding magnates who either directly, or indirectly through the political influence which they exerted, controlled the vast bulk of the wealth of Rome. These men were not all equally selfish or equally vicious. Indeed, the leaders of the revolution were recruited mainly from among them. On the whole, however, events showed that they richly deserved the fate that was in store for them; so that, if there can be little sympathy with the popular program, still less can be said for that which called itself conservative.

Recognizing the gigantic dislocations which had been caused by the Great Wars, but too timid to attack the social and political evils which were their outcome, the senatorials, even when led by a Scaevola[5] or an Aemilianus,[6] displayed no quality higher than moral courage. Meanwhile, in the utter absence of political wisdom, a Nasica prepared to defend legality with clubs and brick bats, as a Popilius was ready to prostitute legal machinery to merely partisan purposes. It is impossible and unnecessary to recount in detail the sordid story of aristocratic demoralization. As Rome staggered down the bloody pathway of revolution, the same theme was re-enacted again and again by the senatorial oligarchy with variation at first on a basis of law and professed respect for republican principles. Presently, however, as the bitterness of faction became intensified, they showed themselves ready to translate dynasty which, by its readiness to resort to violence, exposed itself not so much as the champion of constitutionalism as willing to subvert in its own interests the law of the constitution.

Such, for example, was Sulla who, by his methods, was unwittingly to furnish the revolution with a weapon soon to be turned against the senate itself. Sulla may be called the first deliberate and conscious exponent of the gospel of terrorism. Quick to apply the lessons of the revolution as taught by radicals and conservatives alike, he sought to establish the domination of the oligarchy on a basis of force. At the same time, he himself contributed more than one idea of his own, including "the march on Rome" and the proscription through which he aimed to crush the revolution by the systematic extermination of its leaders. The permanence of his arrangements was

---

5. Valerius Maximus, 3.2.17; *Cunctisque censentibus ut consul armis rem publicam tueretur, Scaevola negavit se quicquam vi esse acturum.*

6. Appian, *Civil Wars*, 1.19; Velleius Paterculus, 2.4. Scipio Aemilianus was probably assassinated in 129 BC for having used his influence to remove judicial powers from the hands of the Gracchan land commissioners and restore them to the magistrates.

to be ensured by the disenfranchisement of the children of the proscribed, the enfranchisement of thousands of their ex-slaves, and the establishment of a host of soldier-settlements on confiscated lands through the Italian peninsula.

But Sulla's chief contribution to the revolution was the idea of the "dictatorship." It was this which served as an inspiration to men like Pompeius Magnus, whose life was to provide an illustration of how far a canny and unprincipled careerist might go within a system which he chose to manipulate to his own profit, regardless of consistency or decency if without actual malice. The historical movements of the period following Sulla's retirement were for some years confused and ambiguous, in keeping with the character of those who directed them, and of these Pompey may well stand as a type. In his earliest command, the Spanish, to which he had been sent for the purpose of crushing the remnants of the democracy, this youth "stormed 876 towns between the Alps and the Pillars of Hercules." This meant widespread slaughter and pillage in the interest of his troops. It meant the alteration of municipal constitutions, the confiscation of lands, the installation of dependents in positions of power and influence—in short, the effective reorganization of the Spanish peninsula with an eye to future political possibilities in Rome. By these means Pompey acquired that reputation for efficiency which he was later to capitalize in the Pirate Wars as the mopper-up of wastage discharged into the Mediterranean from an industrial system based on slavery and, subsequently, in the war with Mithridates, as the organizer of victory in the East. But the Senate, if they learned to respect, also learned to fear him: for it was from Spain that he addressed the insolent letter to the administration, in which he threatened to descend on Italy if subsidies were not immediately forthcoming for his troops. In fact, it was already possible to see in the boy-imperator, the future generalissimo of the East and moderator of the commonwealth envisaged by Cicero's dream.

Thus alleged friends, no less than avowed foes, contributed to the ruin of the republic, while conditions steadily moved from bad to worse. Gracchan food-control, astonishingly moderate at first, resolved itself into the dole. Projects for the relief of debtors through "soft" money expanded into the demands of later radicals for a "clean sheet and a new deal." Throughout, the pathetic situation of the proletarian and debtor class served as the occasion for developing schemes of domination and power by revolutionary leaders of all factions; and it is hardly possible to distinguish between the political aspirations of these men and their desire for personal aggrandizement. There was also a growing eagerness on the part of all factions to consolidate their position; and, as the secret of this was now discovered to lie in military power, a scramble for public office and, through it, for provincial commands in which the fullest potentialities of the terrible military *imperium* might be effectively developed. These tendencies may be illustrated by the events which led up to the conspiracy of Catiline.

Sulla's arrangements represented a final attempt to establish in Rome a government based on *principle*, though the principles involved were anything but acceptable to all but the narrow oligarchy designated as the beneficiary of his political testament. And, even in the case of his own supporters, men like Crassus and Pompey could find no opportunity for the exercise of their talents within the four corners of the scheme. The result, as might be surmised, was the speedy and utter collapse of Sulla's arrangements.

But the evil which men do lives after them. Sulla had purchased power by the corruption of the troops and, with the aid of the troops, he had established his ascendancy. In his effort to support the framework of his constitution, he had created powerful and greedy interests at the expense of interests no less greedy, although for the moment they were stripped of power and, indeed, excluded by force from their legitimate heritage. His methods served as an example, charged to the full with evil omen and malignant suggestion to friend and foe alike. In that degenerate and demoralized age, many must have thought what only Pompey dared to express—*Sulla potuit: ego non potero*?

Thus, in a brief decade after his death, all that was of positive value in the political reconstruction of the dictator had followed him to the grave. The year 66 BC saw Pompey, his favorite lieutenant, armed with military power such as he himself had never dreamed of, setting forth like a new Agamemnon to complete the work in the East which he himself had left unfinished. But at what a price had this vast mobilization of military and financial strength been procured? The tribunate was restored, if not to the proud position which it occupied in the conception of Gaius Gracchus, at least as a formidable weapon of political obstruction and agitation—a weapon which could be picked up by any politician of wealth and ambition, and used to the destruction of society. Pompey himself, the former darling of the *optimates*, now stood at the head of a coalition of big business men, the magnates of the Italian towns, and the starving proletariat of the capital—a coalition united by nothing but a common contempt for the paralyzed government of the aristocracy, and a common desire to ensure, through the championship of Pompey, the establishment and maintenance of security on the Mediterranean and the prestige of the empire on the frontiers.

Such was the service to which Pompey for the moment had lent the might of his sword; not that at this or any other time in his career one may detect any motive for his conduct except the *libido dominandi* characteristic of his day and generation. And throughout his triumphant progress through the East, both political friends and political foes in the capital constantly asked themselves this question: what will the conqueror do when he has finished his work in the Orient, and returns to Rome to join the ranks of the great unemployed? From what they knew of his character, all parties had reason to suspect that he would not be satisfied with taking his place alongside those glorified nonentities who filled the senatorial benches, but would by fair means or foul seek for another extraordinary command by which, in the name of public service and efficiency, the great man might be enabled to dazzle the Roman world with a display of his talents. Furthermore, it was actually known that Pompey was intriguing for such a command, and that he had already fixed upon Egypt as the future stage of his ambition. Egypt—the sick man of the contemporary world—sadly needed the services of the efficiency expert; and a project to seize and exploit the rich heritage of the Ptolemies would without doubt enlist the unqualified support of the powerful financial groups—those harpies of the last age of the republic.

Pompey's friends might wonder and fear; but an imminent necessity compelled his enemies to act. The democrats had never in their hearts accepted as their leader this new Elisha on whom the mantle of the prophet had fallen. His rivals in the ranks of the aristocracy had never really been willing to subject their interests and ambitions to the domination of the new *prince (princeps volentibus vobis)*. Consequently, all parties sought to discover some makeweight to counterbalance Pompey's undoubted ascendancy, especially among the troops. The emergency was desperate, and politics (or war) never made stranger bed-fellows than it did at this moment. For instance, Cicero thought at one time of defending the disreputable and discredited Catiline on a charge of extortion, as a means of conciliating him to the moderate group, although he knew that to procure his acquittal, he would have to prove that black was white. On the other hand, Caesar and Crassus, themselves too respectable openly to espouse the cause of this déclassé patrician—a man who in the days of Sulla's proscriptions had been seen on the streets of Rome carrying in his hand the decapitated head of one of Sulla's victims—nevertheless were not unwilling to fish in the muddy pool of Roman politics. These two politicians, the one boasting of Trojan and indeed of divine descent, but linked by family tradition and personal ambition to the party of the gutter—the other, though by birth an aristocrat, prominent for qualities that exhibited him rather as the leader of the financial blood-suckers—both of these secretly backed Catiline, at least in the early stages of that desperado's career.

Their object was clear; and it had nothing to do with the interests of Catiline. They were willing to play with fire, because when a conflagration breaks out, there is always need of a fireman.[7] In the political explosion which was always a possibility with such inflammable material lying about, there was more than a hope that his services might likewise be required; and a dictatorship, such as that which Sulla had enjoyed, would enable him to stand up against his old colleague and rival, if not actually to supplant him.

Therefore, Crassus and Caesar possibly fomented the first abortive "conspiracy" of Catiline in 66 BC, although all parties seem to have agreed that, the less said about that obscure episode in Roman politics, the better for all concerned. Whether there still survived in the nephew of Marius any tradition of the positive revolutionary program it is difficult to say. Of Crassus it may be affirmed with assurance that he had not and was incapable of framing a program of salvation for the state. And with regard to Caesar, the probability is that as yet he had formulated no definite policies although, from his attitude as recorded by Sallust, it is possible to discern the generally liberal and democratic bent of his mind. But Caesar was above all things a realist, and his sense of reality must have taught him the lesson which Cato never learned, that it is necessary to possess power in order to exercise it; that mere idealism was like a voice crying in the wilderness. It is probable, therefore, that at this period Caesar's modest ambition contented itself with the prospect of climbing to the next rung of the *cursus honorum*, the praetorship, especially if he had learned anything from the incidents of 66 BC.

The march of events therefore continued, and it is difficult to obtain precise information as to the part which Crassus and Caesar played in them. In 65 BC, by a decree of the Senate, all *peregrini* were excluded from home— a reactionary step which exhibited the fears of a weak government. Catiline, after his defeat in 66 BC, appeared rather in the role of a wire-puller than as the nominal head of the revolutionary groups, although in 65 BC Sulla and Antonius, who had been ejected for bribery from the consulship, were glad to combine with him in a desperate scheme to murder their successors and seize the reins of power. It was at this moment that Cicero thought of defending Catiline, over whose head hung a charge of maladministration, the fruit of a proprietorship which he had just concluded in Africa. His trial, when it was held, resulted in acquittal.

A critical period in Catiline's career opened with his candidature for the consulship in the summer of 64 BC. It was the weakness of the *populares* that their ranks contained so many men who could ill afford to wait. On success at this election Catiline staked not only his fortune and his prospects but also his respectability. The defeat which he suffered at the hands of Cicero left him all but desperate, though he was destined to make a final bid

---

7. Cf. the Reichstag fire.

for office in the following summer. Repudiated finally at the polls, he had no recourse except to raise the standard of revolution and the remarkable fact is that he was able to prosecute his designs for so long before the administration dared to challenge him to open conflict. Such was the inflammable material lying about—the misery and discontent arising from the wars, the wretched position of Sulla's victims, the restlessness and the need of the veterans and of ruined farmers become banditti, not less than of déclassé nobles impoverished by extravagance and debt; men such as those of whom Caesar later remarked that *what they needed was a civil war.*

The conspiracy of Catiline was the flash of lighting which, by illuminating the whole sky, gives final warning of the approaching storm. It revealed not merely the leading actors in that melodrama, but also the dim outlines of those more sinister figures operating in the background, whose methods had involved the state in such a catastrophe. Thus, indirectly, it provided inspiration for the historian Sallust, who was presently to give the world an account of the progress of the revolutionary spirit, offering a dynamic and moving interpretation of Roman history from the time when, the earlier inhibitions of religion having lapsed and the temptations of power being multiplied, the unleashed forces of individual aggrandizement were to culminate in the struggle for power of which the conspiracy was merely a significant illustration. In the Caesar of the *Catiline,* Sallust outlined the type of new Roman magnate who, by means of their personal magnetism with which he was endowed and the lavish bounty which he dispensed, drew to his person the elements of a Roman Tammany. But Caesar was not, on that account, to be confused with the forces of red revolution. On the contrary, Sallust already recognized in him the superman whom he was later (in the possibly spurious letters *de Ordinanda Republica*) to hail as the very incarnation of the spirit of popular imperialism towards which the destiny of Rome so clearly pointed as he was also to prescribe for the dictator a program of reform and reconstruction, in which emphasis was laid on the elements of concrete welfare and satisfaction which the latter was to provide.

Above all, the conspiracy focused attention upon the consul Cicero, both as a man of action and as a political philosopher—a man who, despite notorious defects of his character and his ideals, was nevertheless destined to play such an important part in the final tragedy of the republic and, through his books, to exert such portent and far-reaching influence upon generations to come. Cicero was undoubtedly a creature of contradictions. The stern prosecutor of Verres, the upright and energetic proconsul, he was yet at bottom devoid of a sense of imperial responsibility, or rather without a vision of the meaning and potentialities of the Empire. Self-styled savior of his country in 63 BC, seven years later he was to be its conscious if reluctant betrayer. He was the enemy of Catiline and Clodius, but the friend of Milo and Caelius Rufus. In the civil wars he was to exhibit himself as the imperator who was too proud to fight. It is easy by the multiplication of such examples to prove Cicero an opportunist and a trimmer; and equally easy to be contemptuous of the eclectic idealist, the ready and skillful Platonizer, and to pour scorn on the bewildered character of Roman speculation as found in his writings. Those writings were, indeed, little more than a mélange of skillfully compounded doctrine adapted from the Greek schools and prepared for publication in the spare time of a busy lawyer and politician. The student must nevertheless respect the character of a man who closed his career as he opened it, with a resolute attack on despotism and an impassioned appeal for freedom and justice. He must likewise respect the amazing energy in translation and paraphrase which was intended to help the Romans in some degree to grasp the significance of their own past and perhaps (if the Augustan settlement was in fact a partial realization of Cicero's political ideal) even to plot the course of their own imperial future. All of which Cicero achieved with such striking power of verbal invention that in later times to be a Latin was to be a Ciceronian, and the faults of the man were forgotten in the glory of the writer.

In 66 BC, Cicero had emerged from the practice of law to exhibit himself as a supporter of the new imperialism of the fully developed capitalist state, which by his persuasive rhetoric he helped to deliver into the hands of Pompey. At the time of the Catilinarian conspiracy, through a combination of personal vanity and real or pretended fear, he put himself at the head of the conservative movement, or perhaps made himself its catspaw, using his personal influence with the financial groups and the Italian bourgeoisie to align them with the Senate for the last time in a solid bloc to destroy the revolution. The chief element among his supporters consisted of those who, three years before, had backed the extraordinary commands of Pompey in the East, the crowd which manipulated the gambling in shares of the companies of public contractors (*societates publicanorum*) which trembled with the slightest breath of news from the provinces,[8] and whose interests Cicero never failed to advocate in the Senate. To these he appealed in the name of the sacred union of Italy (*consensus Italiae concordia ordinum*) which in so many ways recalled the broken ideals of the younger Drusus.

Cicero looked on his election to the consulship as evidence that aristocratic exclusiveness was now breaking down, when it was in reality merely an indication of the momentary panic of the oligarchy at the prospect of Catiline's return at the polls. He also banked heavily upon the fact that,

---

8. Cicero, *ad Atticus*, 1.19.4; *is enim est noster exercitus, ut tute scis, locupletium.*

through the admission of the municipalities to citizenship, Italy as a whole was now brought into the scale. His hopes seemed to have been realized for a moment when the financier Atticus paraded his gleaming equestrian cohorts in defense of the Senate. But Cicero was speedily to be undeceived. In the swift reaction from the events of December, he witnessed at once the crumbling of his league for peace and freedom and the fading of his bright political dream. This he attributed to the apathy of the bourgeoisie, with their mind on nothing but their wretched money-bags, to the selfishness of the financial classes who preferred a readjustment of the terms of their Asiatic contract to the common good, and above all to the stubborn blindness of the aristocracy under the leadership of Cato, the pedant whose friendship was to be fatal to the republic.

The disruption of Cicero's party, though made possible for the reasons just stated, was in fact brought about by the formation of an infinitely stronger combination of elements, the *societias potentiae* produced through the coalition of Caesar, Crassus and Pompey. Of this coalition, the basis lay in the extraordinary provincial commands which gave the three leaders anoverwhelming preponderance of effective military force, together with the control of the political situation in the capital by a systematic debauchery of the electorate and the use of puppet tribunes in a fashion which constituted a veritable burlesque of constitutionalism. This situation was, beyond doubt, mainly the work of Caesar, who was able to bring it about by judiciously biding his time, and to confirm it by a series of the most dexterous tricks which the history of politics records.

The formation of the coalition represented the utter and final defeat of the older Roman conservatism, which speedily disintegrated into its component parts. A decade later when, having seduced Pompey from his association with Caesar and made him their military champion, the oligarchical die-hards provoked the crisis which led to the civil war, they were doomed to fight their battle alone. Indeed, large sections of the Senate itself refused to follow the example or bow to the threats of the intransigents, despite their fear of death and confiscation; while the financial class, led by the banker Atticus, refused to budge, and the Italians conscripted to fight for the possessing aristocracy, deserted in droves to the standard of the greatest of demagogues, now embarked on a new role.

As for Cicero, he had shown himself not altogether wide of the mark in his reading of the will of Italy; and, having once grasped the futility of the principle of consent, he fell back on the notion of a protectorate or principate, *quiddam praestans et regale,* to act as a balance-wheel within the framework of the constitution. Prepared at first to accept his old hero Pompey as Moderator of the Commonwealth, he saw the vision fade, as the latter made himself the stool-pigeon of the Roman dynasts who had no other aim than to transform the republic into the narrowest and most exclusive of political monopolies. Then, after Pompey's miserable end, he turned with reluctance to the Dictator Caesar, whose speedy fall he had earlier predicted, and gave to his regime a qualified approval, at the same time urging upon him a program of reconstruction acceptable to the Italian bourgeoisie. When, finally, the *Nova Concordia* of Caesar and, with it, the policy of "cooperation" gave place to his later schemes, Cicero hailed his assassination with savage glee which typified the depth of resentment felt by Italians of all classes at their first taste of Oriental despotism. It was in this spirit, also, that Cicero met his heroic death, vainly striving to break the domination of Antony.

Thus, beneath the apparent incongruities of his career, one may detect an attitude on the part of Cicero which was thoroughly consistent. Himself through and through an Italian bourgeois, with an unshakable faith in the fundamental soundness of the bourgeoisie from whom he was sprung, Cicero preached the gospel of a regenerated commonwealth, expressing itself in terms of class-concord, but resting on the enlarged basis made possible by the inclusion of the Italian municipalities within the body politic. This gospel was aristocratic, as befitted a people who thought in terms of property, status, and tradition. It thus implied the notion of the class-state as an instrument for the promotion of human happiness, through the provision of outlets for individual self-expression, at the same time as a rigorous social discipline imposed upon its members the highest existing standards of civilized decency. It was, in other words, a typical conservatism of the better type. To the aristocracy of this republic, Cicero was prepared to confide the administration of Rome and the empire, and he endeavored to show both by precept and example that in this way a sound and generous imperial order was possible. It was with a view to finding assurance for the sentiments of humanity and justice required to support such a regime that he explored the philosophers with feverish activity, hoping to discover a fresh sanction for politics in the religion and morality of the Greek schools. To this end, also, he sought to water the barren sands of Roman materialism with an idealism derived in the main through the Academy from Plato. And, if his own hopes were doomed to disappointment, his gospel was nevertheless to triumph over Caearism in its original form and perhaps within the very camp of the enemy through the "conversion" of Caesar Augustus.

Thus far we have traced the course of the revolution from its beginnings in the land-bill of Tiberius Gracchus, seeking to put together the ingredients of the democratic program as it slowly developed. That program was to be epitomized in the life and work of Julius Caesar. Caesar has been the subject of such unending controversy that it is with extreme diffidence that one attempts an appraisal of his career. Denounced through the ages, notably by Machiavelli, as worse that Catiline, he has been hailed by Mommsen as the prototype of all those who forge elements of a new society by the method of blood and iron. Thus he has been variously described as the greatest political architect and the greatest political destroyer in the history of antiquity. And certainly there is an element of acute paradox in his life and character. He was at once the most and least Roman of all the Romans. He was descended from the bluest blood of the city, heir to the Trojan legend which he was not unwilling to capitalize in the cults of *Venus Genetrix* and *Venus Victrix*. Yet he was utterly detached, not less by temperament and training (the atheist *pontifex maximus*) than by the circumstances of a career spent largely amid foreigners on the frontiers and in the provinces; and he showed himself capable of subverting the republic in order to erect on its ruins a world monarchy of the Hellenistic type, and ready to find support for his schemes equally among the barbarous Gauls, or in effete and decadent Egypt; and even to turn to his purpose the fierce religions nationalism of the Jews.

Caesar was a practical exponent of that *real politik*, the philosophic analysis of which is contained in the fragmentary works of Sallust, with its implied moral that in politics there is no morality. Utterly contemptuous of what he could not see, and seeing only what could be discerned (so to speak) with the naked eye, as is shown by his famous argument with Cato on the punishment of the Catilinarians, Caesar weighed and balanced the complex forces, psychical and physical, with which he had to deal, and which it was his purpose to use for his own ends (*dominatio*, τυραννις etc. which he quotes). And the sole principle which one can detect in his conduct is that of self-assertion, the *dignitas* to which he so constantly alludes.

Moreover, as an ancient writer observes, Caesar was the only one of the revolutionaries to approach, cold-sober, the task of subverting the republic. This is illustrated at first by his career as a politician, during which he embarked on the formation of a faction, a course imposed upon him by the tactics universally employed by his great political opponents and rivals. This work culminated in the *societas potentiae*, the coalition of which he really pulled the strings, and it yielded him his great command in Gaul with its opportunities for profit and distinction.[9]

The next phase of Caesar's career embraced his work as general and organizer during the conquest and annexation of the Gauls. Here one may

---

9. Sallust, *Bellum Catilinae*, 54.4; *magnum imperium, exercitum, bellum novum exoptabat, ubi virtus enitescere posset.*

note the speed and daring which characterized his unique military genius; as well as the startling methods (an improvement upon all existing practice) by which he developed the efficiency of his troops at the same time as he secured their devotion to himself.[10] The solid work of conquest and organization was accompanied by continuous propaganda in which he exhibited himself as a great servant of the state, the man who had forever disposed of the Gallic peril, as well as by preparations for a future, the nature of which could only be surmised. For in the second *quinquennium* of his command, Caesar embarked on the wholesale corruption of the Roman world, the city itself, Italy and the subject provinces, as well as the client kings beyond the frontiers; so that he was in fact the portent and menace which he appeared to be in the eyes of Scipio, Lentulus, or Marcellus.

It is perhaps unnecessary to credit Caesar with a clear prevision of the enormous significance of his acquisitions in Europe, any more than with the deliberate planning of the civil war. The ordinary practice of the day suggests that his immediate aim was the development of sufficient power to outweigh that of Pompey. Nevertheless, his means became ends in themselves—the establishment of a firm bulwark on the Rhine against the rising tide of barbarism, the creation of a new Italy within the enlarged frontier, based on the settlement of impoverished Italians in the fresh and relatively undeveloped plains of Gaul, and their fusion with the native Celts in whom Caesar presently perceived the material for a great potential civilization of the Greco-Roman type.

Despite, however, his efforts at self-justification, it was not this aspect of his work which impressed his countrymen. The amazed oligarchy was struck with terror both by what he had done and what he might attempt. Thus the second *quinquennium* was marked by successive efforts to destroy him, by prematurely terminating his command, as well as by preventing his election to a second consulship, and by bringing him to book for the irregularities which he had committed since his first. The failure of all these schemes provoked the stampede of January 1, 49 BC, in which the die-hards of the oligarchy forced a fearful and reluctant Senate to declare Caesar a public enemy, thus precipitating the Civil War.

Caesar was not slow to accept the challenge, which gave him an opportunity at once of asserting his own claims (*dignitas*) and of vindicating the majesty of the people infringed in the persons of the tribunes who had vainly endeavored to sustain his cause. In other words, he treated the Senate for what it was, merely a "faction" in no wise competent to speak in the name of the Roman people. Yet he entered upon armed conflict with

---

10. See Suetonius, *The Life of Julius Caesar*.

reluctance, for he saw as Pompey could never see the consequences of his acts, and especially the implications of an imposed rather than a negotiated settlement. During the struggle he aimed consistently to prove that he was no Sulla, by his policy of studied clemency in the face of savage atrocities perpetrated by the senatorials and their barbarian allies. At the same time, he shook himself free from the influence of his own disreputable left wing; passing the famous bankruptcy act in which he sought to mediate between the claims of debtor and creditor in a fashion altogether new and refreshing in Roman history.

Caesar's success in the Civil Wars made possible the fulfillment of his program as a statesman. It is an exaggeration to describe that program (with Mommsen) as one of regeneration. What Julius accomplished was rather a work of reconstruction, inasmuch as all the ideas which inspired it fell within the ambit of Greco-Roman or Hellenistic culture, which hardly contemplated even in a metaphorical sense the notion of rebirth. Thus, in the matter of domestic reform, Caesar executed the political testament of the great revolutionaries from the time of Gracchus, just as in the conquest of Gaul he had fulfilled the dream of Marius and the new democratic imperialism. And, in both cases, he displayed himself in a role characteristic of Mediterranean culture, for he proved to be one of the greatest exponents of rationalization in the history of antiquity. This was shown by his measures which ranged from the scientific reform of the calendar to the steps taken for the reorganization of Italy on cosmopolitan lines, as well as for the extension of Italian civilization to the western provinces.

There existed, however, fatal limitations to the possibilities of reform which were, as Caesar himself had foreseen, the inevitable consequences of a victorious peace. It is unnecessary to dwell upon the factors which ultimately drove him toward complete military autocracy expressed in the form of the perpetual dictatorship. These were not less the untrustworthy character of his own supporters than the behavior of the conquered aristocracy, which oscillated from stubborn intransigency to disgusting subservience. Caesar did all he could, by the general amnesty which he extended to exiles as well as by such a gracious gesture as the restoration of the statues of Sulla and Pompey, to conciliate his enemies and to dispel the impression that the basis of the new regime was force and fear. Yet, despite his efforts, he failed to obtain the cooperation which he sought. Moreover, his own liberalism had inescapable limits; and cynics recalled the professions of loyalty to tribunician sacrosanctity with which he had embarked on the war, when Caesar brushed aside the impertinent interference of Metellus in the spring of 49, and still more, when he deposed the malicious Flavius and Marullus five years later. Finally, Caesar was fully conscious of the dilemma in which he was placed by his usurpation of senatorial prerogatives and by his assumption of personal responsibility for the administration, which was so bitterly resented, for example, by Cicero. "How can I fail to be hated," he declared, "when men of Cicero's distinction must wait for hours in my anteroom for the privilege of an interview?"

Such were the bitter fruits of a conflict the issues of which had already, in Caesar's lifetime, begun to be idealized by the protagonists on either side. Thus, for example, the noble death of Cato had served, as nothing in his life, to cast a halo over the agony of the republic whose hero and martyr he had become; so that it became necessary for Caesar to abandon for once his congenital and deliberate clemency, pursuing the other in death with a vindictiveness which he had never exhibited against him while he lived. So, too, it became obvious that rationalization, which is the application of scientific method to politics, had its limits; as Caesar himself perceived toward the close of his life, when he found himself seeking for a formula of government more compelling than either the record of his past or the promise of his future achievement.

It was then that he embarked on the final subversion of republicanism, the fabric of which had been crumbling with progressive rapidity since the outbreak of war. "The republic," he declared, "is merely a name, without substance or appearance"[11]; and, as if to signalize his contempt for the system, he appointed Caninius consul for the last day of the year 45 BC. "He was," observed Cicero with bitter cynicism, "a most wide awake official, for during his tenure of power he never slept." It was then, too, that Caesar accepted that accumulation of excessive honors which raised him above the level of mere mortality, scaling the heights of Olympus (*viam adfectabat Olympo*) in a manner which represented a complete departure even from his earlier pretensions, when he had merely sought for himself a place beside the Roman kings.

For, while it might with justice be claimed that, as the ancient kings were the legitimate heads of a free people and the natural protectors of the commons, Caesar's work was accordingly not one of destruction but of fulfillment, such a claim could not possibly be made on behalf of one who aspired to be associated with the glories either of the Trojan line or the line of Alexander. What Caesar at one time thought of Alexandrianism may be judged from his own scathing comments on the situation which he found to prevail in the Egyptian capital; in view of which the details of his lapse toward a world monarchy of the Hellenistic type might seem incredible, were they not so largely supported by contemporary evidence. He renounced

---

11. Suetonius, *The Life of Julius Caesar*, 77.

all the political inheritance of the civilized West and all the glorious hopes and ideals with which Greece and Rome had enriched the world, flirting with oriental mysticism which represents the suicide of reason, in a vain endeavor to avert the collapse of his regime. For it was, indeed, beyond the capacity of Caesar, epicurean, atheist and master of political realism as he was, to discover a workable formula of government for the future. And this he himself admitted when he declared that, in satisfying the claims of honor and glory, he had finished his life's work.

Thus the career of Caesar was not so much a model as a warning. It is true that, just as he had gathered up and expressed the past of the revolution, so also, in the tragedy of his death, he epitomized the whole imperial future. Yet the work of the liberators, many of whom had been his devoted followers almost to the end, was not altogether in vain. Despite such popular manifestations as the funeral in the forum and the spontaneous apotheosis of power in the person of Caesar, the deed of the regicides sufficed to postpone for centuries the final orientalization of the empire. It drove Rome back to the native channels of legitimacy, thus inspiring the Augustan settlement which brought the great Roman revolution to a close, while at the same time it made possible the reorganization necessary for present and future tasks of the Eternal City.

6

Niccolò Machiavelli[1]

To GIVE EXPRESSION TO a body of ideas in such a way as to associate them forever with one's name is to become a classic. This is a sufficiently rare distinction, but it is in a peculiar sense the achievement of Niccolò Machiavelli. An obscure under-secretary to the Florentine republic, preoccupied during his brief career with the strictly local and ephemeral questions of contemporary Italian politics, and today (four hundred years after his death) he looms forth as one of the most significant figures in the history of European literature. For generations, he lived in the popular imagination as a devil incarnate, who had stolen the mantle of Beelzebub himself. "He gave name to our old Nick," said Butler[2] perhaps as a joke, but the joke was taken seriously by Macaulay.[3] While critical scholarship is doubtless right in referring the name to *Nyke*, a water-goblin of Norse mythology, it is none the less probable that, by the familiar process of syncretism, the Machiavelli of popular tradition became identified with and gave color and body to what must have been little more than the shadow of a name. Marlowe introduced Machiavelli in his own person to the English stage:

> Albeit the world think Machiavel is dead
> Yet was his soul but flown beyond the Alps
> And, now the guise is dead, is come from France

---

1. [Charles Norris Cochrane, "Niccolo Machiavelli," Charles Norris Cochrane Fonds. University of Toronto Archives, B2003-0011/004 (06).]

2. Butler, *Hudibras*, 3.1.1314.

3. Meyer, *Machiavelli and the Elizabethan Drama*, 178.

To view this land, and frolic with his friends[4]

There he was destined to enjoy a long and ignoble career as the stage villain of Elizabethan drama, exhibiting himself Proteus-like in the varied roles of Barnabas, Richard III, Iago, and other characters. Common usage, derived from popular tradition and the stage-character, has made of his name a standard term—although a term of opprobrium: the word "Machiavellian" is sufficient to designate the mingled qualities of craft, hypocrisy, jealousy and malice, mobilized in pursuit of mean and selfish ends. The books of Machiavelli have been repeatedly edited either in whole or in part, and they have been repeatedly translated into most of the languages of Europe; so that their titles, if not their contents, are familiar to all. The modern reader is confronted also by a swelling volume of critical studies, dealing with every conceivable aspect of his work—his sources, his relation to contemporary life and thought, the influence which he has exerted on literature, on speculation, and on practical politics from his day to our own. Thus Machiavelli takes rank with the great thinkers and writers of all time, and he has earned for himself in this world at least the immortality which his enemies denied him in the next. He has even enjoyed a belated revenge on those who sought to proscribe his name and annihilate his influence in his native city; the cenotaph erected in Santa Croce to commemorate his memory bears the proud and defiant inscription *Tanto nomini nullum par elogium*: "What eulogy can be adequate for such a name?"

In order to illustrate modern views of the significance of Machiavelli, it may perhaps be permissible to cite two recent and divergent estimates, both of which are familiar to the English reader. Lord Acton declares of him that, in recording the experience of his own epoch, he also foretold the secret of men since born. "Machiavelli," he concludes, "is the earliest conscious and articulate exponent of certain living forces in the present world. Religion, progressive enlightenment, the perpetual vigilance of public opinion, have not reduced his empire, or disproved the justice of his conception of mankind. He obtains a new lease of authority from causes that are still prevailing, and from doctrines that are apparent in politics, philosophy and science. Without sparing censure, or employing for comparison the grosser symptoms of the age, we find him near our level, and perceive that he is not a vanishing type, but a constant and contemporary influence."[5] Such is the verdict of the great nineteenth-century Catholic historian on the man whose name was one of the first to be placed on the *Index*, and whose works

---

4. Marlowe, *The Jew of Malta*, quoted in Meyer, *Machiavelli and the Elizabethan Drama*, 39.

5. Acton, introduction to *Il Principe*, xix.

were totally and utterly condemned by the Church. In sharp contrast with this is the judgment of liberal idealism, as expressed by Lord Morley in his brilliant but ill-balanced essay. Morley traces at length the "sinister renown" of Machiavelli through the centuries. "In all the great countries all over the West" he says "this singular shade is seen, haunting men's minds, exciting, frightening, perplexing them, like some unholy necromancer, bewildering reason and conscience by riddles and paradox."[6] Nevertheless, with an optimism which is surely the product of dogma rather than experience, Morley undertakes to exorcise the fiend and to dissipate the spell which he has cast upon the minds of men. To the spirit of Machiavelli, he opposes the spirit of Midlothian; and, in the refulgent light of that great revelation, he finds that Machiavellism is but sophistry, and that what Machiavelli put aside, whether for the sake of argument or because he thought them in substance irrelevant, are nothing less than the living forces by which societies subsist and governments are strong. Thus Machiavelli was even in the fifteenth century as great an anachronism as was Julian the Apostate in the fourth, and, since faith in progress under Liberal guidance was still undimmed at least when Morley wrote, the *Life of Gladstone* is doubtless a still greater anachronism today. For this reason, or possibly because he realized that the ideas of Machiavelli presented an insoluble difficulty to idealistic liberalism, Gladstone refused entirely to discuss him; for when his biographer on one occasion raised the name of Machiavelli in conversation, the great man peremptorily checked him with the remark, "I prefer not to discuss the subject."[7]

Machiavelli and Machiavellism cannot, however, be dismissed in any such cavalier fashion as Gladstone proposed. Like the works of Darwin in our own day, and for very much the same reasons, the writings of Machiavelli have provoked question and controversy, ever since the contemporary Cardinal Pole launched the first attack upon them, declaring that they were traced by the finger of Satan, and branding their author as the enemy of the human race.[8] Ecclesiastics and scholars divided on the issue, and their disputes (more especially upon the side of Machiavelli's detractors) have produced some of the choicest invective of all literature. Cardinal Pole affirmed that if the devil himself reigned in the flesh and had a son to whom he proposed to leave his Kingdom, the precepts which he would give him would be precisely those of the *Prince*. The churchmen took pleasure in retailing the horrors of the atheist's death-bed. "*Blasphemans evomuit improbum spiritum,*" says the Jesuit Raynaud. Apparently the blasphemy consisted

---

6. Morley, *Machiavelli*, 5.
7. Morley, *Life of Gladstone*, 2:515.
8. Pole, *Apologia Reginaldi Poli ad Carolum V*, 136.

in saying that he would rather be in Hell with Plato, Seneca, Plutarch and Tacitus, than join the company of these poor spirited wretches whose home was the Kingdom of Heaven.[9] The reference to Tacitus, Plutarch, Seneca and Plato indicates that the spiritual affinity of Machiavelli with the classics had been already noted when the passage was written. Others accused him of plagiarizing wholesale from the classics, and especially, be it noted, from Aristotle *Politics*, Book 5.[10]

If the Catholic controversialists were roused to the attack by Machiavelli's criticisms of the Church, the Protestants were no less stirred by his supposed aspersions on the Book. Centillet, the first Protestant critic, denounces him as an audacious atheist, vomiting the blasphemy that Moses, by his own qualities and the strength of his own arms, made himself leader of the Hebrew people. The opponents of French absolutism labeled him as the devil who stands by the ear of princes, whispering precepts of tyranny; although, as has been remarked, such precepts, if needed, could easily have been supplied from the pages of the Old Testament. But in many ways the most interesting, if not the most instructive, attack on Machiavelli from the non-Catholic position is that which flowed from the pen of the juvenile Frederic, who was later to distinguish himself as the partitioner of Poland and the founder of the militarized kingdom of Prussia. Frederic describes Machiavelli as a monster, the declared enemy of humanity, whose pen drips with poison, and he undertakes to provide an antidote for the incoherent and horrible system which Machiavelli has had the impudence to obtrude upon the world. His attack—it can hardly be called an argument, although it received the enthusiastic *endorsation* of Voltaire—appears to move on two levels (1) that of absolute idealism and (2) that of policy. On the first level, it is largely shadow boxing, and involves the negation of history and science.[11] On the second, it is marred by the uncritical acceptance of the characteristic social and political dogmas of the eighteenth century. As a whole, the *Examen* is vitiated by reason of the fact that it deals with the *Prince* in isolation from the other writings of Machiavelli; and the observations in ch. xxvi, in which Frederic defines diplomats as "privileged spies" and urges the justice

---

9. See Bayle, "Machiavel."

10. *Sua omnia vaferrimus hic nequitiae doctor, dissimulato plagio ex Aristotele fortasse transcripsit. Eo tamen discrimine, quod hic impie ac impudenter omni principi commendet, quae non nisi Dominis ac Tyrannis convenire longe rectius ac prudentius ante scripserat Aristoteles.* Conringius, *praefatione suae librae de principe*, quoted in Farneworth, *Works of Nicholas Machiavel*, 1:486.

11. See Frederick II, "Preface to His *Examen*," 2:180: "The names of good Princes alone should be recorded in history, and those of others suffered to perish with their crimes. This indeed would greatly diminish the number of histories but the world would be the better for it." This is the link between Frederick the Great and Agnes Macphail.

and expediency of preventive war, themselves sink to a Machiavellian (or Bismarckian) level.

These criticisms are based on little more than a travesty of Machiavelli, and they represent almost as serious a misapprehension of his thought as for instance that of Marlowe when he makes him say:

> I count religion but a childish toy
> And hold there is no sin but ignorance.
> Birds of the air will tell of murders past;
> I am ashamed to hear such fooleries.
> Many will talk of title to a crown;
> What right had Caesar to the Empery?
> Might first made kings, and laws were then most sure
> When, like the Draco's, they were writ in blood.[12]

Such as they are, however, they serve to show that for more than two centuries, criticism of Machiavelli was dominated by prejudice and blinded by passion. Indeed, as Burd remarks, it is only within recent years that Machiavelli has come to be examined calmly and judiciously in his proper setting, that is to say in the light of history. There is perhaps no better gauge of the originality of his ideas than the difficulty which men have had in attaining this point of view.

In describing the ideas of Machiavelli as original, we do not wish to claim for him absolute novelty either of thought or expression. That, indeed, is a claim which he would never have dreamed of making for himself. Absolute originality, by the way, is a philosophical conception, and it should be left for philosophers to deal with. But if it be granted that originality consists in a radical departure from the conventional, then Machiavelli was in a real sense a pioneer, for he was among the first to shake himself free from the ideas and molds of thought which had dominated speculation for a thousand years. And of this he himself was fully conscious when, in his preface to the *Discourses on Livy*, he penned the following noble words:

> Albeit the jealous temper of mankind, ever more disposed to censure than to praise the works of others, has constantly made the pursuit of new methods and systems no less perilous than the search after unknown lands and seas;[13] nevertheless, prompted by that desire which nature has implanted in me, fearlessly to undertake whatsoever I think offers a common benefit to all, *I enter upon a path which, being hitherto untrodden by any*, though it involve me in trouble and fatigue, may yet earn

---

12. Marlowe, *Jew of Malta*, 271.
13. The passage was written within twenty years of the discovery of America.

me thanks from those who judge my efforts in a friendly spirit. And, although my feeble discernment, my slender experience of current affairs, and imperfect knowledge of ancient events, render these efforts of mine defective and of no great utility, they may at least open the way to some other who, with better parts and sounder reasoning and judgment, shall carry out my design, whereby if I gain no credit, at all events I ought to incur no blame.[14]

In these words Machiavelli proclaimed his belief that history rather than dogma is the real teacher of mankind, and threw out a hint of the future development of the historical principle. They are sufficient to mark him as the real founder of the modern science of politics.

This of course does not embrace his entire claim to literary distinction. Like most of the artists, philosophers and statesmen who were his contemporaries, Machiavelli dabbled a little in the pool of pure literature, and his achievements were by no means contemptible. The *History of Florence* forms, of course, the historical basis for his speculations in the *Discourses* and the *Prince*; and, as such, it is essential to his work as a political scientist. From the standpoint of literature, however, it is noteworthy as an example of national biography. It has been called the first of its type; but this is hardly the case for, in its composition, Machiavelli had the models of Livy and Tacitus constantly before him. The *Art of War* is an interesting attempt to revive the form and achieve the effect of the philosophic dialogue of classical times. Of his dramatic efforts, the *Mandragora* has been pronounced the ripest play in the Italian language. The novellete *Belphegor* represents an amusing satire, in which the devil himself is glad to take refuge in Hell from the terrors of matrimony. One sentence may be quoted to illustrate Machiavelli's whimsical and cynical humor. Describing the wife whose mad career of insolence and extravagance proved insupportable to *Belphegor*, he says:

> Everybody was fully convinced that the woman was really possessed of a devil, and that her distemper was not owing to capours or to any shim-sham of that sort; for she talked Latin, disputed in philosophy and discovered the private failings and infirmities of several godly people.[15]

These literary efforts deserve mention because they represent the first flights of Machiavelli's genius. They illustrate also the versatility of the Renaissance mind, in sharp contrast with the unhappy tendency to specialization

---

14. Machiavelli, *Discourses*, 3–4.
15. Machiavelli, *Marriage of Belphegor*, in *Works* (1762), 2:170.

which is equally characteristic of modern times. Their environment—a method which in the nineteenth century was described as the characteristic prejudice of the Renaissance, but which from another standpoint might well be regarded as its saving feature.

The true distinction of Machiavelli is, however, in the field of political speculation; and, in relation to the problems of politics, he represents, as we have said, a violent departure in outlook and method from the ideas which were current in his day. To measure the greatness of his achievement, it is necessary to take into account two factors (1) the condition of Italy and Europe, and (2) the condition of political thought, as they were when he began to write.

The conditions of Italy at the dawn of the fifteenth century is sufficiently familiar. It would be difficult to exaggerate the anarchy and demoralization of that unhappy country, which was still paying in blood and tears for the political and spiritual empire which, in Roman times, it had imposed upon the world. Divided into warring principalities, within each of which contending factions struggled for control, the peninsula was at the same time the victim of foreign aggression—preyed upon in turn by the sovereigns of Spain, France and Germany, and threatened by the barbarous empire of the Turk. To quote from the *Examen*:

> The story of Cadmus, who sowed the teeth of a serpent which he had killed, and from whence a race of men sprung up, who fought each other till they were all killed, is a lively representation of what the Italian princes were in Machiavelli's time . . . Whoever reads the history of Italy from the end of the fourteenth to the middle of the fifteenth century, will find nothing else but one continued series of cruelty, sedition, violence, confederacies to destroy each other, usurpation, assassinations, in a word, an assemblage of such enormous crimes that the very idea of them alone inspires one with horror.[16]

In this case, at least, the rhetoric of Frederic does not surpass the truth.

Meanwhile, what of the condition of political thought? Until Machiavelli's day, men still lived in the afterglow of the Roman world, all the more brilliant by contrast with the gathering blackness. Dreaming still of a revival of the majesty of the Christian empire, they divided merely on the issue of whether Pope or Emperor should wear the crown and bear the sword of universal dominion. For thought still writhed in the trammels of mediaeval rationalism—a vicious circle of absolutes from which it was well-nigh impossible to escape. And thus continued the interminable debate of Guelf

---

16. Frederick, *Examen*, in *Works*, 1:680.

and Ghibelline, in which men argued from the books, and sought to deduce the formulae of government from first principles, whether those of Holy Writ or the hardly less sacrosanct texts of the Justinian Code. So far as the affairs of the actual world were concerned, their arguments were as lofty and as barren as the metaphysical speculations castigated by Bacon.

Perhaps the first stirrings of revolt against the current ideas are to be found in that startling phenomenon of Machiavelli's own day and Machiavelli's own city, viz., the missionary revival of Savonarola, with his message that no good could come to Florence save from the fear of God and the reform of manners. With this attitude Machiavelli, of course, had no sympathy; and, when the flame of religious fervor lit by Savonarola was presently quenched in blood, he was free to make his gloomy and cynical observations which led Morley to remark that if Machiavelli had been at Jerusalem two thousand years ago, he would have found nobody of any importance in his eyes, save Pontius Pilate and the Roman legionaries.[17]

Savonarola had preached that there could be no salvation for the Florentines apart from God: Machiavelli urged rather the truth of the ancient proverb that God helps those who help themselves. "He who told us," he argues, "that our sins were the cause of our being overrun by enemies, told the truth; but they were not the sins he imagined."[18] In other words, Machiavelli revolts from the spirit of religion which is so close to the spirit of fatalism, and begs his countrymen to consider whether their woes are not the result of their own vice and folly, and that of their rulers. Accordingly, moved by that robust faith in nature and in their own powers, which prompted the Elizabethan mariners to trust themselves on the uncharted ocean and which is the quintessence of the Renaissance spirit, he puts first causes to one side, and proceeds to analyze these secondary factors as he saw them—the results being the generalizations which are to be found in the *Discourses*, the *Prince*, and the *Art of War*. In so doing, he marked himself as one of the first and greatest of the humanists of modern times. His achievement then, was to introduce into the discussion of politics a new method; and in his case, as is usual, the method is the man. To recognize this is the first step toward a true appreciation of Machiavelli; the opposition which his work has excited has arisen almost entirely from the failure to understand the scope and limitations of his position and to meet him on his own ground. It is the fundamental defect of Dyer's book, *Machiavelli and the Modern State*, that he seeks to connect him with Dante and the great mediaevalists and finds

---

17. Morley, *Machiavelli*, 48.
18. Machiavelli, *Prince*, 98.

in his work a "residuum of Mediaeval mysticism."[19] Machiavelli was one of the least Mediaeval of all men, and any "residuum of mysticism" to be found in his thinking is that which comes from the classics, and which the Greek intellect had failed to dissolve.

Any adequate treatment of Machiavelli, therefore, involves an examination of the outlook and method of humanism; and to this task, the rest of the essay must be devoted.

The Greeks, in their search for truth in morals and politics, had in their day marked out two clearly defined paths of attack—the one metaphysical and the other physical, the one ideal the other real, the one the method of philosophy, the other the method of science. The method of philosophy involves the attempt to view phenomena *sub specie aeternitatis*; and, in the white radiance of eternity, time, space, and matter tend to merge in the great First Cause. This is a standpoint shared by many in both ancient and modern times. The Turkish aphorism "God makes the crops grow, why use manure?" is the counterpart among a barbarous and primitive people of the lofty sentiment of Plato "We are but the puppets of God." It is, however, not the characteristic attitude of the West; the true source of which lies rather among the Greek sophists and scientists; and the earliest illustrations of which are to be found in the Protagoran dictum, "Man is the measure of all things," and the generalizations of the early Hippocratics. The essence of science consists in the exclusion of what the Hippocratics described as the "general hypothesis," i.e. the effort to relate phenomena to a universal principle. Normally and politically, therefore, the scientific attitude (which is the attitude of humanism) expresses itself, in Bishop Creighton's words,[20] in human society organizing itself apart from God. Accordingly, science recognizes the impossibility of deducing the end of man, and confines itself to examination of his history. Essentially limited and partial in outlook, it proceeds by the method of abstraction, and such abstraction gives rise to concepts like "matter" and "energy" in the natural sciences, just as in the human sciences it gives rise to the equally abstract conceptions of the "economic" or the "political" men. In politics, the philosophical standpoint (the synoptic vision) is best illustrated by Plato; while the method of science is represented by Thucydides. In Aristotle, both points of view are presented, although not perhaps reconciled. The body of the *Politics* is devoted to an examination of society in the light of final causes; while the old books 4–6 (Newman's books 6–8) are just as obviously written from the scientific and historical point of view. The passages are so important that I quote them:

19. Dyer, *Machiavelli and the Modern State*, xv.
20. Quoted by Figgis, *Political Aspects*, 50.

> The emphatic announcement at the outset of the [fourth] book of the multiplicity of the problems of Political Science strikes us as something altogether new ... Aristotle here suddenly becomes aware that Political Science has a *technical* as well as an *ethical* side; he insists that the statesmen, like the physician or the general, must be able to make the best of the material which happens to be at his disposal, nay, that he must understand how to construct any constitution that may be demanded of him, *even if it is not the best that circumstances admit* ... *The [fifth] book goes so far as to advise a tyranny how to maintain itself in power.* Another obvious difference between the two groups of books is that the one is far fuller of historical detail then the other...[21]
>
> [Thus] *in Aristotle's hands, Ethics and Politics show an inclination to draw away from each other* ... Plato had studied the inferior constitutions only to show how fatal they are to justice and happiness; Aristotle studies them because *it is the business of* πόλίτιχος *to know how to construct the inferior forms of state.*[22]
>
> The principle that *the constitution of a state is dependent on its social conditions* had probably never been enunciated with anything like equal clearness before.[23]

The triumph of the church was the triumph of metaphysics, and, for a thousand years, the metaphysical standpoint dominated European speculation. (Broadly speaking. It has been suggested that Marsilius of Padua almost escaped). We have already noted the revulsion of Machiavelli from that standpoint; we have now to add that, in revolting from it, he fell back on the alternative method of science. According to this latter method, the factors to be considered were twofold, viz., man (or rather men) and nature or the environment, and the relations of these as revealed in history and experience. In this connection, the first and most important thing to notice is the assumption of a stable natural order, the existence of which is a necessary postulate of science, because it alone makes possible the successful formulation of laws or rules of human behavior.

In two striking passages, Machiavelli reveals his faith in the existence of such an order:

> The wise are wont to say, and not without reason, or at random, that he who would forecast what is about to happen should look

---

21. Newman, *Politics of Aristotle*, 2:xxiii–xxiv; emphasis added.
22. Ibid., 397.
23. Newman, *Politics of Aristotle*, 1:518. See also Cochrane, *Thucydides*; Aristotle is perhaps tacitly indebted to Thucydides.

> to what has been; since *all human events, whether present or to come, have their exact counterpart in the past. And this, because these events are brought about by men, whose passions and dispositions remaining in all ages the same naturally give rise to the same effects*: although doubtless, the operation of these causes takes a higher form, now in one province and now in another, according to the character of the training wherein the inhabitants of these provinces acquire their way of life.[24]
>
> Manners and institutions differing in different cities, seem here to produce a harder and there a softer race; and a like difference may also be discerned in the character of different families in the same city . . . These qualities we cannot refer wholly to the *blood*, for that must change as a result of repeated inter-marriages, but must ascribe rather to the different *training* and *education* given in different families. For much turns on whether a child of tender years hears a thing well or ill spoken of, since this must needs make an impression on him whereby his whole conduct in after life will be influenced.[25]

The proposition that history repeats itself is one which has been frequently and properly denounced in modern times. And it might be urged in respect of these messages, that they commit Machiavelli to such a view. But the exact repetition of events depends upon the recurrence of precisely the same conjuncture of circumstance—in other words upon a metaphysical theory of cycles which is (as we shall subsequently attempt to show) not an essential element of Machiavelli's thought. His real notion is that of Thucydides rather than Polybius. He specifically admits the variability of conditions and by conditions he means the cultural as well as the material environment. In response to variations in these conditions, the different potentialities of human nature are actualized; and the result is, if not progress, at any rate change. Within these limits, however, it is possible to find regular recurrence or succession of similar facts; and it is this which makes possible the generalizations of political science. Also men are alike, but conditions vary; the latter alone are susceptible of study and alone worth studying; because they alone may be modified by the political architect.

The two factors—human nature and the environment—are designed by Machiavelli respectively as *virtù* and *fortuna*; and of these I shall first discuss *fortuna*, which I have had the temerity to translate as "environment." The principle passages in which Machiavelli expounds his views on this subject are the *Prince* ch. xxv and the *Life of Castruccio Castracani*, which

---

24. Machiavelli, *Discourses*, 475–76.
25. Ibid., 481–82.

has been called a study of luck. Dyer observes that Machiavelli studiously evades all mention in his writings of the Will of God and of Divine Power, instead of which he introduces mystical references to Fate, Fortune, Heaven, and the Heavens; and he accuses him of a vague and crude belief in the influence of supernatural agencies upon sub-lunary events.[26] He notes also what he describes as a tendency to personify natural forces.[27] Now it must be admitted that Machiavelli exposes himself to the danger of being interpreted as a mystic, e.g., in the passage in which he declares that it is better to be adventurous than cautious because, as he says, "Fortune is a woman, and if you wish to keep her under it is necessary to beat and ill-use her; and it is seen that she allows herself to be mastered by the adventurous rather than by those who go to work more coldly. She is, therefore, always, woman-like, a lover of young men, because they are less cautious, more violent, and with more audacity command her."[28] ("Live dangerously." This, by the way, is the precept of Mussolini, to which his practice also appears to conform.) In the *Castruccio*, we find fortune contrasted with prudence, which is of course a leading element of *virtù*. "It seems," says Machiavelli, "as if Fortune had a mind to show the world that it is she alone, and not Prudence, that makes men great, by exerting her power at a time when Prudence cannot be said to have any share in it."[29] Castruccio, as a foundling of immature years had, as we say, the good fortune to be adopted by the Lord of Lucca, and to this circumstance he owed the training in arms which afterwards made him the leading condottiere of his generation. "But Fortune, now beginning to grow jealous of his glory, put a stop to his career, at a time when he would certainly have accomplished the great designs he had been long revolving in his mind."[30] The fact is, as Machiavelli proceeds to explain, that he caught cold after the dust and sweat of a successful engagement, and the ensuing fever killed him. These passages, and others like them[31] are rhetoric; in Machiavelli's day, scientists had not yet learned the perils which lurk in metaphor. Such a concept as that of fortune was particularly ambiguous, because of the associations which the word had dragged down with it from antiquity. But if one looks behind these associations, one finds that in Machiavelli the word connotes circumstances—the given—the environmental condition

---

26. Dyer, *Machiavelli and the Modern State*, 51.
27. Ibid., 13.
28. Machiavelli, *Prince*, 207.
29. Machiavelli, *Castruccio*, in *Works*, 1:749.
30. Ibid., 767.
31. Machiavelli, *Discourses*, in *Works*, 3:321; "Fortune throws a mist before people's eyes, when she would not have them obstruct her designs."

which largely make men, and with which *virtù* is everywhere required to cope. In other words, the distinction between *virtù* and *fortuna* is precisely the distinction developed by Aristotle in the *Politics* and elsewhere between ἀρετη and τυχη. "Nevertheless not to extinguish our free will, I hold it to be true that fortune is the arbiter of one half of our actions, but that she still leaves us to direct the other half or perhaps a little less."[32] Burd[33] refers this passage to Marsillio Ficini.[34] He evidently does not notice, however, that this passage reflects exactly the Aristotelian differentiation, on which it is doubtless based. Aristotle had said, "The good man would endure poverty, illness, and other ill-fortune nobly, but good Fortune lies in the opposites."[35] And again, "The cause of the external goods of the soul is spontaneity and fortune, but no one ever becomes just or temperate (the internal goods) from fortune or as a result of fortune."[36] So much for the treatment of environment, which Machiavelli evidently takes over from Aristotle—a mean between the fatalistic view that circumstance determines everything, and the contrary assertion that "character is fate."

The discussion of environment has already revealed to some extent Machiavelli's conception of *virtù*. With regard to human nature, the first and most important assumption, and an assumption which he shared with Aristotle, is that man is in a real sense a cause, i.e., that the human will is free; with the no less important corollary that it is the voluntary action of individuals and combinations of them which makes events, rather than the illimitable web of evolution, the Zeitgeist, the national idea, the group mind, or any other figment of the mystical imagination. This, as we have already observed has been noticed by nineteenth century critics, and branded as "the classical prejudice of the Renaissance." In reality it was their own blind spot. Where do ideas come from if not from individuals, and what is the group mind except, as the Roman lawyers said, a *consensus*? It is indeed the very thing which gave vitality to the Elizabethan drama, and it is essential to sound views of history and political science, no less than to imaginative literature. There can be no tragedy where there is no struggle; and there can be no struggle unless the will is free.

---

32. Machiavelli, *Prince*, 203.

33. Burd, *Il Principe*, 355–56; his long and interesting note on ch. xxv. is off the rails.

34. Burd, *Il Principe*, 358; "Ingenium ac Fortuna divisum in nobis habent imperium: hoc quidem in animi cultum plurimum dominatur. Haec vero quam plurimum in rebus externis."

35. Aristotle, *Politics*, 1332a19.

36. Ibid., 1332b27.

Morley declares that Machiavelli saw in human nature nothing but cunning, jealousy, perfidy, ingratitude, and credulity, and yet sought on such foundations to erect an enduring society. We may refuse to admit that this is a fair statement of Machiavelli's opinion, without denying that he recognizes fully the vicious tendencies of unrestrained human nature.[37] Moreover, the view that men are prone to evil is not so shocking as it appears to liberal idealism. It is in fact none other than the theological doctrine of original sin; and, as such, has been endorsed by St. Augustine and the Church. It is a view, however, which Englishmen have been reluctant to accept (so far at least as they themselves are concerned) ever since Pelagius journeyed from Britain to Rome armed with the contrary thesis; although the Ecclesiastics of that day proved it by burning his books and proscribing him as a heretic. Nor is it quite the view of classical humanism, for humanism could never have admitted the corollary that divine grace is alone sufficient to repair the fault brought by Adam upon all his descendants. Machiavelli indeed shared with Aristotle the humanist position that men are potentially capable of good as well as evil; that the secret of actualizing the good lies in preventing them from giving way to their tendencies toward evil; and that the prevention of such tendencies is the function of government. This function he deemed eternal, for he found no evidence for the dogmas of human equality or human goodness which make government either usurpation or an excrescence. In thus distinguishing between force and that sublimation of force which is power, Machiavelli marked the gulf that separates him from the philosophic anarchists of modern times. In placing the seat of that power in the coercive might of the state, he proclaimed himself a believer in the political organization of society. I cite some of the relevant passages:

> Few men can resolve to be either perfectly good or totally bad.[38]
>
> Men usually rise from one degree of ambition to another. They endeavor first to secure themselves against oppression, and then to oppress others.[39]
>
> [The legislator] must *assume* that all men are bad, and will always, when they have free rein, give vent to their evil inclinations... Men never behave well unless compelled, and whenever they are free to act as they please, and are under no restraint, everything falls at once into confusion and disorder. Wherefore

---

37. See *Discourses*, 1.42; etc.
38. Machiavelli, *Discourses*, in *Works* (1762), 2:71.
39. Ibid., 113.

it has been said that, *as poverty and hunger are needed to make men industrious, so laws are needed to make them good.*[40]

Careful consideration of this fact [that men easily become corrupted] should make those who frame laws for commonwealths and kingdoms more alive to the necessity of placing restraints on men's evil appetites, and depriving them of all hope of doing wrong with impunity.[41]

At least by implication, Machiavelli admits the existence of bravery,[42] loyalty,[43] and wisdom.[44] In *Prince* chapter 17 it is asserted of men in general that while they are ungrateful, fickle, false, cowardly and covetous, as long as you succeed, they are yours entirely. *Prince* chapter 26 declares that glory and riches are the end which every men has before him.

As Machiavelli never looked forward to a day when government would become superfluous, so he hardly looked back to a time when it had not existed. Frederic, indeed, complains that Machiavelli "omits to examine into the origin of civil empire in general."[45] Had he done so, he could have found that it implies a contract, the breaking of which renders the prince a tyrant. "Thus he would have subverted his own system." In so saying, Frederic reveals a characteristic dogma of the eighteenth century and, at the same time, betrays his own ignorance of Machiavelli. For the *Discourses* open with a discussion of the origin of civil society; and, while it is true that Machiavelli has little to say on the subject, and that little can hardly be called original, (it is in all probability lifted from Polybius), nevertheless his remarks are sufficient to show his disbelief in the fallacious contract notion, and to reveal his opinion that morals and law, as well as government, belong to the very warp and woof of society, and have existed since the beginning of human history:

> Diversities in the form of government spring up among men by chance. (i.e. with changes in environmental conditions) For, in the beginning of the world, its inhabitants, being few in number, for a time *lived scattered after the fashion of beasts; but afterwards, as they increased and multiplied, gathered themselves into societies and,* the better to protect themselves, began to seek who among them was the strongest and of the highest courage, to whom, making him their head, *they rendered obedience.* Next

---

40. Machiavelli, *Discourses* (1883), 20.
41. Ibid., 136.
42. Machiavelli, *Prince*, ch. 19.
43. Machiavelli, *Prince*, ch. 22.
44. Machiavelli, *Prince*, ch. 23.
45. Frederick, *Examen*, in *Works*, 2:188.

arose the knowledge of such things as are honorable and good, as opposed to those which are bad and shameful. For observing that when a man wronged his benefactor, hatred was universally felt for the one and sympathy for the other, and that the ungrateful were blamed, while those who showed gratitude were honored, and *reflecting* that the wrongs they saw done to others might be done to themselves, to escape they resorted to making laws and fixing punishments against anyone who should transgress them; and in this way grew the recognition of Justice. Whence it came that afterwards, in choosing their rulers, men no longer looked about for the *strongest*, but for him who was the most *prudent* and the most *just*.[46]

Machiavelli then proceeds, on the basis of Polybius, to outline the cycle revolving within which all states are and have been governed, and concludes that for the sake of stability, the ideal form is a mixture of the first three forms, monarchy, aristocracy and democracy.

The *synoicismus* or "consolidation" by which the city-state comes into existence is dealt with in the following passage:

All cities have been found either by the people of the country in which they stand, or by strangers. Cities have their origin in the former of these two ways when the inhabitants of a country find that *they cannot live securely if they live dispersed in many and small societies,* each of them unable, whether from its situation or its slender numbers, to stand alone against the attacks of its enemies; on whose approach there is no time left to unite for defense without abandoning many strongholds, and thus becoming an easy prey to the invader. To escape which dangers, *whether of their own motion* OR *at the instance of greater authority among them,* they restrict themselves to dwell together in certain places, which they think will be more convenient for them to live in and easier to defend.[47]

With these statements, contrast the dictum of a modern "realist." The differences are self-evident. "The state, completely in its genesis, essentially and almost completely during the first stages of its existence, is a *social institution, forced by a victorious group of men on a defeated group, with the sole purpose of regulating the dominion of the victorious group over the vanquished,* and securing itself against revolt from within and attacks from abroad. *Teleologically, this dominion had no other purpose than the economic*

---

46. Machiavelli, *Discourses* (1883), 13–14.
47. Ibid., 6.

exploitation of the vanquished by the victors."[48] Its subsequent development shows the same motive at work. "Its purpose, in every case is found to be the political means for the satisfaction of needs. At first, its method is by exacting a ground rent, so long as there exists no trade activity the products of which can be appropriated. Its form in every case is that of dominion, whereby *exploitation is regarded as 'justice' maintained as a constitution, insisted on strictly and in case of need enforced with cruelty.*"[49]

Machiavelli evidently takes no stock in the proposition *homo homini lupus*. And, if he nowhere quite specifically describes man as a *social animal*, he nevertheless implies that morals are social, so that the moral act has no significance apart from its context. This is a point to be kept in mind in discussing the famous maxim regarding "good faith,"[50] which is perhaps the crux of Machiavelli's whole position.

Elsewhere he notes, "As poverty and hunger are needed to make men industrious, so laws are needed to make the good."[51] In this passage, Machiavelli indicates his belief that the nature and purpose of government is, in keeping with its origin, to protect against his own evil tendencies no less than against external enemies. This function it is powerless to discharge unless it is armed with preponderant force in the community. As he notes, "The chief foundation of all states, new as well as old or composite, are good laws and good arms; and as there cannot be good laws where the state is not well armed, it follows that where they are well armed they have good laws."[52] Machiavelli here affirms, with an exaggerated emphasis which has been noted as a characteristic of the *Prince* as opposed to his other writings,[53] the truth of the Aristotelian maxim, that virtue is never without strength. (σώματα οἰκετικα, οργανα ἔμψυχα) He elsewhere argues the thesis which he here merely states; and, while still maintaining the position that influence is not government, puts the relation of Arms and Laws in a more acceptable light:

> If we consider the nature of government and the institutions of the ancients, we shall find a very strict and intimate relation between these two conditions [the civil and the military—in Machiavelli's day divorced]; and that they are not only compatible

---

48. Oppenheimer, *The State*, 15.
49. Ibid., 85.
50. Machiavelli, *Prince*, ch. 18.
51. Machiavelli, *Discourses* (1883), 20.
52. Machiavelli, *Prince*, 97.

53. *The Prince* is a call to action. It bears much the relation to the *Discourses* and the *Art of War* as does the *Communist Manifesto* to Karl Marx's *Das Kapital*.

> and consistent with one another, but necessarily connected and united together, For all the arts and sciences which have been introduced into society for the common benefit of mankind, and all the ordinances that have been established to make them live in the fear of God and obedience to human laws, would be vain and insignificant, if not supported and defended by a military force, which, when properly conducted and applied, will maintain these ordinances and keep up their authority, though perhaps they may not be altogether perfect and without flaw in themselves. But the best ordinances in the world will be despised and trampled under foot, if they are not upheld as they ought to be by a military power.[54]

No one, however, has been more acutely conscious than Machiavelli of the danger and difficulty involved in organizing a military force in due subordination to the civil power. To one who lived in the Italy of the *White Company*, it was obvious that while the existence of such a force was an indispensable support to the majesty of the state nevertheless, to maintain it was to hold a wolf by the ears. The chief dangers arose, of course, from the common practice of employing mercenary troops—a practice which Machiavelli denounced with all the emphasis at his command[55]—but he was also alive to the demoralizing character of the military life.

> But surely he cannot be called a good man, who exercises an employment that obliges him to be rapacious, fraudulent and cruel at all times, in order to support himself, as all those must be of course who make a trade of war ... *War makes thieves, and Peace hangs them.*[56]

Indeed, the whole argument of the *Dell'arte della guerra* is directed to finding a way of harnessing Mars, so to speak, in the service of society.

That war itself should ever be abolished, never, of course, entered the mind of Machiavelli. He has been accused of neglecting the economic motive in human life: but he recognizes at least that it is a powerful factor in making for strife among people. Speaking from the standpoint of the aggressor, he writes, "There are two sorts of war. The one is occasioned by the ambition of Princes or Republics for power and domination, the other is when a whole people are compelled to quit their country either by famine or sword, and go in search of new habitations in another—The most numerous migrations have been chiefly from Scythia, where the inhabitants are

---

54. Machiavelli, *Art of War*, in *Works* (1762), 2:viii.
55. See *Prince*, chs. 12–13; *Art of War*; and *Discourses* 2.20, etc.
56. Machiavelli, *Art of War*, in *Works* (1762), 2:7–8.

generally so numerous and the country so sterile, that it was not able to sustain them."[57] He also claims, "It has always been, and indeed ought to be, the main end and design of those who wage war, to enrich themselves and impoverish their enemies; nor is there any other reasonable motive to contend for victory and conquest, but the aggrandizement of one nation, and the depression of another."[58] But in waging war morale counts for more than money.[59]

Nevertheless, he never holds up war as a nation ideal and his pages are full of condemnations of imperialism and its exponents:

> I say that Caesar and Pompey and almost all the Roman generals who lived after the Second Punic War, owed their reputation to their abilities rather than their virtue.[60]
>
> It cannot be called talent to slay fellow-citizens, to deceive friends, to be without faith, without mercy, without religion; such methods may gain empire, but not glory.[61]

Machiavelli thought mainly in terms of defense from the perils of war and imperialism; and by this path he was led to his conception of a civic militia, and of the national as the natural basis of the state. And here his model was clearly that of the early Roman commonwealth, in which he thought he saw the due subordination of the military to the civil spirit, and the might of the state employed only to protect the life of the people.[62]

But the state implies the organization of a people for justice, no less than for defense and with Machiavelli, the general is always subordinated to the statesman:

> The disorders of our ancestors are not to be imputed to the nature of the men, but to the iniquity of the times, which now being altered, afford this city fair hopes of better fortune; the malevolence of which may easily be frustrated by the institution of wholesome laws, by a prudent restraint of ambition, by prohibiting such customs as tend to nourish and propagate faction, and by substituting others that may conduce to maintain liberty and good government.[63]

---

57. Machiavelli, *Discourses*, in *Works* (1762), 2:191.
58. Machiavelli, *History of Florence*, in *Works* (1775), 4:268.
59. Machiavelli, *Discourses*, 2.10.
60. Machiavelli, *Works* (1775), 3:26.
61. Machiavelli, *Prince*, 65.
62. Machiavelli, *Prince*, 207; "That war is just which is necessary, and arms are hallowed when there is no other hope but in them."
63. Machiavelli, *History of Florence*, in *Works* (1775), 4:173.

Political justice was to him the maintenance of liberty and good government; good government with liberty, if possible; if not, without it.

To Machiavelli, as may be supposed, the task of the statesmen was not easy, nor were his problems simple. In words which might have served as a warning to the late Baldwin administration, he expressed his profound disbelief in "safety first" as a maxim of government:

> Never let any government imagine that it can choose perfectly safe courses; rather let it expect to have to take very doubtful ones, because it is found (even) in ordinary affairs that one never seeks to avoid one trouble without running into another; but prudence consists in knowing how to distinguish the character of troubles, and for choice to take the lesser evil.[64]

He thought in terms of the least possible evil rather than in those of the greatest possible good. That men are bad, and therefore government is good, looks like a simple proposition; but to find the particular good to counteract the particular evil is the problem, and this is what makes government a difficult and, it may be added, occasionally a dirty business:

> The prince need not make himself uneasy at incurring a reproach for those vices without which the state can only be saved with difficulty, for if everything is considered carefully, it will be found that something which looks like virtue, if followed, would be his ruin; whilst something else, which looks like vice, yet followed brings him security and prosperity.[65]

The grim necessity of exacting the death penalty, the awful responsibility of waging war—these are still facts of modern society and they are still the duties of the administrator. It is indeed, the existence of just such facts which today prompts many—and those perhaps not the least ignoble spirits—to withdraw their allegiance from a system which makes such exorbitant demands upon their loyalty. In Machiavelli's day, the demands were not less stern but more, for beneath men's feet there yawned the great gulf of anarchy; and thus it was that those who, like him, saw in anarchy worse evils still, were led to pledge their fealty to the state, grim and forbidding as she was. Accordingly, he commends the murder by Romulus of his brother in the myth which typifies the cruel necessity of government: "Romulus, though he put his brother to death, is yet of those who are to be pardoned, since what he did was done for the common good and not from personal

---

64. Machiavelli, *Prince*, 177.
65. Ibid., 119.

ambition."[66] (St. Augustine, it should be remembered, gave a qualified approval to the same act.)

He also defends the slaying of the sons of Brutus: "To meet these difficulties and their attendant disorders, there is no more potent, effectual, wholesome and necessary remedy than to slay the sons of Brutus."[67] It was better he thought, that some should die, rather than that the people perish. It should be remembered that Machiavelli published his vindication of authority, the year after he had himself been imprisoned, racked, and exiled by the then Florentine government.

If true to its functions, government can hardly hope to achieve popularity. Severity may be occasionally necessary, and by its necessity it is justified: "Severities may be called properly used, if of evil it is lawful to speak well, that are applied at one blow and are necessary to security."[68] But to suppose that Machiavelli recommends cruelty from a light-hearted callousness, or a thirst for blood, is unworthy of such a serious thinker. Yet the exercise of authority is always to some extent a test of relative strength, and this is especially apparent in crises, as for instance, when the state is menaced by conspiracy. In such cases, it is the duty of government to temporize, until it is sure that it has power to strike.[69]

In view of these facts, he concludes, it is much safer to be feared than loved, if respect and devotion are incompatible; and perhaps the best that the statesman can hope for is that in failing to win the love of his subjects, he may at least avoid their hatred.[70] This indeed is the surest guarantee of government: the best possible fortress is not to be hated by the people.[71]

In order to accomplish its duty, government must be strong and, in a crisis, absolute, and unified in the person of one man.

> We must take it as a rule to which there are few if any exceptions, that no commonwealth or kingdom has ever had salutary institutions given it from the first or has its institutions recast in an entirely new mould, unless by a single ruler ... For this reason the wise founder of a commonwealth, who seeks to benefit not himself only or the line of his descendants, but his state and

---

66. Machiavelli, *Discourses*, 43.
67. Ibid., 67.
68. Machiavelli, *Prince*, 68.
69. Machiavelli, *Discourses*, 3.6.
70. Machiavelli, *Prince*, ch. 17.
71. Ibid., ch. 20.

country, must endeavor to acquire an absolute and undivided authority.[72]

The model for such provisional and temporary absolutions Machiavelli found in the Roman dictatorship and without some such safeguard, he declares, a city can hardly pass unharmed through extraordinary dangers.[73] He approves also of the occasional grant of discretionary power to the Roman Consul, especially in the field.[74] Even in normal times, the existence of a power of obstruction, such as that which was granted to the Roman tribunes, is a source of weakness.[75] Strength depends among other things upon a sound principle of succession. Machiavelli perceived that the anarchy of the third century was the result of failure to devise ways and means for the transmission of sovereign power. Of the prerogatives of sovereignty, the details are nowhere laid down; and, indeed, they must necessarily vary in different states; but it is noticeable that Machiavelli appears to include in them the censorial power. This is going to an extreme, in so far as it tends to assimilate the authority of the state to that of the *pater familias*. Here also, no doubt, Machiavelli was influenced by his classical prepossessions; but his view was determined in part by the nature of his problem. In the anarchy of the fifteenth century, the question was not so much the limitation of sovereignty as its rehabilitation; and, in any case, political science recognizes the legitimacy of censorship as a means of enforcing social utility, even though philosophy may deny it in the sacred name of individual freedom. So that, if we do not sympathize with Machiavelli in this respect, we can at least understand him.

This being the case, it may perhaps be regarded as surprising that Machiavelli concerns himself with any sort of limitation of sovereignty. Yet to him nothing is more apparent than that, while government must be strong in order to be successful, its immense power for harm makes it necessary that it should ordinarily be limited. This is in keeping with his views of human psychology; his distrust of human nature in subjection implies an even greater distrust of human nature when entrusted with power. He notes, "When an uncontrolled authority is given, (even regularly and by public vote), no security is afforded by the circumstances that the body of the people is not corrupted; for in the briefest possible time absolute authority will make a people corrupt and obtain for itself friends and partisans."[76]

72. Machiavelli, *Discourses*, 42.
73. Ibid., 1.34.
74. Ibid., 2.33.
75. Ibid., 1.50.
76. Ibid., 115.

Absolute power is corrosive; but there is also another argument against it: "As mankind are liable to be corrupted, good men too often become bad by a long continuance of power."[77] There is no magic in the purple to protect the wearer from the temptations which beset the ordinary man. While Machiavelli, therefore, was an authoritarian, he was no absolutist. Absolutist, indeed, the humanist can hardly be, for he sees his problem not in terms of abstract forces, but rather in terms of human beings, with all their weal and woe the subject of his thought. Thus the Hobbesian notion that the will of the sovereign is in itself enough to render legitimate the acts of government. (*sic volo, sic iubeo, sit pro ratione voluntas*) is quite out of keeping with Machiavellism, and with the classical tradition upon which it is based. For to him, as to the Greeks, "political obligation," as has been said, "was not grounded in any right to rule, inherent in the state as such, irrespective of the manner in which power was used, but rested upon the value of the end for the attainment of which the state was the necessary means."

Yet for Machiavelli, as a realist, there existed no "natural rights"—that feeble barrier with which philosophy has vainly endeavored to stem the encroachments of sovereign power. Machiavelli simply assumed that the limits of sovereignty were determined by what the state could do for the subject. What it could do, it ought to do, because the more it did, the stronger it was. Hence he asserts that no grievance should go unredressed, because it is dangerous to allow them to do so.[78] So also he prescribes the duty of humanity and generosity in the treatment of the subject.[79] Indeed, expediency dictates the obligation of positive beneficence; no prince or commonwealth ought to defer favors which will win the devotion of the people until they are extorted by necessity.[80] Such favors include the encouragement of agriculture and commerce.[81] But above all, government should respect the property, the security and the honor of the subject:

> He will never be hated as long as he abstains from the property of his citizens and subjects and from their women.[82]
>
> And a prince should guard himself, above all things, against being despised and hated.[83]

---

77. Machiavelli, *Reform of Florence*, in *Works*, 4:266.
78. Machiavelli, *Discourses*, 2.28.
79. Ibid., 3.19–22.
80. Ibid., 1.32.
81. Machiavelli, *Prince*, ch. 21.
82. Ibid., 131.
83. Ibid., 126.

This last precept marks the distinction between *imperium* and *dominium*, a distinction slurred over in absolutist theory. The precepts as a whole show that Machiavelli recognized the difference between social good and social evil, just as he recognizes also the difference between ability and virtue, in the sense of moral excellence.

The basis of his position is that justice generates social strength, and issues in the creation of civic spirit without which, as has been said, all political organization is but the forcible suppression of anarchy. Such civic spirit implies a strong and active "will for the state." Born of the sense of utility—common advantages shared by ruler and ruled—it is reinforced also by the sanction of religion. Machiavelli contrasts the fear of God to the fear of the Prince, and pins his faith on the fear of God.

> A kingdom without the fear of God must either fall to pieces or must be maintained by the fear of some prince who supplies that influence not supplied by religion. But since the lives of princes are short, the life of this prince also, and with it his influence, must soon come to an end; where it happens that a kingdom which rests wholly on the qualities of its prince lasts for a brief time only; because those qualities, terminated with his life, are rarely renewed in his successor.[84]

Hence he urges the fostering of religion as a positive duty of government, recognizing, like Polybius, that what holds the state together is not merely a sense of utility but also what we may call a social conscience. This, indeed, is in itself almost adequate; as may be seen from the note on ecclesiastical principalities:

> Ecclesiastical principalities can be held without capacity or good fortune; for they are sustained by the ancient ordinance of religion, which are so all-powerful, and of such a character that the principalities may be held no matter how their princes behave and live. These princes alone have states and do not defend them, they have subjects and do not rule them; and the states, though unguarded, are not taken from them, and the subjects, although not ruled, do not care, and they have neither the desire nor ability to alienate themselves.[85]

But Machiavelli while recognizing the binding nature of the tie which exists between ruler and ruled in ecclesiastical states, does not conceal his contempt for the quality of ecclesiastical government. He cannot, however,

---

84. Machiavelli, *Discourses*, 52.
85. Machiavelli, *Prince*, 87.

be called a secularist, in as much as he would have liked to borrow so far as possible the support of religion for the civil state; but failing that, he was willing to do without it; for he believed most firmly that it was possible to organize and maintain a stable political association on the basis of service, by meeting the real needs and gratifying the real aspirations of the people for whom it was designed.

> And let no one impugn this statement with the trite proverb that he who builds upon the people, builds on the mud . . . granted a prince who has established himself, who can command, and is a man of courage, undismayed in adversity, who does not fail in other qualifications, and who, by his resolution and energy, keeps the whole people encouraged—such a one will never find himself deceived in them, and it will be shown that he has laid his foundations well.[86]

This is Machiavelli's answer to Lord Morley.

But if the strength of the state is indicated by its ability to meet these conditions, its weakness is measured by its failure to do so; and failure is revealed progressively in faction, or civil strife and conspiracy, and revolution. Machiavelli, like Aristotle, writes more from the positive than the negative standpoint, and is concerned rather with the creation and preservation of the state than its destruction. Incidental passages, however, indicate something of the character of those pathological conditions which, in the last analysis, result in the annihilation of the body politic.

We may start with the proposition that no government (except that of Plato's Republic) can hope to satisfy all the people all the time. "As Princes cannot help being hated by someone, they ought, in the first place, to avoid being hated by everyone; and when they cannot compass this, they ought to endeavor with the utmost diligence to avoid the hatred of the most powerful."[87] That is to say, no government can hope to be without opposition.

> Those are much mistaken who think that any Republican government can continue long united. Differences and divisions for the most part are prejudicial to Republics; and yet it is certain, there are some which are of service to them. Those, indeed, are hurtful that are attended with parties and factions; but when this is not the case, they tend to the benefit of the Commonwealth. As it is impossible, therefore, for any legislator or founder of a Republic entirely to prevent feuds and animosities in it, it ought

---

86. Ibid., 77.
87. Ibid., 151.

to be his chief care to provide against their growing up into factions.[88]

In thus distinguishing between that kind of opposition which takes the form of a difference of opinion and which is actually a tonic to the state, and that which expresses itself in what he calls "party" or "faction," Machiavelli foreshadows the future development of government by public opinion. The distinction between this and faction is clearly brought out in a speech of certain deputies to the Florentine Signiory, the tone of which recalls very forcibly the Thucydidean analysis of faction:

> The common disease of the other cities in Italy has at last invaded ours, and is continually eating deeper and deeper into its vitals. For after this province had shaken off the yoke of the emperors, all its towns for lack of restraint, ran into extremes, and from liberty degenerated into downright licentiousness, making such laws and instituting such governments as were rather calculated to foment and support factions, than maintain freedom. From this source are derived all the defects and disorders that they labour under. No friendship or union is to be found amongst the citizens, except betwixt such as are accomplices in some wicked design either against their neighbours or their country. All religion and fear of God are utterly extinguished. Promises and oaths are no further binding than they serve to promote some private advantage, and taken, not with any design to observe them, but as necessary means to facilitate the perpetration of villanies, which are even honoured and applauded as good conduct and policy if they meet with success.
>
> From hence it comes to pass, that the most wicked and abandoned wretches are admired as notable industrious men; whilst the innocent and conscientious are laughed at and despised as fools. And certainly there is no sort of corruption that may not be found in the cities of Italy, nor any people in the world so thoroughly disposed to receive the infection as those of Florence. The young men are indolent and effeminate; the old, lascivious and contemptable. Without regard to age or sex, every place is full of the most licentious brutality, for which the laws themselves, though good and wholesome, are yet so partially executed that they do not afford any remedy. This is the real cause of that selfish spirit which now so generally prevails, and of that ambition, not of true glory, but of dishonourable preferment. Hence proceed those fatal animosities, those

---

88. Machiavelli, *History of Florence*, in *Works* (1775), 2:3.

seeds of envy, revenge and faction, with their usual attendants, execution, banishments, depression of good men and exaltation of evil. For the good, confiding in their virtue and uprightness, have not recourse to any base means, like wicked men, to advance, or even so much as defend themselves, so that they generally fall miserable victims to the cruelty and oppression of tyrants, and die in poverty and disgrace. Such dreadful and pitiable examples, both give rise and strength to parties: for the evil will *naturally* form one side, either out of *avarice* or *ambition,* and the good, another, out of *fear* and *necessity*; and what is still more dangerous, the authors and ringleaders of them varnish over their pernicious designs with some sacred title, for being in reality enemies to all liberty, they more effectually destroy it, by pretending to defend the rights, sometimes of the Nobility, sometimes of the Commons: since the fruit which they expect from a victory, is not the glory of having delivered their country, but the satisfaction of having conquered the other part and secured the fort of the state to themselves. And when they have once obtained that, there is no sort of cruelty, injustice, or rapine, that they are not guilty of. From thence forward, laws are enacted, not for the *common good,* but for *private ends*; from that time both war and peace are made and alliances concluded, not for the honour of the public, but to gratify the humour of particular men. And if the other cities of Italy are full of these disorders, certainly ours overflows; our laws, our statutes, and civil ordinances are made to indulge the caprice, or serve the ambition of the conqueror, not to promote the true interest of a free people: so that one faction is no sooner extinguished but another is lighted up. A city that endeavours to support itself by parties instead of laws, can never be at peace; for when one prevails, and is left without opposition, *it necessarily divides again*; the people not being able to defend themselves by the ordinary laws which were at first made for their preservation. The truth of this is sufficiently confirmed both by the ancient and modern dissensions, that have happened in our own city.[89]

It is evident that Machiavelli recognized the radical distinction between what we now call free government—the system in which citizens, united by similarities of outlook and temperament, combine in parties to make their opinions effective within a given political order—and faction, which sets itself to subvert that order by methods which confuse legitimate propaganda with violence and fraud. This is a distinction which is slurred

89. Ibid., 169–71.

over in the more recent apologetic of fascism. Mussolini declares that force involves consent, and consent is the very essence of force. "In the long run," he says, "the consent which a government enjoys is best measured pragmatically by its force, rather than by election schemes and other devices of so-called public opinion."[90] Such sophistry is the product of an anti-intellectualism which is far removed from the rational empiricism of Machiavelli, and from the classicism on which it is based. From the standpoint of Machiavelli, fascism, like sovietism, would certainly have been classified as faction. For Machiavelli, as we have seen, believed in the reality of human freedom and of choice as the free expression of personality. Thus, in politics, he recognized the difference between voluntary adhesion to principle, and submission to brow-beating and the strong arm. It was, indeed, the ground of his faith in republicanism, that the republican system made it possible to oppose the administration without attacking the state. At the same time, he saw that no government—commonwealth or principality—could hope to eliminate force entirely from the body politic by completely satisfying everybody. There were always elements, greater or less in numbers and power, to whom the ideal of the whole appealed less than their personal interests pursued at the expense of the common interest, and whom the ugly motives of fear, hatred, contempt or jealousy prompted to conspiracy and revolution. And just as revolutionary activity implied an appeal to force or fraud, so its suppression always involved a test of relative strength:

> I cannot conclude this discourse without advising all Princes and Republics, upon the discovery of a conspiracy against them, carefully to examine into the nature of it, and to compare the strength of the conspirators with their own, before they proceed to punish them; and if they find them many and powerful, not to take any notice of the matter, till they are sufficiently able to crush them; otherwise, they must be inevitably ruined themselves. They should, therefore, have recourse to dissimulation upon such occasions, lest the conspirators, when they find themselves discovered, should grow desperate, and proceed directly to execution ... But when conspiracies are weak and in their infancy, they may and ought to be suppressed as soon as possible.[91]

His advice might have been drawn from those pages in which Tacitus describes how Tiberius countered the conspiracy of Sejanus; and no doubt the theory of conspiracy as a whole is derived from Aristotle, *Politics* Book

90. Schneider, *Making the Fascist State*, 109.
91. Machiavelli, *Discourses*, in *Works* (1762), 2:294.

5, just as it is confirmed and reinforced by lessons he takes from the later history of Rome and Italy. The *History of Florence* is, indeed, a mine of information on the subject.

Conspiracy is usually the work of a few highly placed and powerful malcontents; the strength of revolution is derived from numbers. The economic motive of revolution (Machiavelli, as we have noted, has been accused of neglecting the economic factors in history) is illustrated by the amusing speech put into the mouth of a demagogue in fourteenth century Florence.

> All families have the same original, are of equal antiquity, nor has nature showed any partiality in the formation of mankind. Let both sides be stripped naked, and both will be found alike. Clothe yourselves in their robes, and them in your rags; and then you will appear the nobler, and they the plebeians: *for it is poverty alone that makes the real difference between us* . . . Neither conscience nor the fear of infamy, ought to terrify you; for those that succeed in their attempts (let them have used what means soever) are never upbraided with them, or called by ignominious names: and as for conscience, you have no reason to give yourselves any trouble about it. When famine, and racks, and dungeons, are sure to be your portion, what greater terrors can there be in Hell? Consider the course of this world, and you will find the rich, the great, and powerful, have arrived at all their wealth, and grandeur and authority, either by *force* or *fraud*; and when once they are in possession of them, you see with what ostentation they gild over the foulness of their usurpations, with the unjust, but glorious titles of conquest and good policy. Observe, on the other hand, what generally becomes of these who are either too stupid or too pusillanimous to follow their examples: they are buried in poverty and obscurity, or wear away their lives in slavery and contempt. *Honest servants are servants forever: and good men are always poor:* whilst the bold and resolute soon free themselves from bondage, and the fraudulent and rapacious from indigence and distress. God and Nature have given every man the means of making his fortune: and it is sooner and more easily done by force or circumvention, than by honesty and plain dealing. Hence it is that we see mankind in general is more prone to rapine than industry, to evil than good. Hence it is that we devour each other, and he that is weakest is at all times sure to come off the worst. Force therefore, is always to be used, when there is an opportunity;

and what fairer opportunity than the present can we ever hope for from the hands of Fortune?[92]

One may doubt whether Machiavelli himself shared all the ideas which he attributes to this champion of the self-conscious proletariat. His own views of revolution and of its causes are better expressed in a reflective passage written in his own person.

> All republics, especially such as are not well constructed, undergo frequent changes in their laws and manner of government. *And this is not owing to the nature either of liberty or subjection in general, as many think*, but to downright oppression on the one hand, or unbridled licentiousness on the other. For the name of liberty is often nothing more than a specious pretence, made use of both by the instruments of licentiousness, who for the most part, are commoners, and by the promoters of slavery, who generally are the Nobles; each side being equally impatient of restraint and control. But when it fortunately happens, which is indeed very seldom, that some wise, good and powerful citizen, has sufficient authority on the commonwealth, to make such laws as may extinguish all jealousies betwixt the Nobility and the People, or at least so to moderate and restrain them, that they shall not be able to produce any bad effect: in such case, that state may properly be called free, and its constitution looked upon as firm and permanent. For, being once established upon good laws and institutions, *it has no further occasion*, like other states, for the virtue of any particular man to support it. Of such laws and principles, many of those ancient commonwealths, which so long subsisted, were formerly constituted: and for want of them, others have often varied, and still vary, their form of government from tyranny to licentiousness, and from licentiousness to tyranny... Much evil may easily be done in the former, and hardly any good in the latter: the insolent having too much authority on the one, and the ignorant and inexperienced on the other; and both must be upheld by the spirit and fortune of one man alone, who yet may either be suddenly taken off by death or overpowered by adversity.[93]

Subject to the general conditions just outlined, there arise two main forms of political associations: "All states, all powers, that have held or hold rule over men have been and are either republics or principalities."[94]

92. Machiavelli, *History of Florence*, in *Works* (1775), 2:136.
93. Ibid., 165.
94. Machiavelli, *Prince*, 7.

These are (a) the principality (the word is used generally) and (b) the commonwealth. To the examination of these the *Prince* and the *Discourses* are severally devoted, and it is nothing less than fatal to a true understanding of Machiavelli to read them in isolation.

It has been noticed that Machiavelli thinks of the state in motion rather than at rest. This is true, and it is perhaps the most remarkable illustration of his classical prepossessions that he does so. Aristotle had said, "The state is natural, and yet he who first created it was the greatest of benefactors."[95] To Machiavelli, as to him, the raw materials are, at least within limits, amenable to human control. Those limits are determined by the malleability of the material, and it is because this is limited that different forms of political association arise.

> The capacity of a founder is known in two ways; by his choice of a site or by the laws which he frames ... Since to be safe they must be strong, they are compelled to avoid barren districts and to plant themselves in more fertile regions; where the fruitfulness of the soil enabling them to increase and multiply, they may defend themselves against any who attack them, and overthrow any who would withstand their power ... And as for that languor which the situation might breed, care must be had that hardships which the site does not enforce, shall be enforced by the laws.[96]

The factors are twofold (a) the "site," the material environment which to a great extent imposes on the inhabitants definite economic and social conditions of life and (b) the human material which the legislator has at his disposal. The former is, in the words of Aristotle, the gift of τύχη, in those of Machiavelli, of *Fortuna*; the latter are designated respectively as ἀρετή and virtue. Whether a Principate or a commonwealth is to be created will depend on the disposition of the people.[97] On the other hand, to establish a commonwealth, it is necessary to slay the sons of Brutus.[98] A free government cannot exist where the people is either servile, or dependent, or corrupt, or where there exist any considerable body of citizens who are above the law and feared by the magistrates.[99]

In the order of priority, the Principate naturally comes first. Machiavelli's *Prince* is a development of the thought contained in the *Discourses*

---

95. Aristotle, *Politics*, 1253a30–31.
96. Machiavelli, *Discourses*, 8.
97. Ibid., 3.55.
98. Ibid., 3.3.
99. Ibid., 1.49.

I.9–10 and *The History of Florence* IV.165 (already cited in our discussion of revolution). Concentration of power—the institution of a monarch—is essentially the cure for pathological conditions—either a crisis such as the crisis met in Roman history by the appointment of a dictator, or the anarchy which precedes the creation of a new state. The state itself issues from an act of consolidation, the work of genius combined with power, like that associated with the name of Theseus in early Athens. In this connection one may note the daring collocation of Moses, Cyrus, Theseus, and Romulus, which occurs in several passages and which so offended the Protestants.

> Whoever reads the Bible with attention will see that Moses, in order to establish his laws, was obliged to put many people to death, who opposed him out of envy. (Machiavelli quotes Exodus 32:27) "Thus saith the Lord God of Israel, Put every man his sword by his side, and go in and out from gate to gate, throughout the camp, and slay every man his brother, and every man his companion, and every man his neighbor; and the children of Levi did according to the words of Moses, and there fell of the people that day about three thousand men."[100]

The murder by Romulus of his brother had its parallel in the history of the Jewish people. Machiavelli saw this; what his critics took as dogma, he read as literature and as the material for political science.

After the genesis of the prince, there naturally follows the question of his function. And here comes a point which may be surprising to the reader of the *Prince* only: the function of the autocrat, according to Machiavelli, is to lay broad and deep, the foundations of freedom.

> [The founder or reformer of a state] ought to be so prudent and moderate as to avoid transmitting the absolute authority he acquires as an inheritance to another; for as men are, by nature, more prone to evil than good, a successor has used to worthy ends. Moreover, though it be one man that must give a state its institutions, once given they are not so likely to last long resting for support on the shoulders of one man only, as when entrusted to the care of many, and when it is the business of many to maintain them. For though the multitude be unfit to set a state in order, since they cannot, by reason of the divisions which prevail among them, agree wherein the true well-being of the state lies, yet when they have once been taught the truth, they never will consent to abandon it.[101]

100. Machiavelli, *Discourses*, in *Works* (1762), 2:344.
101. Machiavelli, *Discourses*, 42.

Machiavelli has no use for hereditary power. He distrusts the ability of the political Atlas long to carry the burden on his shoulders. He believes profoundly that those communities are strongest in which the many help to sustain the political fabric.

With regard to the nature of monarchical administration, little need be said. Of all the writings of Machiavelli, the *Prince* is easily the most familiar. In fact, it is the only one of his books which has ever been in any sense popular; and the precepts of government which it contains have been taken to represent the thought of Machiavelli generally, although they are in reality merely prescriptions for the abnormal conditions which call the autocrat into being. Two or three points may, however, be noted. In the first place, Machiavelli, like Aristotle, recognizes several types of principalities—the hereditary, the new and the mixed. Of the new, he recognizes that some may be acquired by talent,[102] other by fortune,[103] others by sheer wickedness[104] while still others are elective, the civil principality the ruler of which is elected by the people;[105] the ecclesiastical principality, the ruler of which is the vice-regent of God.[106] Generically, these autocrats represent the Aristotelian substitution of personal authority for the rule of law; specifically the policy of the different types and governed by the conditions which have called them into existence, and to which their administration must necessarily conform. We may leave to Frederic his task of weighing the individual precepts, approving or condemning them as they measure up to his particular standard of morality. In general, they may be said to reflect the thought of the classical realists, especially of Aristotle in his last three books.[107] There is absolutely not a precept which cannot be paralleled from classical literature, and hardly any which cannot be paralleled in Aristotle himself. And Aristotle himself embodies the whole of them in his general recommendation to the despot that he should "let his disposition be virtuous or at least half-virtuous; and if he must be wicked, let him be half-wicked only."[108] It was Aristotle too, who observed that virtue is relative to the constitution. The good citizen, still less the good ruler, is not necessarily the good man.

---

102. Machiavelli, *Prince*, ch. 6.
103. Ibid., ch. 7.
104. Ibid., ch. 8.
105. Ibid., ch. 9.
106. Ibid., ch. 11.
107. Cochrane refers to Newman's edition of the *Politics* where the books are reordered.
108. Aristotle, *Politics*, 1315b9–10.

It was Burke who declared that we do not take the medicine of the state as its daily food; and Machiavelli had laid it down that autocracy is the cure for a special pathological condition of the body politic. He declares:

> Let not anyone finding Caesar celebrated by a crowd of writers, be misled by his glory; for those who praise him have been corrupted by his good fortune and overawed by the greatness of that empire which, being governed in his name, would not suffer any to speak their minds openly concerning him. But let him who desires to know how historians would have written of Caesar had they been free to declare their thoughts, mark what they say of Catiline than whom Caesar is more hateful, in proportion as he who does is more to be condemned than he who only desires to do evil. Let him note also what praises they lavish upon Brutus, because being unable, out of respect for his power, to reproach Caesar, they magnify his enemy. And if he who has become prince in any state will but reflect, how, after Rome was made an empire, far greater praise was earned by those emperors who lived within the laws, and worthily, than by those who lived in the contrary way, he will see that Titus, Nerva, Trajaro, Hadrian, Antoninus and Marcus had no need of praetorian cohorts, or of countless legions to guard them, but were defended by their *own good lives, the good-will of their subjects,* and the *attachment of the senate* . . . From the study of this history we may also learn how a good government is to be established; for while all the emperors who succeeded to the throne by birth, except Titus, were bad, all extra good who succeeded by adoption; as in the case of the five from Nerva to Marcus. But so soon as the empire fell once more to the heirs by birth, its ruin recommenced.
>
> Let a prince therefore look to that period which extends from Nerva to Marcus, and contrast it with that which went before and that which came after, and then let him say in which of them he would wish to have been born or to have reigned. For during those times in which good men governed, he will see the prince secure in the midst of happy subjects, and the whole world filled with peace and justice. He will find the senate maintaining its authority, the magistrates enjoying their honours, rich citizens their wealth, rank and merit held in respect, ease and content everywhere prevailing, rancor, licence, corruption and ambition everywhere quenched, and that golden age restored in which everyone might hold and support what opinions he pleased. He will see, in short, the world triumphing, the sovereign honoured and revered, the people animated with love

> and rejoicing in their security. But should he turn to examine the times of the other emperors, he will find them wasted by battles, torn by seditions, cruel alike in peace and war; many princes perishing by the sword; many wars foreign and domestic: Italy overwhelmed with unheard of disasters: her towns destroyed and plundered; Rome burned: the capital razed to the ground by Roman citizens: the ancient temples desolated, the ceremonies of religion corrupted; the cities rank with adultery, the seas covered with exiles, and the islands polluted with blood. He will see outrage follow outrage; rank, riches, honours and above all, virtue imputed as mortal crimes; informers rewarded; slaves bribed to betray their masters, freedmen their patrons, and those who were without enemies brought to destruction by their friends: and *then he will know the true nature of the debt which Rome, Italy, and the world, owe to Caesar: and if he possess a spark of human feeling, will turn from the example of those evil times, and kindle with a consuming passion to imitate those which were good.*[109]

Thus does Machiavelli anticipate the famous judgment of Gibbon, that the Antonine period was the happiest in the history of the human race; and for much the same reasons. For he too believed in the ideal of security, and thus he eulogizes the comfortable, affluent and somewhat smug civilization of the second century. Despotism, on the other hand, he treats as entirely temporary and provisional in character, and, in the last analysis, justified only when it succeeds in making itself superfluous. The savage denunciation of Caesarism may be based on ignorance of the later phases of republican history, but it shows in the most vivid light what Machiavelli thought of autocracy as a principle of government, and it marks the real cleavage which, at any rate in the most recent phases of his administration, has come to exist between the Florentine and his most recently professed disciple. Dazzled by his own rise and by the vision of the corporative state, Mussolini flouts the value which Machiavelli held most dear when he declares, "Let it be known once and for all that fascism knows no idols and worships no fetishes: it has already passed over and if necessary will turn once more and quickly pass over the more or less decayed corpse of the Goddess Liberty."[110] For in truth, Machiavelli in modern, like Thucydides and Aristotle in ancient times, believed most profoundly that the distinction between the commonwealth and all other forms of government was radical. He had not read his Livy and his Tacitus in vain.

109. Machiavelli, *Discourses*, 46–49.
110. Schneider, *Making the Fascist State*, 342.

But the commonwealth, as it was infinitely the most precious of all forms of government, was also the most difficult to establish. We have already noted that it presupposes moral qualities in the citizen such as are not usually to be found. It is only when they exist that it is possible, in the world of Tacitus, to associate the insociables, authority and freedom. Yet to do so is to make possible what Machiavelli (again following Aristotle) regards as more effective, and, at the same time, more valuable than any form of personal government, viz., the reign of law. For Machiavelli, in the true classical tradition, thinks of freedom mainly from the legal point of view; the free state is the law-state. The free state is that in which there exists, liberty of accusation coupled with the prohibition of calumny.[111] In other words it depends upon the recognition of a body of private rights and the development of a judicial system to enforce them rather than upon machinery of democratic control.

Not that this latter is unimportant. Power either acquired or exercised irregularly is pernicious to liberty.[112] And it was the surrender of control over great spheres of actions to commissions which was fatal to the Roman republic. For this reasons, and also because of their superior (κριτίκα δύναμις) the masses should be entrusted with the ratification of all legislative proposals. It is true that they are easily carried away by grandiose ideas,[113] but though they are sometimes mistaken in general, they seldom or never err in particulars.[114] Yet the limit of legislative enactment should be clearly recognized; and there is especial danger in retroactive measures.[115]

The greatest problem in a commonwealth is the repression of those elements, which in the words of Aristotle, being superior in some respects, claim to be superior in all. Machiavelli has no illusions regarding the dangers threatened by the subterranean influences of wealth and power. He quotes with approval the remark of old Cato that no city can be deemed free which contains a citizen who is feared by the magistrates.[116] "A very few desire freedom that they may obtain power, but all the rest of the people, whose number is countless, only desire it that they may live securely."[117] "The ambitions of the oligarchs, however, are pernicious. I maintain that the ambition of the great is so pernicious that, unless controlled and counteracted in a

---

111. Machiavelli, *Discourses*, 1.7–8.
112. Ibid., 1.34.
113. Ibid., 1.53.
114. Ibid., 1.47.
115. Ibid., 1.37.
116. Ibid., 1.29.
117. Ibid., 169.

variety of ways, it will always reduce a city to speedy ruin."[118] The trouble comes again from the fact that human nature is prone to evil. "Men usually rise from one degree of ambition to another; endeavouring first to secure themselves from oppression, and afterwards to oppress others."[119] Yet the overweening ambition of citizens can, and ought to be repressed, in various ways,[120] so that the establishment and maintenance of a commonwealth is not a hopeless task. Its vitality will be measured, as we have already suggested, by its civic spirit—the willingness of the citizen to go into public life[121]—to forget private grievances where the public good is concerned[122]—and to serve the public interest in any capacity, high or low.[123] Thus civic spirit—or patriotism—is recognized as an adequate substitute for either the fear of God, which ensures obedience in an ecclesiastical polity, or the fear of the prince, which in a tyranny is the sold guarantee of political obligation.

Of the superiority of the commonwealth over these other forms, Machiavelli entertains not the slightest doubt; and those critics are beyond question right who designate him a Republican. Apart from the frequent encomiums on Brutus and Cassius—the heroes and martyrs of the Republican idea—the fierce condemnation of Caesarism is in itself sufficient to show where his heart lay. "Of all princes existing or who may have existed, few indeed are or have been either wise or good,"[124] is a sentiment which finds confirmation in the dictum, "I believe that if her kings had not been expelled, Rome must very soon have become a weak and inconsiderable state."[125] The faults of the people are due mainly to the Prince,[126] according to those laws of imitation which lead men to ape their professed superiors. Machiavelli here grasps a secret which is at once the glory and the peril of all aristocratic forms of government. When Prince and People are compared, it turns out that the people are usually wiser and more constant than the Prince.[127] And also that they can be more fully relied upon than he to maintain the obligations of public faith.[128] Freedom releases human

118. Ibid., 120.
119. Machiavelli, *Discourses*, in *Works* (1762), 2:113.
120. Machiavelli, *Discourses*, 1.52.
121. Ibid., 1.48.
122. Ibid., 3.47.
123. Ibid., 1.56.
124. Ibid., 175.
125. Ibid., 70.
126. Ibid., 3.29.
127. Ibid. 1.58.
128. Ibid., 1.59.

energies,[129] and hence generates that superior vitality of republics which enables the commonwealth to endure longer and with more sustained good fortune than the principality,[130] and makes it harder to overthrow.[131] The excellence of a state is measured by the well-being of the subjects, and while the commonwealth cherishes the ideal of the whole and hurts merely this man or that, the Principality (or Aristocracy) thinks in less catholic terms, and helps merely this man or that to the general detriment of the whole.

> We know by experience that states have never signally increased, either as to dominion or wealth, except where they have lived under a free government. The cause is not far to seek, since it is the well-being, not of individuals, but of the community which makes a state great; and, without question, this universal well-being is nowhere secured save in a republic. For a republic will do what so ever makes for its interest; and though its measures prove hurtful to this man or that, there are so many whom they benefit, that these are able to carry them out, in spite of the resistance of the few whom they injure.[132]

Is there a general formula which will explain the rise and fall of states? This is a question which confronts the practical politician no less than the theoretical philosopher; because on the answer to it, depends the possibility of manipulating the forces upon which the life and well-being of societies depend. Machiavelli, therefore, was confronted with the problem; and it is maintained by at least one critic that, in the answer which he offered, he gave way to a "vague, half-popular half-scholastic mysticism," which operated like a species of intellectual inertia or paralysis upon his otherwise keen and alert mind.[133] Here, then, Dyer finds a puzzling residuum of unrealized mediaeval mysticism, in the conception of *natura naturans:* of a vague, impersonal force working in men and through men; carrying societies through a cycle of change, and keeping them in being by periodical and providential reversions to their earliest and worst rudimentary constitution.

We may observe to begin with that this, if it is the case, is not so much a going-over to the schoolmen as, through them, to Plato and Polybius, from whom the theory of cycles is derived. And certainly there are passages in Machiavelli which lend support to the view that he at least flirted with

129. Ibid., 2.2.
130. Ibid., 3.9, 1.57.
131. Ibid., 1.25, 1.55.
132. Ibid., 198.
133. Dyer, *Machiavelli and the Modern State,* xv.

the theory of cycles. "No state or religious establishment can last long unless it be frequently reduced to its first principles."[134] Elsewhere he comments:

> In the changes that are incident to all governments they often degenerate into anarchy and confusion; and from thence emerge again into good order and regularity. And since it is ordained by Providence that there should be a continual ebb and flow in the things of this world; as soon as they arrive at their utmost perfection, and can ascend no higher, they must of necessity decline; and on the other hand, when they have fallen, through any disorder, to the lowest degree that is possible, and can sink no lower, they begin to rise again. And thus there is a constant succession of prosperity and adversity in all human affairs. Virtue is the mother of peace, peace produces idleness, idleness contention and misrule, and from thence proceed ruin and confusion. This occasions reformation and better laws; good laws make men virtuous; and public virtue is always attended with glory and success. It has therefore been well remarked, that arms are prior to letters, and that in new states and governments there have always been warriors and soldiers, before the rise of scholars and philosophers.[135]

The question arises whether this undigested Polybius, artificially incorporated, represents Machiavelli's real thought; and this, I think, is not the case. His working concepts, as we have seen, are rather the "human nature" and "environment" of Aristotle and of modern biological science. These give rise to two general types of political association, but there is no *necessary transition* from one to the other. The Prince, like Aristotle's tyrant, is recommended to lay the foundation stones of liberty, but he may rather choose to govern like a Caesar. On the other hand, the existence of a commonwealth presupposes certain intellectual and moral qualities, as well as a favorable environment, and its maintenance is secured as long as these conditions subsist. All forms of government, moreover, depend on what Machiavelli calls a certain concentration of *virtù*; their well-being and progress upon the degree to which *virtù* exists. In other words, the human qualities necessary to support the political fabric are, for political science, taken as ultimate though they may be developed to a higher degree when material conditions are favorable, by means of the proper inner environment of culture and discipline. For instance, he notes:

---

134   Machiavelli, *Discourses*, in *Works* (1762), 2:267.
135. Machiavelli, *History of Florence*, in *Works* (1775), 2:213.

> Plutarch, a very grave author, and many others, are of opinion that the Romans were more indebted to their good fortune than their virtue for the largeness of their empire; . . . Livy himself seems to incline to this opinion, since he seldom introduces any Roman speaking of virtue, but he makes him say something of fortune also. But I confess I am not of that opinion myself; nor do I think it can be properly supported by anyone else; because, if no other commonwealth ever made so good progress as the Roman, it is well known that no other commonwealth was so well constituted for that purpose; for as the valour and excellent discipline of their soldiery were the chief causes of their acquiring so extensive a dominion, so their wise *conduct* and the *institutions* established by their first lawgivers were means of preserving what they got . . . I am therefore of opinion that any other Prince or People endued with the same degree of *virtue* and *courage,* and observing the same wise measures, would likewise have the same good fortune that the Romans did.[136]

This almost amounts to saying that character is fate; it certainly includes the notion that institutions make character. And since the idea of necessary progress has gone to the limbo of discarded dogmas along with the notion of degeneracy, or of cyclical change, it may be regarded as scientific realism in the modern sense of the word.

The character thus created will of course be relative to the constitution; and Frederic is doubtless right when he says the Machiavelli's Prince is like Homer's gods, who are represented as strong and powerful, but seldom or never as equitable or just.[137] But in truth the idea that in politics there is no morality was no discovery of Machiavelli. It is merely one of the more explosive doctrines to be found in classical literature, and even Poincaré's bright school boy was able to see that it was the lesson of Sallust's Catiline. Machiavelli, indeed, does not press the doctrine nearly so far as it had been pressed two thousand years before; nor we may venture to assert, as far as it has been pressed since.

It is ridiculous to suppose that he recognized no distinction between relative good and evil, even in politics: "It cannot be called talent to slay fellow citizens, to deceive friends, to be without faith, without mercy, without religion; such methods may gain empire, but not glory."[138] Thus the notion of *virtù* does not exclude that of "moral excellence." It is equally absurd to suggest that he makes a hero of Césare Borgia. As a matter of fact, he repre-

---

136. Machiavelli, *Discourses*, in *Works* (1762), 2:165.
137. Frederick, *Examen*, in *Works*, 2:316.
138. Machiavelli, *Prince*, 65.

sents him as one who acquired power not as a result of talent, but through the gift of fortune, and through the malignity of fortune, coupled with his own mistaken policy, lost it, although the measures he took in the intervening time are certainly offered for imitation to new princes.[139]

I do not wish to assume the function of devil's advocate, nor do I complain of the tragedy of Machiavelli—that his reputation has been murdered by a phrase—but to those who like Morely denounce him for preaching the unblest gospel that "whatever policy may demand, justice will allow,"[140] I should suggest the following considerations:

1. Even in ethics, the moral act must be judged, as Plato himself has shown, not in isolation but in its context.

2. Unless we adopt the synoptic standpoint of Plato (and the Hebrew prophets) then politics is a different thing from ethics, with different standards and different rules. Those standards and those rules are dictated by the subject matter: and the greatest tragedies of history have been occasioned by the confusion of the two.

3. Machiavelli states the verdict of history: it remained for the nineteenth century to attempt to justify that verdict.

Machiavelli declares, "I have never endeavoured to throw a veil of honesty over a foul deed, nor to calumniate anyone that was worthy of praise; by meanly insinuating that it was done to serve some vile purpose."[141] Thus does Machiavelli dissociate himself from any attempt to prove that *Die Weltgeschichte ist das Weltgerichte*—a sin of which Acton specifically accuses (among others) Ranke, Coulanges, Mommsen, and Carlyle. The Hebrew in his day asked the question: why do the wicked flourish? And the answer of Christ himself was that they leave their reward in this world. Machiavelli is truer to the spirit of Christianity than many of his critics when the refuses to take the view that makes belief in ultimate goodness easy.

Not that he was a good Christian, or at bottom perhaps a Christian at all. It has been argued that his animus was directed against ecclesiasticism rather than against the faith; and that, it was not so much the Pope, he attacked as the Italian prince. It is difficult to assent to this view. Machiavelli's interests were in this world rather than in the next, and his powers were devoted to the question of ameliorating men's woes here rather than to the discovery of how they could be compensated in the hereafter. He saw that

---

139. Ibid., ch. 7.
140. Morley, *Life of Gladstone*, 2:9.
141. Machiavelli, *Dedicatory Epistle*, in *Works* (1762), 1:xi.

the maxim "the meek shall inherit the earth" was the statement of an ideal rather than a fact; that in fact, so far as political salvation was concerned, it was to be achieved not by meekness, or lowliness or self-abnegation but by a revival of the qualities of courage and energy, a strong respect for law and a devotion to duty such as had in ancient times made possible the greatness of Rome. Morley sneers at Machiavelli and his Romans; today we are more cautious, and statesmen everywhere are asking whether these are impossible ideals; whether or not in fact they cannot be generated or regenerated. In so far as Fascism has succeeded in creating a religion of patriotism (I do not say how far it has) Mussolini has realized the dream of the prince in our day. The teaching of "civics" in the schools of America is based upon the same idea.

Because of his moral bias, Machiavelli has been described as the conscience of the Renaissance and of modern times; but it is truer to say that he represents the revival of an old point of view or rather that in his case the old and the new are one. "The wisdom of this world is foolishness to God" was the cry of Christianity; and Medievalism was an attempt (successful or not depending on the point of view) to substitute the divine wisdom for the human, and for the will of man the will of God. But that is hardly the modern attitude, and it was certainly not the attitude of the Greco-Roman world upon which no light of revelation broke. Thus, in the history of the West, Medievalism is an interlude; and Machiavelli, looking forward and backward like Janus, and find in the old world doctrine for the new, demonstrates the essential affinity between us and classical antiquity.

That he studied his classics, with great and persistent attention, there can be no manner of doubt. He himself never sought to conceal the fact, as may be seen from the familiar letter to Vettori, in which he confesses that Hellas is his spiritual home.[142] We may well admit (with Burd) that he knew little or no Greek. That fact simply serves as one argument in favor of the use of translations, viz., that they enforce attention to the matter rather than the form or style of the author studied. Machiavelli's pages are scattered with recollections and paraphrases of his favorite authors, and loaded with direct references to them, especially the writers of history and politics. This fact accounts for the view entertained by some of his critics that he was little more than a mere plagiarist.

It is our contention, however, that he was no vulgar cribber, no more sneak-thief but rather a pirate of ideas. What he needed he took, and what he took he made use of. In other words, he capitalized on his reading; and

---

142. See Morley, *Machiavelli*, 14; he quotes the translation of Symonds, *Age of the Despots*.

this was possible because he got from the classics no mere batch of isolated maxims, but rather a point of view—an outlook and a method by which those maxims were woven into the very texture of his thought and, in the light of it, assumed fresh meaning, and got a new lease of life. For if experience rather than dogma is the real teacher, then the generalizations of experience assume first importance, and the proper method of enquiry is the one which he adopts, viz., the advancing and testing of various theses which are thought to be applicable to the subject in hand. This is a favorite device of Aristotle, and with Machiavelli it becomes the regular system. It is also the method of the Platonic dialogue, not to speak of the Roman school-boys's essays upon which our modern practice of essay writing is probably based.

How then shall we describe Machiavelli? And what is Machiavellianism? I hesitate more and more to attach a label to any man. But Machiavelli has been so much labeled, and the labels have been so misleading, that it is necessary at least to protest against some of them. He has been described as an "absolutist" and his maxims have been taken to justify that "raison d'état" in the name of which so many public crimes have been committed. To us, thinking as we tend to do in terms of a "state" abstracted from the individuals who compose it, it is all too easy to misinterpret Machiavelli in this way. On the other hand, Machiavelli has recently been described and denounced as the first of the pragmatists: i.e. of those who judge the quality of things by the test of survival value. It is, indeed, possible to find an element of the pragmatic in his doctrine, in so far as he appears to have believed that life itself is prior to any of its formulations, whether those of ethics, or economics, or politics. But the extreme anti-intellectualism of modern pragmatism, he certainly does not share. Indeed, if there is any defect in his way of thought, it probably arises from his too great readiness to accept the rationality of events. For enthusiasts, like Savonarola, he had no sympathy; and enthusiasm seems, in fact, strangely out of keeping with his cold and analytic mind. If he must be labeled, it should probably be as a "rational empiricist"; and if he must be pigeon-holed in any school, it should probably be that represented in England by Edmund Burke. Certainly there is much in common between Burke's principle of expediency and the Machiavellian "raison d'état" when this is properly understood.

There are those who argue that nothing can come of empirical methods, the analysis of secondary cause upon which the science of politics—if there be such a thing—depends. For this, they contend, is to bank on purely human foundations, to organize (in Bishop Creighton's words) apart from God. And any society which does so is, in the last analysis, bankrupt, and courts the decadence of Greece and Rome. These are the mediaevalists; for whom the verdict, pronounced by St. Augustine over the corpse of the

Roman Empire, still stands unimpugned—the judgment of God upon all individuals and all societies who attempt on purely human foundations to erect a scheme of life which will endure. It is with these that Machiavelli takes issues; in raising the standard of humanism, he makes himself, as Acton says, the first conscious and articulate exponents of forces dominant in the world. The battle is not, as Morley imagines, between darkness and light, between the forces of reaction and those of progress. It is rather between Medievalism and that modernism which has its roots in classical antiquity, between the claims of the earthly society and those of the society of God. In Machiavelli, we see one of the earliest of modern attempts to develop a view of life and politics according to the method of science. To those who hold that, after all, life is a unity and cannot be thus mutilated except in thought, the question arises: is not the philosophic standpoint—the standpoint of Medievalism—forced upon men by the necessity of reconciling the various claims of the sciences which modernism blocks out? We may admit that the issue is still unsettled, that there is something to be said for the saint as well as for the sinner, and that the task of the future will be to judge the claims of Augustine and Machiavelli.

7

The Mind of Edward Gibbon

The Mind of Edward Gibbon (I)[1]

MY SUBJECT IS THE mind of Edward Gibbon. I shall not concern myself (except incidentally) with his life and achievement as a member of what Goldsmith called the "commonwealth of polite letters." Nor shall I undertake to assess the value of his work, in the sense in which it has been examined and passed *magna cum laude* by Bury, to rank with that of Thucydides and Tacitus. My object is rather to consider the principles in terms of which Gibbon envisages human nature and human history, and which thus determine his attitude to the problems raised by the collapse of ancient civilization. This means that our attention will be directed not so much to his thinking as to the preconceptions (whether implicit or explicit) which govern his thought. And we shall argue that while, of course, his general outlook was that of the so-called Age of Reason, his specific presumptions were those of what its exponents (oddly enough, from our modern standpoint) called "experimental science"; furthermore that, when Gibbon claims to speak as a philosophic historian, he consciously and deliberately aligns himself with this particular movement of thought, finding in it the clue to an understanding of "that memorable series of revolutions which, in the course of about thirteen centuries, gradually undermined, and at length

---

1. [Cochrane originally published this piece in two parts. This part was published as "The Mind of Edward Gibbon (I)," *University of Toronto Quarterly* 12.1 (1942–43) 1–17. See below, 227–47, for part 2.]

destroyed, the solid fabric of human greatness";[2] "the greatest perhaps, and most awful scene in the history of mankind."[3]

I

By "experimental science" was meant, of course, the method of enquiry which, initiated by Locke with the publication of his *Essay on the Human Understanding*, was to culminate in the philosophic skepticism of Hume. This method had its origin in the work of the great seventeenth-century philosophers, Descartes and Bacon. Descartes had proclaimed the independence and self-sufficiency of the human reason as an instrument for the investigation of truth; Bacon, the doctrine that this instrument should be devoted to the practical end of wresting her secrets from nature. And the *Novum Organon* bore its first fruits with Newton's formulation of the laws of motion. The success of Newtonian physics was accepted as a magnificent vindication of the new method as applied to the study of nature; it remained only to exploit the possibilities of that method in order to achieve an equally valid science of the mind. And it was precisely this task which, in his celebrated essay, Locke undertook. By so doing, he started one of the most powerful intellectual impulses of his own and the following century.

Locke was fully alive to the difficulties which lay in his path. "The understanding, like the eye," he declares, "whilst it makes us see and perceive all other things, takes no notice of itself; and it requires art and pains to set it at a distance and make it its own object." The permanent value of Locke's undertaking remains, of course, a matter of debate. Its historical importance, however, is beyond question. What this was may be gathered from the words of Locke's editor:

> Discarding all systematic theories, he [Locke] has from actual experience and observation, delineated the features, and described the operations of the human mind, with a degree of precision and minuteness not to be found in Plato, Aristotle or Descartes. After clearing the way, by setting aside the whole doctrine of innate notions and principles, both speculative and practical, the author traces all ideas to two sources, sensation and reflection; treats at large of the human understanding in forming, distinguishing, compounding and associating them; of the manner in which words are applied as representations of ideas; of the difficulties and obstructions which arise from

2. Gibbon, "The Author's Prefatory Notes," in *Decline and Fall*, 1:lvi.
3. Ibid., 3:2441.

the imperfection of these signs; and of the nature, reality, kinds, degrees, casual hindrances and necessary limits, of human knowledge; . . . a work of inestimable value, as a history of the understanding, not compiled from former books, but written from materials collected by a long and attentive observation of what passes in the human mind.[4]

The *Essay*, which appeared in 1690, was saluted as "one of the noblest, the usefullest and the most original books the world ever saw,"[5] embodying "discoveries . . . particularly that great and universal law of nature, the support of so many mental powers, which produces equally remarkable effects in the intellectual as that of gravitation does in the material world, viz. the association of ideas" (notice the parallelism).[6] But its chief significance lay not so much, perhaps, in these discoveries, important though they were in their influence on subsequent thought, as in the method by which they were arrived at. This method was heralded as "at its first appearance, absolutely new and directly opposite to the notions and persuasions then established."[7] It was "to quit every arbitrary hypothesis and trust to fact and experience,"[8] or, in Locke's own words, by a "historical, plain method . . . to give an account of the ways whereby our understandings come to attain those notions of things we have . . . and to set down measures of the certainty of our knowledge, or the grounds of these persuasions which are to be found amongst men"[9]; since (as he adds) "it is of great use to the sailor to know the length of his line, though he cannot with it fathom all the depths of the ocean. It is well that he knows that it is long enough to reach the bottom at such places as are necessary to direct his voyage, and caution him against running upon shoals that may ruin him."[10]

Locke's work was part of a progressive secularization of thought which, beginning slowly and tentatively in the sixteenth and seventeenth centuries was ultimately to invade every field of human interest including history, where the problem was to interpret the story of mankind in the light of "experimental science." The difficulty was that, in order to do so, this story had to be envisaged in terms of "those universal and invariable truths" of human nature which experimental science was to discover, rather

---

4. Locke, *Essay Concerning Human Understanding*, 26.
5. "Anonymous Editor," *Works of John Locke*, 1:xxx.
6. Ibid., xvii.
7. Ibid., xii.
8. Ibid., xv.
9. Locke, *Works*, 1:2.
10. Ibid., 5.

than in terms of Christian anthropology. This, however, was accomplished by drawing a distinction between primary and secondary causes, and by concentrating on the latter as alone susceptible of "experimentation" or (as we should now say) of "observation." The new secularism was, indeed, to stimulate a vigorous movement of reaction, of which Bossuet's *Discourse on Universal History* remains a characteristic product. Bossuet, however, was on the defensive, and, while his effort to restate traditional Catholic doctrine was not without its influence even on the mind of the youthful Gibbon, it was none the less a popular failure as compared with the work of lesser men who wrote in the spirit of their time. Thus Gibbon, in speaking of his early conversion to Catholicism, observes with reference to Bossuet: "I surely fell by a noble hand."[11] But over against this we may set the influence of Middleton's *Free Enquiry*, a book which was read by Gibbon while still an undergraduate at Magdalen during the spiritual crisis of his adolescence, and which contributed to shake his faith in the historicity of miracles, as these were currently accepted in the Church. To the remarkable success of Middleton's work Hume bears grudging witness when he says that, on his return from Italy in 1747, he had the mortification to find all England in ferment on account of it, while his own performance (the *First Enquiry*) was entirely overlooked and neglected. Gibbon was later to record his judgment of Middleton in a passage of his *Journal*, dated February 1764. "This man was endowed with penetration and accuracy. He saw where his principles led, but did not think proper to draw the consequences."[12] That task, we may suspect, was reserved for the historian himself.

What experimental science offered was the picture of a world (potentially at least) devoid of mystery; and there is a curious but instructive illustration in Gibbon's *Memoirs* of how it helped him in his pilgrimage from "superstition to skepticism."[13] He is speaking of "the book, as well as the man, who contributed the most effectually to my education," the work of an otherwise obscure teacher, a certain M. de Crousaz, "whose philosophy had been formed in the school of Locke."[14] "His system of logic," Gibbon continues,

> may be praised as a clear and methodical abridgment of the art of reasoning, from our simple ideas to the most complex operations of the human understanding. This system I studied, and meditated, and abstracted, till I had obtained the free command

11. Gibbon, *Miscellaneous Works*, 29.
12. Ibid., 545.
13. Ibid., 30.
14. Ibid., 37.

of a universal instrument, which I soon presumed to exercise on my Catholic opinions... And I still remember my solitary transport at the discovery of a philosophical argument against the doctrine of transubstantiation: that the text of scripture, which seems to inculcate the real presence, is attested only by a single sense—our sight; while the real presence itself is disproved by three of our senses—the sight, the touch and the taste. The various articles of the Romish creed disappeared like a dream.[15]

The significance of this confession is emphasized by the fact that, while indeed it records an experience of early youth, it was written by Gibbon at the mature age of fifty-two; and there is no ground for supposing that his estimate of Locke's sensationalist logic as the "universal instrument" had changed in the interval. On the contrary, the *Memoirs* makes it clear that he accepted without question the experimental method which "has exploded all innate ideas and natural propensities."[16] In speaking of his early intellectual gymnastics he says: "I defended Locke's metaphysic: the origin of ideas, the principles of evidence and the doctrine of liberty"[17]; even though the Whig elements in that doctrine were not entirely to his taste, as having been "founded in reason [i.e., *a priori*] rather than experience."[18]

In claiming for Gibbon an immediate affiliation with the spirit of experimental science, both in its earlier Lockean version and in the form it was to take with Hume, I do not mean to deny or minimize the importance of other and more general influences in the formation of his mind. "I reviewed, again and again," he tells us, "the immortal works of the French and English, the Latin and Italian classics ... Homer and Xenophon were still my favourite authors [in Greek]."[19] Gibbon was a persistent and assiduous reader. In this habit he revealed his adherence to a cardinal article of eighteenth-century faith, the need for invoking "art" (*studium et doctrina*) to supplement the deficiencies of "nature" (*ingenium*). "By long and laborious exercise," he prepared himself for the character to which "from early youth" he aspired, "the character of an historian."[20] The question is what he got from his studies, whether classical or modern, to qualify him for the role. And first, as to the classics.

15. Ibid., 37–38.
16. Ibid., 19.
17. Ibid., 46.
18. Gibbon, *Memoirs*, 95.
19. Gibbon, *Miscellaneous Works*, 89.
20. Gibbon, *Memoirs*, 130.

II

Speaking of his earliest published work, the French essay on the study of literature, which appeared in 1761 when he was twenty-four, Gibbon says, "I was ambitious of proving by my own example, as well as by my precepts, that all the faculties of the mind may be exercised and displayed by the study of ancient literature."[21]

The *Essay*, as he reviews it in the light of his maturity, was not without merit. "Some dawnings of a philosophic spirit," he observes, "enlighten the general remarks on the study of history and of man."[22] Yet this verdict was qualified by an interesting admission: "Alas! my stock of erudition at that time was scanty and superficial; and if I allow myself the liberty of naming the Greek masters, my genuine and personal acquaintance was confined to the Latin classics."[23] This deficiency was presently in some degree to be repaired. Gibbon began the study of Greek at nineteen and, without the help of a tutor, worked through about half the *Iliad* and a large portion of Xenophon and Herodotus. "But my ardour, destitute of aid and emulation, was gradually cooled and, from the barren task of searching words in a lexicon, I withdrew to the free and familiar conversation of Virgil and Tacitus."[24] It was not until 1781, after completing the third volume of the *Decline and Fall*, that he returned energetically to the study of Greek. Then, in the interval of suspense before resuming his labors, he read, "with new pleasure" he tells us, "the *Iliad* and the *Odyssey*, the histories of Herodotus, Thucydides and Xenophon, a large portion of the tragic and comic theatre of Athens, and many interesting dialogues of the Socratic school."[25]

The list is significant, not less for the names omitted than for those included. In particular, it is noteworthy that there is no reference to Aristotle. In the *Decline and Fall* the work of Aristotle is mentioned but once, and then only in connection with the rise of Arab science. There, in characteristic vein, the author alludes to "the philosophy of the Stagirite" as "alike intelligible or alike obscure for the readers of every age."[26] Gibbon, with most of his contemporaries was, of course, like Aristotle a naturalist, but his naturalism (both in spirit and content) was derived from another and quite different source. Nor should the interest which he found in the Socratic

---

21. Ibid., 55.
22. Ibid., 59.
23. Ibid., 58.
24. Ibid., 41.
25. Ibid., 103.
26. Gibbon, *Decline and Fall*, 3:1869.

dialogues be taken to imply any assent to what he calls "the specious and noble principles" of Plato and "the philosophers who trod in his footsteps."[27] Platonism, as he saw it, was "so far removed beyond the senses and the experience of mankind" that while it "might serve to amuse the leisure of a philosophic mind, or, in the silence of solitude, might sometimes impart a ray of comfort to desponding virtue," nevertheless produced on the mind an "impression so faint" that it "was soon obliterated by the commerce and business of active life."[28] Classical idealism, whether in its pure Platonic or in its qualified Aristotelian form, and therewith the Christian philosophy which developed over against it, were to remain forever beyond Gibbon's ken.

But if Gibbon's knowledge and appreciation of Greek were limited and imperfect, quite the reverse may be said of his Latin; he has, indeed, been called "the last of the great Latinists." Properly speaking, his Latin discipline began only with his translation from the atmosphere of Oxford, "steeped in port and prejudice,"[29] to the more bracing, if more rigorous, intellectual climate of Lausanne (1752); but once begun, it continued without interruption for the rest of his life. And here the question is not what authors he read (for he read them practically all) but rather the spirit in which he addressed himself to his studies. Gibbon himself answers the question:

> I read with application and pleasure [at the age of eighteen] all the epistles, all the orations, and the most important treaties of rhetoric and philosophy [of Cicero]; and, as I read, I applauded the observation of Quintilian, that "every student may judge his own proficiency by the satisfaction which he receives from the Roman orator." I tasted the beauties of language, I breathed the spirit of freedom, I imbibed from his precepts and examples the public and private sense of a man. Cicero in Latin and Xenophon in Greek are indeed the two ancients whom I would first propose to a liberal scholar; not only for the merit of their style and sentiments, but for the admirable lessons which may be applied to every situation of public and private life ... After finishing this great authority, a library of eloquence and reason, I formed a more extensive plan of reviewing the Latin classics under the four divisions of (1) historians (2) poets (3) orators and (4) philosophers, in a chronological series ... to the decline of the language and empire of Rome, and this plan, in the last twenty-seven months of my residency at Lausanne [January,

---

27. Ibid., 1:361.
28. Ibid.
29. Gibbon, *Miscellaneous Works*, 49.

1756, to April, 1758] I nearly accomplished. Nor was this review, however rapid, either hasty or superficial. I indulged myself in a second and even a third perusal of Terence, Virgil, Horace, Tacitus, etc., and studied to imbibe the sense and spirit most congenial to my own.[30]

This is an interesting piece of self-revelation. To it we may perhaps add another, drawn from Gibbon's *Journal* for October, 1762. He had been studying the *Ciceronianus* of Erasmus, together with such extracts from his letters (about forty-seven pages in all) as relate to the great Ciceronian controversy. He warmly agrees with Erasmus in his attack upon the "blind admirers and copiers of Tully . . . who, at the revival of letters formed, especially in Italy, a very considerable sect," and concludes: "So servile an attachment to any author destroys all freedom and originality of genius and produces only a set of tame writers, who will copy the faults but who will surely never attain to the perfections of their great model . . . We should rather endeavor to speak as Cicero would do if he lived at present than as he did in his time."[31] Yet Erasmus himself, as Gibbon observes, was not exempt from the faults which he denounced in others. His writings are "an incoherent mixture of Roman manners with Batavian ones, a mixture not less ridiculous than their scrupulous antique idiom."[32] He cites, as an example, Erasmus's use of the term *interdictio aquae et ignis* to express the ecclesiastical notion of excommunication. "Perhaps the natural conclusion," he continues, "was that, instead of that ungrateful labour upon a dead language, it would be better to improve and cultivate the living ones. But this conclusion was too much for the age of Erasmus."[33]

The words just quoted will serve to indicate Gibbon's position in the historic literary quarrel of the Ancients and Moderns. It is his declaration of independence from servility to the antiquarianism and traditionalism of Renaissance scholarship and, so far, reveals a fresh and original approach to classical study. Yet with Gibbon the revolt was in no sense radical. All he asserts is the right to converse with the great minds of antiquity as an equal among equals. Gibbon's attitude thus remains at bottom quite unhistorical. In the words of a recent writer, he gazes back at antiquity as though from one mountain-peak of civilization to another, across the vast and formless chasm of the Middle Ages. From this standpoint he looks of course to the great Latin models for what they can teach him of *eloquentia*, a matter of

30. Ibid., 40.
31. Ibid., 448.
32. Ibid., 449.
33. Ibid.

essential importance inasmuch as for him "style is the mirror of the mind"; so that when he himself undertakes to write history, he marries it inevitably to literature. Furthermore, as he studies the diction of his classical authors, he gradually learns to envisage the human situation as they do, i.e., in the spirit of a man of the world. Accordingly, while recognizing the primacy of "diligence" and "accuracy" as virtues of an historian, he does not overlook the propagandist value of history as an instrument for attacking the tyranny of the church, just as Tacitus, for example, had used it to attack the tyranny of the Caesars. In this connection, it may be pertinent to recall Gibbon's extraordinary admiration for the "discerning eye" and "masterly pencil" of an author to whom he more than once alludes as "that great historian," "the first to apply the science of philosophy to the study of facts,"[34] in "an immortal work, every sentence of which is pregnant with the deepest observations and the most lively images."[35] "The expressive conciseness of his descriptions," he adds, "has deserved to exercise the diligence of innumerable antiquarians, and to exercise the genius and penetration of the philosophic historians of our own times."[36] His writings "will instruct the last generations of mankind."[37] The author in question is, of course, Tacitus himself.

We may thus conclude that Gibbon's indebtedness to the classics was not merely formal or stylistic; to a very considerable extent it was ideological; his reading served to color the very substance of his thought, imparting to it much of its characteristically secularist quality. He can thus repeat with sympathy, if with certain qualifications, the classical thesis that the "greatness of Rome was founded on the rare and almost incredible alliance of virtue and fortune,"[38] or pride himself on what he calls "my impartial balance of the virtues and vices of Julian."[39] And herein we may discern the true relationship of Gibbon with the earlier Renaissance tradition of historiography, represented by Machiavelli (which has been emphasized and, indeed, exaggerated by Christopher Dawson). Not that Gibbon consciously and deliberately imitated Machiavelli, though indeed he had read his work and for some time contemplated writing himself on the same theme, the history of Florence. It was merely that he and the Renaissance historians had quarried largely from the same mine. The concepts of interpretation

---

34. Gibbon, *Decline and Fall*, 1:167.
35. Ibid., 1:414.
36. Ibid., 1:167.
37. Ibid., 1:250.
38. Ibid., 2:964.
39. Gibbon, *Miscellaneous Works*, 100–101.

which they utilized were thus formally identical; the difference lay in the significance to be attached to those concepts by Gibbon's day.

III

It is evident from the *Memoirs* that Gibbon subjected himself to an intense and widely diversified discipline in modern literature. To mention the names of but a few men whose work had a direct bearing on his future as an historian, there were Voltaire in France, author of the famous *Siècle de Louis XIV*, and, in England, Robertson and Hume. Of Voltaire and his influence, Gibbon has nothing significant to report, although there are obvious parallels between the two writers. For example, Gibbon's well-known characterization of history as "little more than a register of the crimes, follies and misfortunes of mankind,"[40] is a literal translation from Voltaire's "*un ramas de crimes, de folies et de malheurs.*" On the other hand, the performance of the Scottish historians obviously affected him deeply. "I will assume the presumption of saying," he declares, "that I was not unworthy to read them; nor will I disguise my different feelings in the repeated perusals. The perfect composition, the nervous language, the well-turned periods of Dr. Robertson, inflamed me to the ambition that I might one day tread in his footsteps; the calm philosophy, the careless, inimitable beauties of his friend and rival often forced me to close the volume with a mixed sensation of delight and despair."[41]

There is still another name that should be mentioned, one to whom Gibbon repeatedly alludes as "a celebrated writer of our times." In 1734 Montesquieu had published his *Considérations sur les causes de la grandeur des Romains et de leur décadence*. This work may be regarded as, in certain important aspects, an anticipation, almost indeed a *précis*, of Gibbon's *Decline and Fall*. The theme is identical; so also, in general, is the method of treatment. In his *Universal History* Bossuet, speaking in theological terms, had explained the collapse of Rome as a judgment of God on the sinful pride of mankind and on his claim to independence and self-sufficiency. Montesquieu, on the contrary, following the line taken by Machiavelli in his *Discourses on Livy*, secularized the issue, which he made to depend on the strictly human qualities of virtue and vice. Thus, for him, the greatness of Rome was due to the insight of her early legislators, the practical wisdom of the Senate, the excellence of the citizen body; her decline, to the inordinate growth of the state, to Asiatic luxury, to civil discord, to the frightful tyranny

---

40. Gibbon, *Decline and Fall*, 1:60.
41. Gibbon, *Miscellaneous Works*, 55.

of her earlier emperors, and the sloth, rapacity and bigotry of those who succeeded Constantine.

It is hardly necessary to dwell on the analogy between the point of view here indicated and that of Gibbon in the *Decline and Fall*. Of many possible illustrations, I shall cite but two. The first is Montesquieu's characterization of the Emperor Augustus as a *rusé tyran*, who gently led his people into servitude. With this we may compare Gibbon on the same subject. "A cool head, an unfeeling heart, and a cowardly disposition, prompted him at the age of nineteen to assume the mask of hypocrisy, which he never afterwards laid aside . . . His virtues, and even his vices, were artificial; and, according to the various dictates of his interest, he was at first the enemy, and at the last the father, of the Roman world . . . His moderation was inspired by his fears. He wished to deceive the people by an image of civil liberty, and the armies by an image of civil government."[42] My second illustration is the estimate (now recognized to be in many respects false) of Byzantine history as "a tedious and uniform tale of weakness and misery."[43] In this phrase, Gibbon merely reproduces Montesquieu's judgment regarding the weakness of the Eastern Empire, which he ascribes to universal bigotry, gross superstition, profound ignorance, and the chronic religious dissension which vitiated political life.

To say that Montesquieu attributes the greatness and decline of Rome to moral causes is not, in itself, enough to distinguish him from a Christian writer like Bossuet. The question is rather what standard of moral values he invokes. And this may be readily identified. It is the standard put forward by classical *scientia*; and it comes directly from his classical authorities, Polybius, Livy and, above all, perhaps, Tacitus in his famous indictment of the Caesars. So far as Gibbon reproduces these judgments, it is because his are derived from the same source.

In considering the *Esprit des lois* and its possible influence upon Gibbon, we cannot, however, be satisfied with this simple explanation but must go a step further. *L'Esprit des lois*, published by Montesquieu fourteen years after his *Considérations*, marks a clear advance upon his earlier thinking and, quite as clearly, ranks as a landmark in social studies. Of this advance the author himself was fully conscious, as is evident from the words in which he records his sense of its importance:

> Many times I began, and many times I abandoned this work; a thousand times I flung to the winds the pages I had written . . . I followed my purpose without forming any design; I understood

42. Gibbon, *Decline and Fall*, 1:55.
43. Ibid., 2:1604.

neither the rules nor the exceptions; I found the truth only to lose it again. But, when I once discovered my principles, everything that I was looking for came to me and, in the course of twenty years, I saw my work begin, grow, advance and come to an end . . . I first examined men, and reached the conclusion that, in the infinite variety of their laws and customs, they were not guided only by their fancies . . . I laid down my principles and saw . . . the histories of all nations as nothing but consequences of them, each particular law relating to another law, or dependent on another of greater generality . . . I drew my principles, not from my prejudices, but from the nature of things.[44]

What were those principles which, in the opinion of Montesquieu, made all the difference between success and failure? Montesquieu's "discovery" was that, while law in general may be described as human reason, so far as reason governs the peoples of the earth, positive law, the actual civil and political code of any particular nation, is nothing but an application of this reason to a particular set of circumstances. Such a code must therefore bear a definite relation to the physical features of the country, to its climate, be it cold, hot or temperate, and to the prevalent mode of life, whether agricultural, hunting or pastoral; it must be related to the degree of freedom permitted by the constitution, to the religion of the inhabitants, their inclinations, their wealth, their numbers, their commerce, their manners and customs. Finally, the individual laws must have a mutual inter-connection, in keeping with their origin, with the intent of the legislator, and with the material order in relation to which they are established. The task, then, is to examine all these relationships, which together form an *ensemble* that may be designated *l' esprit des lois*.

If this be Montesquieu's "discovery," it is perhaps not quite as original as he imagined; for both the method and its application had been clearly anticipated in antiquity. It is to be seen in certain early documents of the Hippocratic corpus, especially the treatises on *Ancient Medicine* and *Airs, Waters, Places*; the former is a plea for a rejection of what the writer calls the general, in favor of specific hypotheses subject to observation and verification; the latter, a study of environment as a factor conditioning an illustration of the results to be achieved by applying the Hippocratic method to the interpretation of history. To satisfy oneself of this, all that is required is to study the introductory chapters of Thucydides's first book. But there is no direct reference in Montesquieu either to Hippocrates or Thucydides. We may therefore conclude that he was ignorant of those writers, unless,

---

44. Montesquieu, *Spirit of the Laws*, xlv; [Cochrane's translation].

indeed, he deliberately concealed his obligation to them. On the other hand, it is evident that he had read Aristotle's *Politics*, certain passages of which are clearly animated by the Hippocratic spirit; for example, the classification of societies on a vocational basis. Yet he seldom refers to Aristotle, and then only to point to his deficiencies. In this way he testifies to the effectiveness of the blow struck by Bacon against the Aristotelian system a century before.

We have already referred to the work of Bacon in stimulating investigation into nature upon empirical and utilitarian lines and to its first fruits in the Newtonian cosmology, a universe of matter-in-motion governed by mechanical and, therefore, mathematically calculable law. We have seen, also, how Locke made use of the "experimental method" in order to lay the foundation for an analogous science of the human mind. The new method was to carry all before it. Thus, already by 1748 we find Montesquieu, under the inspiration of "experimental science," declaring that "man, considered as a physical being, is like other bodies in nature, governed by invariable laws; while, as an intelligent being, he constantly violates the laws that God has established and changes those which he establishes himself."[45] On the assumption that human beings, by virtue of their intelligence, are capable of a limited freedom, Montesquieu proceeds to build up his account of law, clearing the ground for a vision of civilization as a conquest of the outer or physical by the inner or moral environment. For though, he argues, the empire of climate is the first of all empires, its dominion is absolute only over savages. In civilized society its power is disputed and, in some degree, neutralized by the moral forces of religion, law, policy tradition, custom, and habit; and these forces, while no doubt generated in response to physical demands, combine to form the "general spirit" of a people and therewith its norms or conventions, the institutions characteristic of a developed social and political order. Accordingly, those institutions are to be explained, not logically (in the light of *a priori* considerations) but historically, i.e., by the "historical, plain method" of Locke, as a consequence of impulses discernible within the minds and hearts of men, such, for example, as fear (the basis of Oriental despotism), honor (Teutonic monarchy) or "virtue" (Greco-Roman republicanism).

But if the new instrument, thus applied to social study, made possible the solution of certain problems, it did so only by creating others not less serious. To what purpose, for instance, was the new cosmology substituted for the traditional Christian picture of a providential order, if it was only to revive, in a new and more terrible form, the ancient Kingdom of Zeus or "natural necessity?" Montesquieu was fully alive to the difficulty, and

---

45. Ibid., 5; [Cochrane's translation].

he confronted it boldly, even if to solve it he had to resort to dogmatism. "It is the height of absurdity," he protests, "to suppose that a blind fatality has produced all that we see in the world."[46] The denial of fate was, at the same time, a denial of fortuity. "Fortune," he declares, "is not mistress of the world";[47] if she has any reality, it is merely as a function of natural (physical and moral) law; from this standpoint, her relationship is that of the particular to the general, as when, for example, a commander wins successive battles only in the end to lose the campaign. In these protests we may discern the attempt of neo-classical science to escape from the implications of its own philosophic starting-point. But its effort to do so was destined to be fruitless until at length it found a way out of the impasse in the skepticism of Hume.

It is apparent from evidence, both direct and indirect, that Gibbon was a close student of Montesquieu, and particularly of *L'Esprit des lois*. Accordingly, there is some danger of exaggerating its influence upon him. We find it difficult to subscribe to the verdict of the French editor (Paris, 1876) when he asserts that Gibbon's work is little more than a paraphrase of Montesquieu's concluding chapters. For us the real interest and importance of *L'Esprit des lois* is that it exhibits the results of Montesquieu's quest for a fresh principle of understanding. It is hardly less significant that he discovers this principle in "experimental science." The relationship of Gibbon to Montesquieu is primarily internal: it lies in the presumptions of a logic which they hold in common. This being so, it is not surprising that they should display a similar attitude in dealing with their material or that their conclusions should, broadly speaking, be similar. Otherwise, the chief significance of Montesquieu, as an influence upon Gibbon, is that he raised certain questions which Gibbon thought it necessary to answer. But, in order to find the requisite answers, Gibbon had to look further afield until, as we shall see, he discovered them in Hume.

The first of such questions concerns liberty and necessity, the problem of free human activity in a mechanically ordered world. This is a problem which, as we have seen, Montesquieu raised but did not solve, or rather perhaps rose only to dismiss as absurd. His interest is entirely in the empirical freedoms, and his one direct reference to what he calls philosophic liberty is to define it as the exercise of the will or, at any rate, the notion that the will is exercised. But the problem was not to be evaded in such cavalier fashion. Hume's solution was to by-pass the ancient philosophic dualism by

---

46. Ibid., 3; [Cochrane's translation].
47. Montesquieu, *Political Theory of Montesquieu*, 164; [Cochrane's translation].

exposing "the narrow extent of science when applied to material causes."[48] "Our idea of necessity and causation," he declares, "arises entirely out of the uniformity observable in the operations of nature, where similar objects are constantly conjoined together, and the mind is determined by custom to infer the one from the appearance of the other."[49] "Beyond the constant conjunction of similar objects, and the constant inference from one to the other, we have no notion of any necessity or connection."[50] Thus did philosophic skepticism cut the Gordian knot and make possible the undiluted humanism of the Age of Reason.

To reject as spurious the classical concept of physical necessity was at the same time to reject its correlate, the classical concept of freedom, regarded as the special power of a spiritual agent to effect results independently of the laws of nature. It was thus, as Hume saw it, a "reconciling project," designed to make possible a science of human nature possessing precisely "the same accuracy of which the several parts of natural philosophy are susceptible."[51] The possibility of such a science rests, he thought, on the uniformities exhibited in human behavior in all nations and ages, and these uniformities he explained as the result of a constant number of psychological impulses, "ambition, avarice, self-love, vanity, friendship, generosity, public spirit":

> These passions, mixed in various degrees, and distributed throughout society have been, and still are, the source of all the actions and enterprises which have been observed among mankind. Would you know the sentiments, inclinations and course of life of the Greeks and Romans? Study well the temper and actions of the French and English: you cannot be much mistaken in transferring to the former most of the observations which you have made with regard to the latter. Mankind is so much the same in all times and places, that history inform us of nothing new or strange in this particular. Its chief use is only to discover the constant and universal principles of human nature, by showing men in all varieties of circumstances and situations, and furnishing us with materials from which we may form our observations and become acquainted with the regular springs of human action and behaviour. These records of wars, intrigues, factions and revolutions, are so many collections of *experiments*, by which the politician or moral philosopher fixes the principles

---

48. Hume, *Philosophical Works*, 392.
49. Ibid., 97.
50. Ibid.
51. Hume, *Abstract of a Treatise on Human Nature*, 6.

of his science, in the same manner as the physician or the natural philosopher becomes acquainted with the nature of plants, minerals, and other external objects, by the *experiments* which he forms concerning them.[52]

So much for the science of human nature, considered as mere description, where all we note is the "constant conjunction" of "actions" with their "proper motives"; but this is important, for on it is founded "our belief in witnesses, our credit in history, and indeed all kinds of moral evidence, and almost the whole conduct of life."[53]

The description of human nature is, however, merely the first step in Hume's "attempt to introduce the experimental method of reasoning into moral subjects." The next question is whether, by following this method, it is possible to arrive at norms or principles of conduct. This question Hume undertakes to solve in his second *Enquiry*. Two problems arise: (1) as to the genesis and nature of the moral sentiments, (2) as to the moral imperative, the "obligation," as he says, "to be virtuous."[54] There is no need to follow his argument in detail. Regarding (1), the moral sentiments, it will be sufficient to recall that he bases morality upon the sentiments of benevolence and self-love which enter into the constitution of human nature, and that he regards these sentiments as universal. "The sentiments which arise from humanity, are not only the same in all human creatures, and produce the same approbation or censure; but they also comprehend all human creatures, nor is there anyone whose conduct or character is not, by their means, an object to everyone of censure or approbation."[55] "Virtue and vice thus become known; morals are recognized; certain general ideas are framed of human conduct and behavior; such measures are expected from men in such situations."[56] "And these principles . . . are social and universal."[57] In civilized man, as opposed to the savage, they are merely generalized. "They form, in a manner, the party of human kind, against vice and disorder, its common enemy,"[58] although, to become effective, they must often be reinforced by the love of fame. And as for (2), the obligation to be virtuous, it

---

52. Hume, *Philosophical Works*, 98.

53. Hume, "Abstract of a Treatise of Human Nature" in *An Enquiry Concerning Human Understanding*, 137.

54. Hume, "An Enquiry Concerning the Principles of Morals," in *Moral Philosophy*, 264.

55. Ibid., 260.

56. Hume, *Philosophical Works*, 342.

57. Ibid., 343.

58. Ibid.

depends upon what Hume calls "just calculation and a steady preference for the greater happiness."[59] This preference is natural since "in all ingenuous natures, the antipathy to treachery and roguery is too strong to be counterbalanced by any views of profit or pecuniary advantage. Inward peace of mind, consciousness of integrity, a satisfactory review of our own conducts; these are circumstances very requisite to happiness, and will be cherished and cultivated by every honest man."[60] He continues: "the hypothesis which we embrace is plain. It maintains that morality is determined by sentiment. It defines virtue to be whatever mental action or quality gives to a spectator the pleasing sentiment of approbation; and vice, the contrary."[61] And in this, the moral judgment, "the distinct boundaries and offices of reason and of taste are easily ascertained. The former conveys the knowledge of truth or falsehood, the latter gives the sentiment of beauty and deformity, vice and virtue."[62] Finally, the whole position is recommended in what must seem to the modern reader strange terms: "To be a philosophic sceptic is, in a man of letters, the first and most essential step toward being a sound, believing Christian."[63]

If it was the sight of the "bare-footed friars singing vespers in the temple of Jupiter" which provided Gibbon with his impulse of curiosity, it was his study of authors like Locke and Montesquieu which led him to formulate as he did the issue so vividly and (to him) so distressingly illustrated by that incredible spectacle.[64] That issue, as he sees it, is one of revolution, "the memorable series of revolutions by which . . . the solid fabric of human greatness was undermined and, at length, destroyed."[65] But, in his attempt to resolve this issue, Gibbon enjoyed the benefit of assistance which had been denied to any of his predecessors. For, if Locke had forged the "universal instrument," if Montesquieu had demonstrated its value as a method of social study, it had remained for Hume to exploit its full possibilities as the basis for a systematic philosophy of human nature. Now, in his essay on the study of literature, Gibbon had asserted that the historian should be, in the best sense of the word, a philosopher, because the first qualification for his task is the power of perceiving the relative importance of facts. And, thereby,

---

59. Hume, "An Enquiry Concerning the Principles of Morals," in *Moral Philosophy*, 264.

60. Ibid. 267.

61. Ibid., 270.

62. Ibid., 274.

63. Hume, *Dialogues Concerning Natural Religion*, 89.

64. Gibbon, *Miscellaneous Works*, 82.

65. Gibbon, *Decline and Fall*, 1:lvi.

he perhaps forecast his own future as the Tacitus of the modern world. But if the need for philosophy is the need of a principle of discrimination, Gibbon found this in the work of a man whose mere letter of congratulation upon the publication of his first volume more than repaid him (as he proudly confesses) for the labors of ten years. In spirit and content, the philosophy of the modern Tacitus was to be that of the skeptical philosopher, Hume. And by accepting the findings of philosophic skepticism, he was enabled to put forward his views and conclusions as scientific fact without even the suspicion that he was dogmatizing. To these facts we may ascribe all that has come to be regarded as most characteristic of Gibbon. On it the strength and weakness of his interpretation depend.

The Mind of Edward Gibbon (II)[66]

In the former of these two articles, we examined the intellectual history of Edward Gibbon in order to discover the influences which contributed to inform his mind and thus equip him for his task as author of the *Decline and Fall*. We tried to estimate his obligations to the Greek and Latin classics and to modern literature, particularly the literature of eighteenth-century thought. The result was to show that, while the development of Gibbon's genius was by no means narrow or one-sided, there was one element which predominated in his intellectual discipline, and it was this which colored, even if it did not wholly dictate, his appreciation of the issue. Gibbon wrote in the spirit and with the resources of philosophic skepticism. It was as a philosophic skeptic that he embarked on his investigation and that he reached his final verdict in the words: "I have described the triumph of barbarism and religion."[67] Accordingly, the next step must be to consider how the skeptical philosophy is applied by Gibbon, and to examine its value as a principle of historical interpretation. We shall begin by raising at once the vexed question of Gibbon's attitude to Christianity.

IV

It is a mistake to suppose, with certain of his critics, that the animus of Gibbon is directed against the church rather than the faith, against historical Christianity but not against the Evangel of Christ. True indeed, he opens his

---

66. [This second part of the essay was published as Charles Norris Cochrane, "The Mind of Edward Gibbon (II)." *University of Toronto Quarterly* 12.2 (1942–43) 146–66.]

67. Gibbon, *Decline and Fall*, 3:2431.

polemic in the celebrated fifteenth and sixteenth chapters by distinguishing between "the pure and humble religion" of the Founder on the one hand and on the other "the inevitable mixture of error and corruption which it contracted in a long residence upon earth among a weak and degenerate race of beings."[68] This, however, is merely a debater's expedient calculated to mask the force of the attack and, if possible, to turn the flank of the defense. In a famous observation on the pagan cults Gibbon had remarked that to the people they were equally true, to the philosopher equally false, and to the politician equally useful. He thus stigmatized them for their purely pragmatic character in a spirit which would have been agreeable to Augustine himself; for it is precisely this charge that Augustine levels against paganism. But while, even for enlightened pagans, the important thing about a god was not his reality but the reality of his cult ("the will to believe"), the Christian on the other hand claimed allegiance for his religion first and foremost because he held it to be true. For him, as distinguished from his pagan contemporaries, everything therefore depended upon the existence of the Deity whom he worshipped, a Deity whom he put forward as *summa substantia*, the "cause" of all being, all order and all life or process in the universe. This claim skepticism rejected, by denying to the concept of substance (whether material or immaterial) any intelligible meaning, and by resolving the concept of cause into a mere inference based on the observable uniformities of sensible phenomena, in the words of Hume, "a native determination of the mind itself to find in the future the same pattern as we have witnessed in our past experience" and thus dependent entirely upon the so-called laws of association, the resemblance, contiguity and constant conjunction of events.[69] This, obviously, was to cut at the very root of Christian faith. Hence, for those like Gibbon, who accepted the skeptical philosophy, that faith took rank as just another variant in the endless series of delusions to which the human spirit was prone; to be accounted for as a product of fear and credulity on the one hand and, on the other, the machinations of designing priests and statesmen who used and abused it as, alternatively, the opiate or stimulant of the masses.

Accordingly, Gibbon's attitude is to be understood, not as the consequence of a "permanent mental lesion" suffered during the spiritual crisis of his adolescence, but rather as an expression of righteous indignation on the part of a thoroughly honest man against what he conceived to be an amalgam of hypocrisy and fraud—a man, however, who was totally unconscious that his own vision was clouded and, we may add, distorted by the spectacles

---

68. Ibid., 1:348.
69. Cf. Hume, *Treatise of Human Nature*, 99.

he wore. In saying this, I do not for a moment question the significance of the religious crisis as a contributing factor. Doubtless it played its part in bringing Gibbon into line with the dominant intellectual tendencies of his day. But I insist that what he thought as an adult was at least as decisive in shaping his attitude as anything that may have happened to his nerves in boyhood—nerves which, by the way, seem to have been thoroughly sound throughout his life. "I believed as I still believe," he wrote, "that the propagation of the Gospel, and the triumph of the church, is inseparably connect with the decline of the Empire."[70]

For a characteristic expression of the skeptical attitude, we need only refer to Hume's essay on the *Natural History of Religions*. The title itself indicates a fresh approach to the question of religious phenomena. Philosophic skepticism looks at them all with equal detachment, and it brands them indiscriminately as manifestations of the sub-rational in human nature, as pathological or animal and, thus, hardly to be understood. As Hume quite simply was to put it: "the whole is a riddle, an enigma, an inexplicable mystery," to be accounted for only as a disease of the human mind.[71] "Examine the religious opinions which have, in fact, prevailed over the world. You will scarcely be persuaded that they are anything more than sick-men's dreams. Or perhaps you will regard them more as the playsome whimsies of monkeys in human shape than the serious, positive, dogmatic asseverations of a being who dignifies himself with the name of rational."[72]

Accordingly, it is not surprising that the attitude of the modern Tacitus towards the Christians differs little from that of his ancient counterpart towards the Bacchanalian conspirators of 184 BC. Thus, while applauding the general spirit of toleration prevalent within the empire, he justifies the exceptional restrictions imposed upon the faithful, on the ground that they were a subversive element in the community. In this he is not, as has recently been argued, disingenuous. He merely reflects the prejudice of philosophical skepticism, as will be evident to anyone who considers Hume's enquiry into morals and the secularization of ethical values to which it points. The values therein put forward, while claiming to be universal, were in fact merely cosmopolitan, the product of "reason and taste," the reason and taste of the eighteenth century. In applying them as he does, Gibbon associates himself with the enlightenment in its effort to "wipe out the infamy," and all the evidence he accumulated of evils within the ancient church) of which there were admittedly many) is just so much grist to the mill. His Christian

---

70. Gibbon, *Miscellaneous Works*, 89.
71. Hume, "Natural History of Religion," in *David Hume on Religion*, 95.
72. Ibid., 94.

antagonists, on the other hand, were quite justified in their instinctive revulsion from his work. What is distressing to a student of the so-called Gibbon controversy is that the opposition they put up was so weak as to deserve Gibbon's contempt. The trouble was that they wasted their strength in attacking secondary objectives such as the historicity of miracles, while wholly neglecting the central question of Gibbon's logic, upon which the issue ultimately depended. The reason for this was that their thinking was governed by an ideology not so remote after all from Gibbon's own, an ideology which was to fill the churches of contemporary England with statues of generals and admirals in place of saints, and to cover the walls with tablets commemorating their largely secular virtues.

V

Christianity presents itself to Gibbon as a type, perhaps the most formidable type, of superstition; and this apparently with little or no sense of its relatively pure and innocuous character in a society filled with the grossest and most shocking forms of pagan *religio*. Our concern is not, however, to institute any comparison between pagan and Christian standards of life or thought, but merely to discover what Gibbon means by superstition. To him superstition was not, as it was for the Christians, the prostitution of the mind and heart to its own fancies (*fantastica fornicatio*). It was rather a resurgence of the infantile and bestial in human nature against the domination of the mind. From this standpoint, it emerged as the monstrous offspring of ignorance, credulity, fanaticism and obstinacy; in other words, as a reversion to barbarism, which we must now briefly discuss.

Gibbon's picture of barbarism, unlike that of the Romantics, involves no idealization of the noble savage. On the contrary, it hardly rises, at any rate on the lowest plane, above the life of animality. "In this primitive and abject condition [Gibbon is speaking of the savages on the Red Sea coast], which ill deserves the name of society, the human brute, without arts or laws, almost without sense or language, is poorly distinguished from the rest of animal creation." Even time, which counts for so much in the life of civilized society, is quite devoid of significance: "Generations and ages might roll away in silent oblivion and the helpless savage was restrained from multiplying his race by the wants and pursuits which confined his existence."[73]

In general, then, the savage or barbarian (Gibbon hardly troubles to distinguish between them) emerges as the hapless victim of natural forces which serve to condition and qualify his existence. How they do so may be

---

73. Gibbon, *Decline and Fall*, 3:1720.

seen from his pages on the Germans and the Scyths. In either case the ultimate determinant is physical and such characteristic differences as manifest themselves in Germanic and Scythian ways of life are thought to depend upon this fact. Thus, for example, the German land is one of great rivers, deep and impenetrable forests, intense and prolonged cold. In the entire world, opines Gibbon, there is nothing like it except, perhaps, Canada. Amid these conditions the German tribes sustain themselves in palisade villages sparsely located in occasional clearings of the forest. The question is: how do these conditions affect their life?

In depicting the Germanic way of life, Gibbon strikes three notes. The first is one of inconsistency. Against a background of drudgery on the part of wives and captives, the old and the weak, appears the lazy warrior, "at once the most indolent and most restless of mankind," seeking either "self-effacing oblivion" in drink and gambling or self-expression, "a more lively sense of his existence," through the violent exercise and violent emotion of waging war.[74] The second note struck is that of improvidence, in which liberty is confused with license, "freedom is gratifying present passion, courage in overlooking all future consequences."[75] Thus incapable of prudence, the German is still less capable of philosophy. Accordingly, as the third note of his life, he is exposed to the "blind terrors of superstition."[76] "As for their religious system, if the wild opinions of savages can deserve that name, it is dictated by their wants, their fears and their ignorance."[77]

By contrast with primitive Germanism, Gibbon offers a quite different picture of the Scyths, though here again the determinants are the same. The mark of Scythian life is a dull uniformity, determined physically by the great open spaces, and it finds expression on the plane of instinct rather than of reason. "The operation of instinct," says Gibbon,

> is more sure and simple than that of reason . . . and the savage tribes of mankind, as they approach nearer to the condition of animals, preserve a stronger resemblance both to them and to each other. The uniform stability of their manners is the natural consequence of the imperfection of their faculties [i.e., the faculties have no chance to develop in such conditions]. Reduced to a similar situation, their wants, their desires, their enjoyments still continue the same; and the influence of food or climate, which in a more improved state of society is suspended or subdued by

74. Ibid., 1:173.
75. Ibid., 1:176.
76. Ibid., 1:180.
77. Ibid., 1:179.

so many moral causes, most forcefully contributes to form and to maintain the national character.[78]

But if this is barbarism, what is civilization? For answer, we shall once more quote the words of Gibbon himself: "The different characters that mark the civilized nations of the globe may be variously ascribed to the use and abuse of reason, which so variously shapes, and so artificially composes, the manners and opinions of a European or a Chinese."[79] And again: "In a civilized state every faculty of man is expanded and exercised, and the great chain of mutual dependence connects and embraces the several members of society. The most numerous portion of it is employed in constant and useful labor. The select few, placed by fortune above the necessity, can however fill up their time by the pursuit of interest or glory, by the improvement of their estate or their understanding, by the duties, the pleasures, or even the follies of social life."[80] A genuinely civilized order is an order which makes this liberty and this diversity possible, by guaranteeing them alike against the subversive forces of anarchy and despotism.

Gibbon's notion of civilized order is thus utterly static and immobile; in this respect, it falls little short of the ideals of classicism put forward by the political theorists of antiquity. "Such is the constitution of civil society," he writes, "that, whilst a few persons are distinguished by riches, by honors, and by knowledge, the body of the people is condemned to obscurity, ignorance and poverty."[81] And again:

> Most of the crimes which disturb the internal peace of society are produced by the restraints which the necessary, but unequal, laws of property have imposed on the appetites of mankind, by confining to a few the possessions of those objects which are coveted by many. Of all our passions and appetites, the love of power is the most imperious and unsociable nature, since the pride of one man requires the submission of the multitude. In the tumult of civil discord the laws of society lose their force, and their place is seldom supplied by those of humanity. The ardour of contention, the pride of victory, the despair of success, the memory of past injuries and the fear of future dangers, all contribute to inflame the mind and to silence the voice of

---

78. Ibid., 1:792–93.
79. Ibid., 1:792.
80. Ibid., 1:173.
81. Ibid., 1:396.

pity. From such motives almost every page of history has been stained with civil blood.[82]

For Gibbon the life of civilization is the life of virtue; its antithesis (superstition or barbarism) is vice. Accordingly, the qualities of the virtuous man are political and social; and (as he puts it in his notes for a revision of the first volume of the *Decline and Fall*):

> The first place in the hall of fame is due and assigned to the successful heroes who had struggled in adversity; who after signalizing their valour in the deliverance of their country, have displayed their wisdom and virtue in the foundation or government of a flourishing state. Such men were Moses, Cyrus, Alfred, Gustavus Vasa, Henry IV of France, etc., and, in Rome, perhaps above all others, Trajan. The thirst of military glory will ever be the vice of the most exalted minds. Late generations and far distant climates may impute their calamities to the immortal author of the *Iliad*. The spirit of Alexander was inflamed by the praises of Achilles; and succeeding heroes have been ambitious to tread in Alexander's footsteps. Like him Trajan aspired for the conquest of the East.[83]

To see virtue with Gibbon as the life of civilization is to see also what he means by vice or degeneracy. Accordingly, we need hardly labor the point. I should like, however, to call attention to one conspicuous example, as it appears in the picture of the Emperor Commodus, son and successor to Marcus Aurelius, the "philosopher-king." It is clear that, to the historian, this example must have been of crucial significance since he takes the accession of Commodus to the purple as the starting-point for the long agony of the decline and fall.

To Gibbon, as to his ancient authorities, Commodus represents the very embodiment of classical vice, and therefore everything to be deprecated in what has apologetically been called "the weaker and darker side" of the classical world; and this despite "the anxious care of a father" to render him worthy of his destiny, "the fond partiality of a parent for the worthless boy to whose monstrous vices of avarice, cruelty and lust he was to sacrifice the happiness of millions."[84] We need not linger over the historian's picture of the Roman Hercules, burlesquing in the arena all that was sacred in the Antonine ideal of public service, the tyrant whose murder was to be hailed

---

82. Ibid., 1:66.

83. "Marginal Notes" from Gibbon's 2nd edition of *The Decline and Fall*, in Bury, 1900 ed. "Introduction," xxxvi.

84. Gibbon, *Decline and Fall*, 1:66.

in the Senate with "effusions of impotent rage," a son so utterly unlike his father that the authors of the *Augustan History* took refuge in the theory that he must be illegitimate and "explained" him in terms of the gallantries of his mother, the Empress Faustina.

The point of Gibbon's criticism will be clearer if we set it over against an interpretation recently offered by another and quite different authority, Dr. Wilhelm Weber, Professor of Ancient History in the University of Berlin. Weber begins by contrasting the characters of Commodus and Marcus. It was the destiny of Commodus, he declares, to disrupt the concept of world harmony for which his father stood, a harmony based upon the universality of mind, "the commonwealth of reasoning men," and to reveal the *virtus Augusti* in a novel and startling light: as a "life lived beyond the world of reason, compounded of the potencies of the body, of instinct and of imagination."[85] This life the historian puts forward as an escape from "the anemic intellectualism of classical society"; and he pronounces it truly creative, pointing the way to a new order, an order founded on "provincialism, militarism and barbarism," according to a logic which "was deeply rooted in the aspirations of the age and, therefore, genuine."[86] As the embodiment of such a logic, the Emperor, "unchecked though he was by any laws of morality, without care whether fair boys or women served his appetites, whether he shed the blood of strangers or of his own kin, breaking any fetters that could enchain him, yet felt himself without guilt or stain, the source of all piety and the creator of all happiness."[87] This was to repudiate and reject the classical ideal of *humanitas* and, therewith, of its corollary *civilitas*, the attitude proper to a citizen in relations to his fellows. It was to substitute for classical *humanitas* a new ideal of *humilitas* or self-abasement, the abasement of the Emperor before the "Most High God" of his imagination, and of all others before the Emperor as the earthly counterpart of this "Most High God." By classical standards the man who proposed such a program would have been deemed guilty of *hybris* or *adrogantia* and thus richly deserving the fate which overtook him. Yet the memory of the Emperor, though it suffered a temporary eclipse with his assassination, was presently to be rehabilitated in the apotheosis he received as *Divus Commodus*, and he was to be hailed as, in truth, "the rising sun of a new world."[88]

The interpretation thus offered contains elements of the fantastic. It exalts the very features of human nature which Gibbon condemns, "the vital

---

85. Weber, "Antonines," 392.
86. Ibid., 389.
87. Ibid., 392.
88. Ibid.

impulses" as opposed to the "life of reason," and to those impulses it ascribes genuine creativity. For it the promise of humanity is fulfilled in the release of vagrant emotions and passions which are identified as a counterpart in the human psyche to the *hormé* operating in the physical world, and it claims that by such release the life of man is "attuned" to the life or movement of nature. Yet despite the exaggeration with which it is put forward, the point of view is not without significance. It had the merit of directing attention to certain aspects of human nature which were persistently ignored or misunderstood by rationalism, whether of the classical or of the neo-classical type. This will be evident when we consider Gibbon's account of the decline and fall and the theory of human nature on which it is based.

VI

We are now in a position to examine Gibbon's work in its deeper and more universal significance, i.e., as illustrating his views regarding the problem of causation in history. And this, incidentally, will serve to reveal his attitude to contemporary civilization, its position and prospects, especially in relation to current ideas of human progress and perfectibility.

The problem is the eclipse of the Roman Empire; *the locus classicus*, the famous appendix to chapter XXXVIII, "General Observations on the Fall of the Roman Empire in the West."[89] To look at this passage is to discover, in the first place, that the historian finds nothing for astonishment in that catastrophe. "The story of its ruin," he declares, "is simple and obvious, and instead of inquiring why it was destroyed, we should rather be surprised that it subsisted so long."[90] He claims, "The decline of Rome was the natural and inevitable result of immoderate greatness."[91] At this last phrase, the reader may, perhaps, rub his eyes. Does it imply, he may ask, a lurking faith in the existence of some principle of limitation hidden in nature, whether conceived theologically like the *nemesis* of the Athenian dramatists, or mechanically, like the law of *tisis* (action and reaction) invoked by Heraclitus and Herodotus? The answer is that it does not. True to the spirit of skepticism, Gibbon proceeds at once to translate his principle of decline into intelligible terms by resolving it into terms of "physical" and "moral" causation. Of purely physical causes, the skeptical philosopher has little to say beyond qualifying his findings, in the manner and language of Hume, by the significant admission that they are valid so long as the face

---

89. Gibbon, *Decline and Fall*, 2:1218–25.
90. Ibid., 2:1219–20.
91. Ibid., 2:1219.

of nature remains the same.[92] In a similar spirit, he rejects the notion of Fortune, at any rate in the sense that this was conceived by the obscurantists of classical antiquity. With these provisos, he turns to moral causes for his real explanation. "The historian," he observes, "may content himself with the observation which seems to be justified by experience, that man has much more to fear from the passions of his fellow-creatures than from the convulsions of the elements."[93] (Was he thinking of the Lisbon earthquake and Voltaire's *Candide*?) This being admitted, what moral causes, apart from the discarded notion of original and actual sin, can he make use of?

There is no need to embark on any lengthy discussion of the moral values of philosophic skepticism and the Age of Reason. It will be sufficient to recall that those values were wholly mundane, and thus, as in Gibbon's own case, beautifully epitomized in his famous characterization of the Antonine Age as "the happiest and most prosperous period in the history of the human race."[94] The predilections of Gibbon were, in this respect, strongly supported by Hume himself, in his contemptuous repudiation of "monkish virtues" as inconsistent with the ideas of men of sense who "judge of things by their natural, unprejudiced reason without the delusive glosses of superstition."[95] Hume thus denounces as vices "celibacy, fasting, penance, mortification, self-denial, humility, silence, solitude," since these have no real utility or social purpose.[96] "A gloomy, hair-brained enthusiast," he concludes, "may after his death have a place in the calendar, but will scarcely ever be admitted when alive into intimacy and society, except by those who are as delirious and dismal as himself."[97] Such were the sentiments of the master; readers of Gibbon will remember how faithfully they are echoed in his work.

We may thus perceive how the method of experimental science serves to determine the issue raised by the collapse of antiquity; to the eye of science, that issue inevitably presents itself as one between "vice" and "virtue," and these in turn, by an identification equally obvious, are equated respectively with barbarism and civilization. And this is precisely the mode in which it is envisaged by Gibbon.

---

92. Ibid., 2:1225.
93. Ibid., 1:792.
94. Ibid., 1:61.
95. Hume, "Enquiry Concerning the Principles of Morals," in *Moral Philosophy*, 258.
96. Ibid.
97. Ibid.

To formulate the issue as Gibbon does is largely to determine its solution. For this purpose, indeed, all that is needed is to put the argument into reverse. In other words, if civilized order be identified with the rule of reason, then its collapse may be explained quite simply as an abdication of reason from the seat of power, its defeat at the hands of passion and instinct, the triumph of the heart, the belly and the loins over the head. But at this point we encounter a serious difficulty: what account can be given of the impulse to disruption and disorder, the impulse which prompts civilized man to smash the work of his own hands? Why and under what conditions does this impulse operate to set in motion the process of decline? The answer offered by Gibbon to this question is deeply significant and reveals the very core of his thought.

Philosophic skepticism had abolished the old gods; it denied, as we have seen, the existence of any cosmic urge or *hormé*, whether theological or physical, working in nature to frustrate and nullify the aspirations of mankind. On the other hand, their modern substitutes (the obscurantist concepts now in vogue) had not yet been invented in Gibbon's day; nor, if they had, could he as a conscientious skeptic have bowed down before them. Having repudiated all but the evidences of sense, the skeptic had nothing to fall back on except what experimental science told him about the human psyche; and, from this standpoint, he did not even possess the light which was to be thrown on the workings of the psyche by modern investigators whose researches have served to illuminate so vividly the darker and more obscure recesses of the human spirit. Accordingly, all that Gibbon could do was to attack his problem from within the limits of the so-called classical psychology. He thus begins, quite in the spirit of Hume, by making certain identifications of more than dubious validity. In the first place, order is identified with the dictatorship of intelligence whose injunctions are uncritically accepted as universal and absolute, and that merely because of their formal character, i.e., because of their claim to be so. Disorder or anarchy, on the other hand, is conceived as animal impulse within the human soul. In the second place, this reasonable order is made to depend on virtue and, at the same time, it is provided with a criterion of value in the concept of "general," social and political, utility, while vice, the release of the passions and so the opposite of virtue, is branded as subjective and particularist. It is further assumed that reason, the principle of order and virtue, is committed to an endless struggle with the principle of disorder, like Plato's chariot driving the furious and unruly steeds of passion. Such is the version offered by experimental science of what had otherwise been diagnosed as "the warfare of the members."

But why should the charioteer flag in his efforts and permit the untamed beasts to escape from control? Gibbon's answer to this question is perfectly clear: this, he suggests, is merely a question of "degeneracy," the refusal of man to carry the awful burden of civilization. "This diminutive stature of mankind... was daily sinking below the old standard, and the Roman world was indeed peopled by a race of pigmies, when the fierce giants of the north broke in and mended the puny breed. They restored a manly spirit of freedom; and, after the revolution of ten centuries, freedom became the happy parent of taste and science."[98]

It thus appears that the question, as Gibbon sees it, is in the first instance one of freedom, and this freedom he envisages empirically as social and political. "A martial nobility and stubborn commons, possessed of arms, tenacious of property, and capable of preserving a free constitution against the enterprises of an aspiring prince."[99] And he adds: "the principles of a free constitution are irrevocably lost, when the legislative power is nominated by the executive."[100] Here, in very truth, breathes the spirit of 1688; more ambiguously, perhaps, the spirit of '76; for it is notorious that Gibbon had little sympathy with the American Revolution and, still less with the revolution in France, in both of which he discerned subversive tendencies, the "demon of anarchy,"[101] "the Gallic frenzy,"[102] "the wild theories of equal and boundless freedom,"[103] "the strange eccentric motions of a democracy, which always acts from the passion of the moment,"[104] "the fatal consequence of democratic principles which lead by a path of flowers into the abyss of hell."[105] In this connection we may perhaps recall his well-known recantation on the subject of Edmund Burke, written after he had read Burke's *Reflections*. "Burke's book is a most admirable medicine," he confesses, "against the French disease, which has made too much progress even in this happy country. I admire his eloquence, I approve his politics, I adore his chivalry, and I can forgive even his superstition [*aliter*, I can almost excuse his reverence for church establishments]."[106]

---

98. Gibbon, *Decline and Fall*, 1:45.
99. Ibid., 1:46.
100. Ibid., 1:47.
101. Gibbon, *Miscellaneous Works*, 153.
102. Ibid., 115.
103. Ibid.
104. Ibid., 155.
105. Ibid., 154.
106. Ibid., 134.

But to Gibbon, a second and not less essential freedom was that of the mind, in words which he translates from Tacitus, the freedom "to think what you like and to say what you think"; with this proviso, of course, that you are qualified by nature and nurture for this particular mode of self-expression. In this respect, he is a thoroughgoing aristocrat of the classical type.

For Gibbon, however, degeneracy involves much more than the loss of political or intellectual freedom, important to civilized order as these may be. Civilized order contains other and not less essential ingredients, like security and prosperity, and the protection of these values may and often does (as he perceived) involve some restriction of liberty and independence, whether of body or mind. Here we are brought face to face with the crux of his position. This is, that civilized society is, after all, subject to a principle of limitation inherent in its very being and transforming its most cherished values and ideals into dangerous, possibly even fatal, liabilities. The principle in question is not, however, cosmic but human, and prosperity itself, for Gibbon perhaps the ultimate goal of secular order, constitutes a menace to the order which creates it, though the peril may lurk unnoticed in the body politic until the virus has done its work. This is as much as to say that civilized society bears within itself the seeds of its own dissolution. And so much Gibbon would apparently admit: History the teacher which provides experimental science with evidence to support and confirm its generalizations (see Hume), offers a conspicuous illustration in the fortune of Imperial Rome. "Prosperity," Gibbon declares, "ripened the principle of decay; the causes of destruction multiplied with the extent of conquest, and as soon as time or accident had removed the artificial supports, the stupendous fabric yielded to the pressure of its own weight."[107] In the Antonine Age, "it was scarcely possible that the eyes of contemporaries should discover in the public felicity the latent causes of decay and corruption."[108] But "this long peace, and the uniform government of the Romans, introduced a slow and secret poison into the vitals of the Empire."[109] If peace and prosperity breed such evils, the prime function of the statesman must be to guard against these symptoms of decay which, if he cannot quite eradicate, he will at least seek to check by keeping alive, so far as possible, the military and political ethos of a primitive polity.

---

107. Gibbon, *Decline and Fall*, 2:1219.
108. Ibid., 1:43.
109. Ibid., 1:43–44.

VII

If we are so far right in our estimate of Gibbon's mind, we must conclude that for him the defense of civilization means, in substance, a defense of the *status quo*. This being so, it is not hard to understand why he should have entertained little sympathy for the idea of progress, the doctrine proclaimed by Turgot in his famous Sorbonne lectures of 1750, that mankind is by some inevitable compulsion driven forever onward toward a goal of "infinite perfectibility."[110] That doctrine left Gibbon, as it left Hume, quite cold. It is, indeed, true that he paid a gesture of respect to what was rapidly becoming the dominant faith of the century when he declared at the conclusion of his *Observations* that "we may acquiesce in the pleasing conclusion, that every age . . . has increased, and still increases, the real wealth, the happiness, the knowledge, and perhaps the virtue, of the human race."[111] But the evidence by which he reaches this pleasing conclusion is, to say the least, inconclusive: the fact that certain rudimentary arts and crafts, like hardy plants, survive the tempest of social and political disintegration, or that cannibalism, "the horrid repasts of the Laestrigons," have never been revived on the coasts of Italy.[112] Gibbon's real concern, however, is not with a hypothetical future of perfect secular felicity but rather with the actualities of contemporary society; it is to discover, if he can, whether the foundations of existing European civilization are secure. And on this point he allows himself no serious doubt. "It may safely be presumed," he ventures, "that no people, unless the face of nature is changed, will relapse into their original barbarism" . . . "the inestimable gifts [of civilization] have been successively propagated, they can never be lost."[113] For, he argues, and here we may discern the underlying materialism of his thought, civilization in its ultimate analysis means the acquisition and transmission of techniques, the techniques of the arts, of war, of commerce, and of religion. Accordingly, he concludes, "Europe is secure from any future irruption of barbarians; since before they can conquer, they must cease to be barbarous."[114] And, "should victorious barbarism carry slavery as far as the Atlantic Ocean, ten thousand vessels would transport beyond its pursuit the remains of civilized society, and Europe would revive and flourish in the American world."[115] Thus, despite his professed skepti-

---

110. See Turgot, *On the Progress of the Human Mind*.
111. Gibbon, *Decline and Fall*, 2:1225.
112. Ibid.
113. Ibid.
114. Ibid., 2:1224.
115. Ibid., 2:1223.

cism, Gibbon after all has his own gods, though their vast potential, whether for good or evil, was in his day but dimly suspected. They are our gods also, the gods of the industrial revolution and of the machine age. From this standpoint, all that is needed for the defense of civilization is to command, if possible to monopolize, the techniques. But, as we are now being painfully reminded, this is a game at which others, in whose purposes and methods we find something lacking, can also play.

VIII

Gibbon's work may be recommended as a salutary corrective to tendencies which were to emerge in subsequent historiography. I am not now thinking of the stuff produced by romanticism in its depraved and diseased form, a sample of which I have already offered in Weber's account of Commodus; but rather of those earlier and purer expressions of the romantic spirit such as are to be found in the so-called Germanic school of history and jurisprudence, represented by Mommsen. Despite its massive proportions, Mommsen's *History of Rome* is vitiated by certain extravagances from which Gibbon is entirely free; the incipient racism of his *Völkerpsychologie* with its unjust disparagement of the Gallic spirit; the worship of power politics coming out in his estimate of Julius Caesar as the one "entire and perfect man"; the apotheosis of process or movement for its own sake, resulting in a picture of Roman history as one long series of conflicts and struggles. Free from such extravagances, Gibbon is free also from the spell of concepts such as "East" and "West" with which his sturdy skepticism remains unsatisfied until he can translate them into intelligible terms, i.e., into terms of physical and moral causation. "The distinction between North and South," he observes, "is real and intelligible . . . But the difference of East and West is arbitrary and shifts around the globe. As men of the North, not of the West, the legions of Gaul and Germany were superior to the south-eastern natives of Asia and Egypt. It is the triumph of cold over heat; which may, however, and often has been surmounted by moral causes." That is to say, he refused to hypostasize the points of the compass.

In this as in other respects, the strength of Gibbon is that of his method, the method of experimental science. His work thus serves to illustrate the results to be achieved when (to recall Locke's metaphor) the mind's eye turns upon itself and makes itself its own object; in other words, the project of a science of history based on a science of human nature. And here the question of importance is not (as is now commonly assumed) whether Gibbon has been out-moded by the substitution of impersonal for personal, of extra-human, physical or material for moral and intellectual causes; whether, in short, it is things rather than men which shape the course of history. Put in this fashion as a flat antithesis, the question indeed seems to be quite without meaning. On the other hand, any attempt to weigh the relative importance of men and circumstances in the determination of events must surely be arbitrary. The study of history is the study of human activity and what confronts the historian when he undertakes to investigate any problem is a total situation in which, whatever be the factors that enter into and condition it, the efficient cause of action is and can be nothing ultimately but the human will. Accordingly, it is no real criticism of Gibbon to denounce his interpretation as "personal" and "dramatic" or to complain, with certain of his modern critics, that he neglects "the great immanent forces that transcend individual emperors and movements of history."

On this point I should like not to be misunderstood. It is a perfectly legitimate enterprise to explore the springs of human activity whether in terms of psychological or physical motivation. It is equally legitimate to explore them on the hypothesis that they are nothing more than a group of conditioned reflexes. Ultimately, however, the question is what happens when the phenomena thus revealed to the eye of science are translated into terms of personal experience. But meanwhile we may freely recognize our debt to Gibbon for exhibiting the results to be achieved by following the logic of philosophic skepticism. These results we shall now try to summarize.

To begin with, the logic of skepticism yields a picture of human nature in which the individual as such possesses meaning only in relation to a hypothetical type. He is (as Aristotle would have put it) Ἀνθρωπός τίς, "a particular man." Thus envisaged, his particularity tends to be lost in his generality; and he emerges as soldier, statesman, man of affairs, tyrant or emperor. From this standpoint judgments about any particular man take the form of whether or not he acts, so to speak, in character; whether he conforms to or departs from the type in question. This type is *ipso facto* static; it has the immobility of a portrait. True indeed, an attempt is made to allow for movement by invoking the notion of "evolving content" as a necessary correlate to the idea or pattern; but the question remains: how far can new wine be poured into old bottles without risking a breakage? To illustrate, we may refer once more to the concept of Augustan excellence (*virtus Augusti*). This excellence is resolved, in the case of Augustus himself, into *virtus* (in the narrower sense of manliness or courage), *clementia*, *justitia* and *pietas*. The question is: how far can his successors afford to depart from these principles and still remain worthy of the empire? Or, to put the point otherwise, to what extent may a system based on Augustan excellence change without ceasing to be itself? Nothing is more interesting than to observe the slow but steady modification during the centuries in these governing conceptions on which depended the immense majesty of the Augustan peace; except perhaps it be the attitude displayed by conservative or reactionary princes (like Julian the Apostate) toward what they branded as "innovation."

Gibbon's naturalism, like that of Hume, has two aspects. It is or claims to be (a) descriptive, offering a picture of the way men do in fact act, and (b) normative, supplying a basis for those judgments of value which constitute the essence of philosophic history. For the latter purpose, its usefulness depends on the role it assigns to reason in human life, whether as a principle of unification within the self or as a principle of concord and association among men. The role thus assigned to reason by the historian is to all intents and purposes absolute. It is in the light of this fact that certain of Gibbon's most characteristic prejudices are to be understood.

Of such prejudices, perhaps the most significant is that in favor of freedom, and especially "freedom of the mind," the "source of every generous and rational sentiment."[116] What destroys this freedom are habits of credulity and submission. Its presence serves to account for those rare moments of felicity in human history when civilization attains a peak such as (according to Gibbon) occurs in the eighteenth century and occurred in its classical counterpart, the Antonine age.

But if Gibbon thus exaggerates the role of reason, he fails to do justice to the affections as an integral element in the constitution of human nature. Like the ancient Stoics, his ideal is that of the *inmota* or *inconcussa mens*, the mind which functions in proud independence of the passions. These passions—love, grief, fear, pity, anger—he treats indiscriminately as manifestations of enthusiasm, an enthusiasm which for him, as for Hume, is inconsistent with mental balance; and when he thinks of them, it is as phenomena which are somehow outside the rational, i.e., the essential self. In this connection, we may recall the picture of Gibbon himself as the half-hearted suitor "who sighed as a lover and obeyed himself as a son," and the amazing analysis which he offers of his own experience.[117] "I understand by this passion the union of desire, friendship and tenderness which is inflamed by a single female, which prefers her to the rest of her sex and which seeks her possession as the supreme or sole happiness of our being."[118]

The prejudices of philosophic skepticism serve to color and to distort its judgments of value. These judgments are (as we have earlier pointed out) based on "reason" and "taste," a reason and taste which, while in fact merely

116. Gibbon, *Decline and Fall*, 2:1152.
117. Gibbon, *Miscellaneous Works*, 48.
118. Ibid., 47.

cosmopolitan, claim to be universal and are by that very claim rendered vicious or defective. For what this means is that skepticism has identified the purely ephemeral values of a specific historical period with the permanent and essential conditions of human life. By this form of idolatry, it blinds itself to the true issues of history, since it sees as "corruption" any departure from the norms or conventions of its ideal society. For the same reason, its judgments are tainted with an inevitable relativity. At the same time, they are circular, since the fact is ignored that the ideals of any historical system are nothing more than the outward and visible expression of the wills which sustain it. The unrealistic character of Gibbon's value-judgments is nowhere more apparent than in his attitude to emperors like Gallienus and in his imperfect sense of the genuine novelty of situations with which that emperor and his contemporaries were required to deal. Accordingly, he fails to comprehend the measure adopted by princes of the third century in their efforts to reconstruct the defenses, as well as to rehabilitate the administrative and fiscal system, of the empire; above all, perhaps, the changes in the theory and practice of sovereignty to be inaugurated under Diocletian and Constantine. In these movements Gibbon saw, as he was bound by his logic to see, a progressive departure from the concept of civilization embodied in Augustan or Antonine Rome and thus nothing but evidences of "decline." At the same time, he failed to identify and diagnose the real sickness of imperial society, overlooking many possibilities—above all, perhaps, the profound confusions of mind and heart which troubled the world of Trajan, Hadrian and Marcus Aurelius, a sort of fifth column which was operating within *Romanitas* to lower the barriers and admit the advancing hordes of barbarism.

To say this is to point to limitations of insight on the part of Gibbon (rather than lack of such information as has since become available) as the true cause of such inadequacies as appear in his work. These limitations were the inevitable result of the method by which he tried to think, and to appreciate their true dimensions, we have only to translate his findings (as I have earlier suggested) into terms of personal experience. To do this is to perceive that in human activity there is not and cannot be any such exact correlation between stimulus and response as had been postulated by Hume. How a man will act in any concrete situation may indeed (but only in the most general way) be anticipated from what is known of his temperament and habits, and that is more than often very little. But it is one thing to say this; quite another to assert that his action can be calculated in advance with any degree of precision or accuracy. I shall say nothing about the risk involved in imputing motives to another in order to "explain" his actions when it is notoriously so difficult to assess one's own. It is more important to notice that the psychology of experimental science fails to allow for growth or development either in the life of the individual or that of the race. For it is based on the assumption that the moral and psychological factors to be taken into account, however numerous and varied, are nevertheless fixed, unalterable and so, subject to classification under the general heads indicated by Hume, as though human nature contained no unsuspected potentialities and the future were to repeat in every detail the pattern of the past; a point of view from which experience loses much of its significance. So much for the anthropology of experimental science. We must conclude that it fails to do justice to the facts of history. But this is precisely what might have been expected from such a project as that of "anatomizing" human nature (to repeat Hume's phrase), since to anatomize human nature is to treat it as though it were dead.

The truth is that just as each and every actor in history is himself and no other so also the historical situation with which he is confronted is, properly speaking, unique. As Heraclitus had put it: you cannot cross the same river a second time, since the very fact that it is the second makes it a different experience, or (in the words of the Christians) Christ died once and for all for our sins. The Roman analogue to Alexander may, indeed, seek to imitate Alexander by overrunning the East; but in so doing, he does not lose, he merely asserts, his character as Caesar, not as the Macedonian king. The experience which we thus describe as unique is, at the same time, organic and cumulative; as such it finds its place in the texture of a total life, the life both of the individual historical actor and of posterity. That is why the meaning of such experience is never exhausted so long as it is studied merely objectively as "behavior"; i.e., in terms applicable to a *historia animalium*. It was a sense that human life consists of something more than a series of repetitive patterns, that its very essence is growth and development, which romanticism appears to have grasped and which it sought, however blindly, to affirm and communicate. It was the same sense to which, in the nineteenth century, Hegel and Marx in turn tried to give meaning by resurrecting the classical concept of Becoming, and by describing Becoming, the one as the genesis of the idea through thesis, antithesis and synthesis, the other as the working of a dialectic in which the *logos* develops in and through the movement of matter. We may, indeed, be skeptical of these Hegelian or Marxist identifications, while nevertheless recognizing that the creative principle in human life is a moving principle, or a principle of motion no less than order and, therefore perhaps, ultimately incalculable in terms of classical science. To have missed this sense of movement or process was perhaps the greatest of Gibbon's limitations. Accordingly, we are not surprised to learn that Rousseau remarked of him, Mr. Gibbon is not my man.

To us, then, the chief weakness of the *Decline and Fall* both as a work of art and as a study of history is that of logic which misconceives the central problem of human nature, the problem of identity in change, and which offers no intelligible account of that sense of orderly movement in which the substance of personality is disclosed; a logic which, at the same time, misconceives the nature both of order and movement, by denying to movement any significance except within the limits of a preconceived and predetermined order. Failing in this, it sees history as essentially atomistic; the theater of a conflict in which the forces of order (i.e., of reason) are pitted against those of disorder and anarchy (the life of vital impulse and emotion), but without the slightest prospect of final victory. If this, indeed, be the meaning of history, then history contains no promise of any substantial increase in wisdom and understanding, and belies all hope of genuine progress both for the individual and the race. It is thus that Gibbon reads history.

Happily, there is no need to accept his depressing conclusion. It is quite possible to reject the findings of experimental science and to make a fresh beginning from a less inadequate starting point. From this standpoint historical investigation will (on the factual level) take the fullest possible advantage of available techniques for discovering and assembling its data; and these techniques, it may be remarked, have improved vastly since Gibbon's day. On the level of presentation, it will seek with Gibbon to measure up to the most exacting standards of logic and artistry. But finally, on the ultimate level of interpretation, it will abandon conventional illusions of scientific objectivity and will seek with the aid of sympathetic imagination, disciplined and controlled by the comparative study of peoples and cultures, to enter into and recover what it can of past experience, so far as this is possible within the narrow limits of human understanding; and this experience it will seek to "represent" in such a way as to convey something, at least, of its meaning to contemporaries. In this formidable undertaking the historian can ill afford to neglect any possible assistance; he will ignore at his peril the rich resources of language and literature.

From this standpoint we may perhaps venture a final judgment on Gibbon. If we have dwelt on his limitations rather than his merits, it is through no petty desire to disparage his immense achievement. On that score the fame for which he labored is secure and it is folly to suppose that he will or ever can be superseded. Indeed, even to ask such a question is to be guilty of the presumption of demanding from him a kind of finality which is in fact denied to man-made reconstructions of historical truth. On the other hand, if we judge Gibbon's work, as indeed we must, to be a significant contribution to the living body of historical thinking, we shall assess it at something like its true worth and recognize that it is timeless because of its very timeliness. What Gibbon has to offer is an insight of priceless value into the mentality of the eighteenth century, by revealing so lucidly and vividly how that century saw its past. Accordingly, the permanent and essential value of his work is as literature. In saying this I do not for a moment admit that it ceases to be history.

Bibliography

Appian. *The Civil Wars*. Translated by John Carter. London: Penguin, 1996.
Adcock, F. E. "The Growth of the Greek City-State." In *Cambridge Ancient History*, vol. 3, edited by J.B. Bury and S.A. Cook. Cambridge: Cambridge University Press, 1965.
Arendt, Hannah. *Love and Saint Augustine*. Edited by Joanna Vecchiarelli Scott and Judith Chelius Stark. Chicago: University of Chicago Press, 1996.
Aristotle. *Analytica Posteriora*. In *The Basic Works of Aristotle*, edited by Richard McKeon. New York: Modern Library, 2001.
———. *The Ethics of Aristotle*. Edited by John Burnet. London: Methuen, 1900.
———. *Metaphysics*. Translated by Hugh Lawson-Tancred. London: Penguin, 1998.
———. *Nicomachean Ethics*. Translated by Terence Irwin. 2nd ed. Indianapolis: Hackett, 1999.
———. *Poetics*. Translated by Malcolm Heath. London: Penguin, 1997.
———. *The Politics of Aristotle*. Translated by Ernest Barker. Oxford: Oxford University Press, 1962.
Auden, W. H. "Augustus to Augustine." *The New Republic*, September 25, 1944, 373–75.
Augustine. *Concerning the City of God against the Pagans*. Translated by Henry Bettenson. London: Penguin, 1984.
———. "Contra Julian." In *Answer to the Pelagians*, vol. 2. Translated by Roland J. Teske. Edited by John E. Rotelle. New York: New City, 1998.
———. *Homilies on the Gospel of John (1–40)*. Translated by Edmund Hill. Edited by Allan Fitzgerald. New York: New City, 2009.
———. "The Grace of Christ and Original Sin." In *Answer to the Pelagians*, vol. 1, edited by John E. Rotelle. Translated by Roland J. Teske. New York: New City, 1997.
———. "On Nature and Grace." In *Answer to the Pelagians*, vol. 1. Translated by Roland J. Teske. Edited by John E. Rotelle. New York: New City, 1997.
———. "On the Spirit and the Letter." In *Answer to the Pelagians*, vol. 1. Translated by Roland J. Teske. Edited by John E. Rotelle. New York: New City, 1997.
———. "On the Way of Life of the Catholic Church." In *The Catholic and Manichaean Ways of Life*. Translated by Donald A. Gallagher and Idella J. Gallagher. Washington, DC: Catholic University of America Press, 1966.
———. *The Retractations*. Translated by Mary Inez Bogan. Washington, DC: Catholic University of America Press, 1968.
———. *On the Trinity*. New York: New City, 2012.

---. "Unfinished Work in Answer to Julian." In *Answer to the Pelagians*, vol. 3. Translated by Roland J. Teske. Edited by John E. Rotelle. New York: New City, 1999.

Bayle, Pierre. "Machiavel." In *A General Dictionary, Historical and Critical*, vol. 7. London: J. Bettenham, 1741.

Bradley, A. C. "Aristotle's Conception of the State." In *Hellenica*, edited by Evelyn Abbott. London: Longmans, Green, 1880.

Bell, Caroline, and Eddie Bell. *Thank You Twice: or, How We Like America*. Edited by Alden Hatch. New York: Harcourt, Brace, 1941.

Byron, George Gordon. "Prometheus." In *The Complete Poetical Works*, edited by Paul Elmer More, 191. Boston: Houghton Mifflin, 1905.

Burke, Edmund. *Reflections on the Revolution in France*. Edited by J. G. A. Pocock. Indianapolis: Hackett, 1987.

Butcher, Samuel H. *Aristotle's Theory of Poetry and Fine Art*. London: Macmillan, 1911.

Butler, Samuel. *Hudibras, Parts I and II and Selected Other Writings*. Edited by John Wilders and Hugh de Quehen. Oxford: Clarendon, 1973.

Caesar, Julius. *Civil War*. Edited and translated by Cynthia Damon. Cambridge: Harvard University Press, 2016.

Camus, Albert. *Christian Metaphysics and Neoplatonism*. Translated by Ronald D. Srigley. Columbia: University of Missouri Press, 2007.

Case, Shirley Jackson. Review of *Christianity and Classical Culture*, by Charles Norris Cochrane. *The Journal of Religion* 24 (1944) 289–90.

Cicero. *De Legibus*. In *On the Republic and On the Laws*. Translated by C. W. Keyes. Cambridge: Harvard University Press, 1928.

---. *Letters to Atticus*. Edited and translated by D. R. Shackleton Bailey. Vol. 1. Cambridge: Harvard University Press, 1999.

---. *On Obligations*. Translated by P. G. Walsh. Oxford: Oxford University Press, 2000.

---. *Oratio de Lege Manilia*. Charleston: Nabu, 2013.

Chapot, Victor. *The Roman World*. Translated by E. A. Parker. London: K. Paul, Trench, Trubner, 1928.

Cochrane, Charles Norris. "The Augustinian Prognostic," Charles Norris Cochrane Fonds. University of Toronto Archives, B2003-0011/006 (16).

---. *Christianity and Classical Culture: A Study of Thought and Action from Augustus to Augustine*. Reprint, with text rev. and corr. Indianapolis: Liberty Fund, 2003.

---. "The Classical Idea of the Commonwealth," Charles Norris Cochrane Fonds. University of Toronto Archives, B2003-0011/004 (13).

---. "Extract from Letter to Hutton." Charles Norris Cochrane Fonds. University of Toronto Archives, B2003-0011/001 (01)–(09).

---. "The Imperfection of Politics," Charles Norris Cochrane Fonds. University of Toronto Archives, B2003-0011/006 (18).

---. "The Latin Spirit in Literature." *University of Toronto Quarterly* 2.3 (1932–33) 315–38.

---. "The Mind of Edward Gibbon (I)." *University of Toronto Quarterly* 12.1 (1942–43) 1–17.

---. "The Mind of Edward Gibbon (II)." *University of Toronto Quarterly* 12.2 (1942–43) 146–66.

———. "Natural Necessity and Human Freedom," Charles Norris Cochrane Fonds. University of Toronto Archives, B2003-0011/006 (17).

———. "Niccolo Machiavelli," Charles Norris Cochrane Fonds. University of Toronto Archives, B2003-0011/004 (06).

———. "Pax Romana," Charles Norris Cochrane Fonds. University of Toronto Archives, B2003-0011/004 (12).

———. "Personality and History," Charles Norris Cochrane Fonds. University of Toronto Archives, B2003-0011/006 (19).

———. "Response to 'Federalism in Antiquity,' by Moses Hadas." In *Approaches to World Peace: Fourth Symposium*, edited by Lyman Bryson, Louis Finkelstein, and Robert MacIver. New York: Harper, 1944.

———. "Revolution: Caesarism," Charles Norris Cochrane Fonds. University of Toronto Archives, B2003-0011/004 (11).

———. *Thucydides and the Science of History*. New York: Russell & Russell, 1965.

Collingwood, R. G. *An Essay on Metaphysics*. Oxford: Clarendon, 1940.

———. *The New Leviathan: or Man, Society, Civilization and Barbarism*. Oxford: Clarendon, 1942.

Cornford, Francis Macdonald. *Thucydides Mythistoricus*. London: E. Arnold, 1907.

Dyer, Louis. *Machiavelli and the Modern State*. Boston: Athenaeum, 1904.

Figgis, John Neville. *The Political Aspects of S. Augustine's "City of God."* London: Longmans, 1921.

Frederick II, King of Prussia. "The King of Prussia's Preface to His *Examen*, or Critical Essay upon Machiavel's *Prince*." In vol. 2 of *The Works of Nicholas Machiavel*, translated by Ellis Farneworth, 178–80. London: T. Davies, 1762.

Friedland, Martin. *The University of Toronto: A History*. Toronto: University of Toronto Press, 2013.

Gibbon, Edward. *The Decline and Fall of the Roman Empire*. Edited by J. B. Bury. 3 vols. New York: Heritage, 1946.

———. *The History of the Decline and Fall of the Roman Empire*. Edited by J. B. Bury. 7 vols. London: Methuen, 1900.

———. *Memoirs*. Edited by Henry Morley. London: G. Routledge, 1891.

———. *The Miscellaneous Works of Edward Gibbon*. Edited by John Sheffield. London: John Murray, 1837.

Gilson, Etienne. *L'Espirit de la Philosophie Mediévale: Deuxième sèrie*. Paris: Vrin, 1932.

———. *The Spirit of Mediaeval Philosophy*. Translated by A. H. C. Downes. Notre Dame: University of Notre Dame Press, 1991.

Herodotus. *The Histories*. Translated by Aubrey de Selincourt. London: Penguin, 1954.

Hesiod. *Works and Days; and Theogony*. Translated by Stanley Lombardo. Indianapolis: Hackett, 1993.

Hobbes. *Leviathan: With Selected Variants from the Latin Edition of 1668*. Edited by Edwin Curley. Indianapolis: Hackett, 1994.

Homer. *Odyssey*. Translated by Robert Fagles. New York: Penguin, 1996.

Hume, David. *An Abstract of a Treatise on Human Nature, 1740: A Pamphlet Hitherto Unknown*. Reprinted with an introduction by J. M. Keynes and P. Sraffa. Cambridge: Cambridge University Press, 1936.

———. *Dialogues Concerning Natural Religion*. Edited Richard H. Popkin. Indianapolis: Hackett, 1998.

———. *Enquiry Concerning Principles of Morals.* Edited by J. B. Schneewind. Indianapolis: Hackett, 1983.

———. *Moral Philosophy.* Edited by Geoffrey Sayre-McCord. Indianapolis: Hackett, 2006.

———. *Natural History of Religion and Dialogues Concerning Natural Religion.* Edited by A. Wayne Colver and John Valdimir Price. Oxford: Clarendon, 1976.

———. *The Philosophical Works of David Hume.* Vol. 4. Edinburgh: Adam Black, 1826.

———. *A Treatise of Human Nature.* Kitchener, ON: Batoche, 1999.

Innis, Harold A. "Obituaries: Charles Norris Cochrane, 1889–1945." *The Canadian Journal of Economics and Political Science* 12 (1945) 95–97.

Jaeger, Werner. *Aristotle: Fundamentals of the History of His Development.* Translated by Richard Robinson. Oxford: Clarendon, 1934.

———. *Paideia: The Ideals of Greek Culture.* Translated by Gilbert Highet. 3 vols. Oxford: Blackwell, 1939–45.

Jerome. *Select Letters.* Translated by F. A. Wright. Cambridge: Harvard University Press, 1933.

Kristeller, Oskar. Review of *Christianity and Classical Culture: A Study of Thought and Action from Augustus to Augustine,* by Charles Norris Cochrane. *The Journal of Philosophy* 41 (1944) 576–81.

Krutch, Joseph Wood. "Was Europe a Success?" *The Nation,* August 15, 1934, 171–72.

Laistner, M. L. W. Review of *Christianity and Classical Culture,* by Charles Norris Cochrane. *American Historical Review* 47 (1942) 314–15.

Lewis, C. S. *Surprised by Joy: The Shape of My Early Life.* Orlando: Harcourt, 1966.

Lindsay, Alexander D. *Religion, Science and Society in the Modern World.* New Haven: Yale University Press, 1943.

Locke, John. *Essay Concerning Human Understanding.* New ed. Vol. 1. New York: Valentine Seaman, 1824.

———. *The Works of John Locke.* Vol. 1. London: Thomas Tegg, 1824.

Machiavelli, Niccolò. *Discourses on the First Decade of Titus Livius.* Translated by Ninian Hill Thomson. London: Kegan Paul, Trench, 1883.

———. *Il Principe.* Edited by L. A. Burd. Oxford: Clarendon, 1891.

———. *Prince.* Translated by W. K. Marriott. London: J. M. Dent, 1908.

———. *The Works of Nicholas Machiavel.* Edited by Ellis Farneworth. 2 vols. London: T. Davies, 1762.

———. *The Works of Nicholas Machiavel.* Edited by Ellis Farneworth. 2nd ed., corrected. 4 vols. London: T. Davies, 1775.

MacIver, R. M. *Social Causation.* New York: Harper, 1964.

Marlowe, Christopher. *The Jew of Malta.* In *The Complete Plays of Christopher Marlowe.* New York: Nelson Doubleday, 1969.

McKillop, A. B. *A Disciplined Intelligence: Critical Inquiry and Canadian Thought in the Victorian Era.* Montreal: McGill-Queen's University Press, 2001.

Meyer, Edward. *Machiavelli and the Elizabethan Drama.* Weimar: E. Felber, 1897.

Mommsen, Theodor. *History of Rome.* Translated by William Purdie Dickson. 5 vols. Cambridge: Cambridge University Press, 2010.

Montesquieu, Charles de Secondat, baron de. *Political Theory of Montesquieu.*

———. *The Spirit of the Laws.* Translated by Anne M. Cohler, Basia Carolyn Miller, and Harold Samuel Stone. Cambridge: Cambridge University Press, 1989.

More, Paul Elmer. *Platonism.* 3rd ed. Princeton: Princeton University Press, 1931.

Morley, John. *The Life of William Ewart Gladstone*. Vol. 2. London: Macmillan, 1903.
———. *Machiavelli: The Romanes Lecture*. London: Macmillan, 1897.
Newman, W. L. *The Politics of Aristotle*. 4 vols. Oxford: Clarendon, 1887–1902.
Niebuhr, Reinhold. *The Nature and Destiny of Man: A Christian Interpretation*. Vol. 1, *Human Nature*. New York: Scribner's, 1941.
Oppenheimer, Franz. *The State: Its History and Development Viewed Sociologically*. Translated by John M. Gitterman. Indianapolis: Bobbs-Merrill, 1914.
Orosius, Paulus. *The Seven Books of History against the Pagans*. Translated Roy Deferrari. Washington, DC: Catholic University of America Press, 1964.
Pelikan, Jaroslav. "Writing as a Means of Grace." In *Spiritual Quests: The Art and Craft of Religious Writing*, edited by William Zinsser. Boston: Houghton Mifflin, 1988.
Plato. *Gorgias*. Translated by Donald J. Zeyl. Indianapolis: Hackett, 1987.
———. *Laws*. Translated by Trevor J. Saunders. London: Penguin, 1975.
———. *The Republic*. Translated by Allan Bloom. 2nd ed. New York: Basic, 1991.
Pliny. *Natural History*. Translated by H. Rackham. Vol. 9. Cambridge: Harvard University Press, 1952.
Pole, Reginald. *Apologia Reginaldi Poli ad Carolum V. Caesarem super quatuor libris a se scriptis de unitate ecclesia*. In *Epistolarum Reginaldi Poli, S.R.E. Cardinalis et aliorum ad ipsum collection*. Edited by A. M. Quirini. 5 vols. Brescia: J. M. Rizzardi, 1744–57.
Ratzinger, Joseph. *Volk und Haus Gottes in Augustins Lehre von der Kirche*. St. Ottilien: EOS, 1992.
Rousseau, Jean-Jacques. *On the Social Contract*. Translated and edited by Donald A. Cress. Indianapolis: Hackett, 1988.
Sallust. *Bellum Catilinae*. Edited by Patrick McGushin. Bristol: Bristol Classical, 1991.
Schneider, Herbert W. *Making the Fascist State*. New York: Howard Fertig, 1968.
Seneca. *Epistles 93–124*. Translated by Richard Gummere. Cambridge: Harvard University Press, 1925.
Stewart, J. A. *The Myths of Plato*. London: Macmillan, 1905.
Suetonius. *The Lives of the Caesars: Books I–IV*. In vol. 1 of *Suetonius*. Translated by J. C. Rolfe. Cambridge: Harvard University Press, 1914.
Tait, M. D. C. "Charles Norris Cochrane, 1889–1945." *Phoenix* 1 (1946–47) 1–2.
Thucydides. *The Peloponnesian War*. Harmondsworth: Penguin, 1954.
Turgot, Anne-Robert-Jacques. *On the Progress of the Human Mind*. Translated by McQuilkin De Grange. Hanover, NH: Sociological, 1929.
Valerius Maximus. *Memorable Doings and Sayings*. Edited and translated by D. R. Shackleton Bailey. 2 vols. Cambridge: Harvard University Press, 2000.
Velleius Paterculus. *Compendium of Roman History*. With an English translation by Frederick W. Shipley. Cambridge: Harvard University Press, 1924.
Vergil. *The Aeneid*. Translated by Robert Fitzgerald. New York: Vintage, 1981.
Weber, Wilhelm. "The Antonines." In vol. 11 of *Cambridge Ancient History*, edited by S. A. Cook, F. E. Adcock, and M. P. Charlesworth. Cambridge: Cambridge University Press, 1936.
Woodhouse, A. S. P. "Charles Norris Cochrane, 1889–1945." *Proceedings and Transactions of the Royal Society of Canada* 40 (1946) 83–87.

www.ingramcontent.com/pod-product-compliance
Lightning Source LLC
Chambersburg PA
CBHW030823230426
43667CB00008B/1351